In-Stage Composite Series

MATHS 5
PLUS

STAGE 3

Harry O'Brien Greg Purcell

OXFORD
UNIVERSITY PRESS
AUSTRALIA & NEW ZEALAND

STUDENT
BOOK

Contents

Contents

The **Maths Plus In-Stage Composite Series** allows teachers to simultaneously develop understanding of the NSW Board of Studies 2002 Outcomes at different levels within a Stage. The series provides a sound foundation for the teaching and learning of mathematics from Early Stage 1 to Stage 3 through the use of comprehensive, student-friendly activities based on the Mathematics K–6 Syllabus.

As far as possible, the teaching and learning activities in both *Student Books* within each Stage are parallel to each other. Occasionally, it was not possible to match Outcomes one-to-one. In these instances an alternative page has been provided in the *Teaching Guide* so that teachers can still treat the same Outcome simultaneously within the group if they wish.

Example

- *Maths Plus Student Book 5* presents teaching and learning activities in a logical sequence that develops initial understanding of the Stage 3 outcomes.

Year 5   **Year 6**

- *Maths Plus Student Book 6* follows the same sequence of Outcomes as *Student Book 5* but builds upon the understanding already gained.

- Teachers of composite classes within a Stage will appreciate the opportunity to focus upon a single Outcome but at different levels of understanding.

Supplementary Resources

The **Maths Plus In-Stage Composite Series** offers a range of interconnected resources that help to reinforce and consolidate understanding of Outcomes developed in each *Student Book*:

- *Mentals and Homework Books 1–6*
  These match one-to-one with the activities presented in the *Student Books*. All strands of the syllabus are represented.

- *Teaching Guide*
  Lesson activities and strategies for whole-class groups as well as remedial and extension groups are outlined as a guide for teachers. Approximately 30 Blackline Masters are provided to support lesson activities.

- A *Program Planner* available from **www.oup.com.au/primary** that allows teachers to customise the teaching and learning program to suit their own needs.

- *Assessment and A–E Reporting Guide*
  Assessment BLMs that allow for A–E grading are a new and exciting addition to this new series.

You will find the **Maths Plus In-Stage Composite Series** an invaluable, comprehensive resource whether you use the series for coursework or you select specific components to support your own teaching.

Find a topic

v

Find a Stage 3 outcome

Find a Stage 3 outcome

Revising 3-digit addition

Learning to trade in an addition sum

Add
1 hundred
+ 1 hundred
equals
2 hundreds

Hund	Tens	Ones
1	¹3	3
+ 1	1	9
2	5	2

Add 1 ten
+ 3 tens
plus 1 ten
equals 5 tens.

Process

9 ones plus
3 ones equals
12 ones.
Exchange
10 ones for
1 ten.
Record 2 in the
ones column.

+

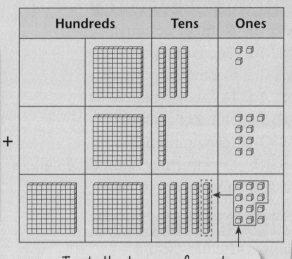

Hundreds	Tens	Ones

Trade the ten ones for a ten

---

1 Complete each addition algorithm.

a
Hund	Tens	Ones
2	2	6
+ 1	3	8

b
Hund	Tens	Ones
3	5	9
+ 2	3	6

c
Hund	Tens	Ones
3	8	4
+ 2	6	6

d
Hund	Tens	Ones
3	5	9
+ 4	0	6

e
Hund	Tens	Ones
3	5	9
+ 2	6	5

f
Hund	Tens	Ones
3	0	7
	2	6
+ 1	4	3

g
Hund	Tens	Ones
2	4	5
3	0	6
+ 4	0	7

h
Hund	Tens	Ones
4	5	6
	2	3
+ 2	9	7

i
Hund	Tens	Ones
8	0	7
	6	7
+		9

j
Hund	Tens	Ones
3	5	7
4	7	3
+	3	8

k
```
  2 6 7 g
  3 0 4 g
  1 6 5 g
+     1 4 g
```

l
```
  2 6 1 cm
      3 7 cm
      5 3 cm
+ 4 1 0 cm
```

m
```
    2 7 °C
    3 5 °C
       6 °C
  2 3 °C
```

n
```
  4 2 5 mL
  3 6 2 mL
      3 7 mL
+ 1 2 4 mL
```

o
```
  $ 7 . 8 5
  $ 8 . 8 5
  $ 0 . 8 6
+ $ 8 . 5 8
```

---

2 Solve the problems.

a At Kingsland primary school there are 248 girls on the school roll and 249 boys. How many children attend the school?

b Mr Green the garden shop owner banked $389 on Monday and $456 on Tuesday. What was his total banking for the two days?

3 Calculate the answers for each multiplication grid.

a	× 6
2	
3	
5	
8	
10	
4	
6	
9	
7	

b	× 7
1	
3	
5	
7	
9	
8	
6	
4	
10	

c	× 8
4	
6	
5	
3	
7	
2	
9	
10	
8	

d	× 5
2	
5	
3	
8	
10	
4	
6	
9	
7	

e	× 9
4	
6	
5	
3	
8	
7	
9	
2	
10	

f	× 4
3	
1	
5	
7	
9	
8	
6	
4	
10	

4 Write a division fact that can be made from the multiplication fact.

a $6 \times 5 = \square$ $\square \div \square = \square$

b $7 \times 6 = \square$ $\square \div \square = \square$

c $8 \times 9 = \square$ $\square \div \square = \square$

d $8 \times 4 = \square$ $\square \div \square = \square$

e $9 \times 6 = \square$ $\square \div \square = \square$

f $7 \times 9 = \square$ $\square \div \square = \square$

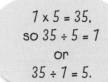

$7 \times 5 = 35$,
so $35 \div 5 = 7$
or
$35 \div 7 = 5$.

5 **School banking**.

Complete the "Total" section of the table to show how much money each person has saved since they started their school banking account.

	a	b	c	d	e	f
	Anne	**Bree**	**Calvin**	**Lauren**	**Mani**	**Jorge**
Monthly banking	$9	$10	$8	$6	$8	$4
Number of months	8	7	7	9	5	8
Total						

6 Create as many multiplication sentences as you can that have a product of 48.

Revising polygons

A **polygon** is a shape made up of three or more straight sides.

7 Give a clear description of each shape by recording its properties.

Shape	Name	Sides	Angles	Types of angles	Lines of symmetry
△	triangle	3	3	acute	3
▭					
⏢					
⬠					
⯃					
⬡					

8 Draw a line to match each description to the correct quadrilateral.

a A parallelogram is a four-sided shape with two pairs of parallel sides. Opposite sides and angles are equal. A square and a rectangle are other examples of a parallelogram.

b A rectangle is a parallelogram with two pairs of equal sides and four angles of 90°.

c A rhombus is a parallelogram with four equal sides and two sets of matching angles.

d A square is a parallelogram with four equal sides and four angles of 90º.

e A trapezium is a quadrilateral with only one pair of parallel sides.

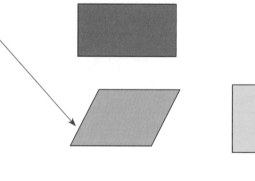
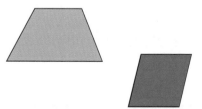

SGS3.2a Manipulates, classifies and draws two-dimensional shapes and describes side and angle properties

WMS3.3, WMS3.2

Longer distances are measured in **kilometres**. There are **1000 metres** in 1 kilometre. Trundle wheels are often used to measure long distances because each revolution equals 1 metre.

9 How many times would a trundle wheel click when measuring 1 kilometre? _____

Measuring one kilometre

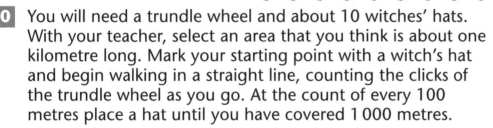

10 You will need a trundle wheel and about 10 witches' hats. With your teacher, select an area that you think is about one kilometre long. Mark your starting point with a witch's hat and begin walking in a straight line, counting the clicks of the trundle wheel as you go. At the count of every 100 metres place a hat until you have covered 1000 metres.

10 x 100 m equals 1 km.

Mark out a 1 kilometre cross country course

11 In your school, mark out a cross country course that is about 1 kilometre. You may need to write some distances in chalk on the ground or mark distances with markers.

Use a stopwatch to record how long it takes your group members to run your course.

12 Use the map of New South Wales and the distances from Sydney to calculate the distances between these places.

Town	Distance from Sydney
Kingscliff	840 km
Coffs Harbour	558 km
Port Macquarie	407 km
Newcastle	162 km
Sydney	
Wollongong	78 km
Bega	446 km
Merimbula	456 km

a

Kingscliff Port Macquarie	
Distance	

b

Bega Wollongong	
Distance	

c

Coffs Harbour Newcastle	
Distance	

d

Port Macquarie Newcastle	
Distance	

e

Merimbula Wollongong	
Distance	

Map of New South Wales showing: BRISBANE, Gold Coast, Kingscliff, Ballina, Iluka, Moree, Burke, Narrabri, Inverell, Armidale, Arrawarra, Coffs Harbour, Nyngan, Tamworth, Port Macquarie, Dubbo, Halidays Point, Nelson Bay, Newcastle, West Wyalong, The Entrance, Hay, Wagga Wagga, SYDNEY, Narrandera, Yass, Wollongong, Albury, Bega, Merimbula

13 Use a street directory to help you name locations about 1 km from school, less than 1 km from school and more than 1 km from school. Measure some of the distances to check your accuracy.

Less than 1 km	About 1 km	More than 1 km

Last year, the following **strategies** were taught. Use them to solve the questions on this page.

1 Use the split strategy to add and subtract these numbers.

> Add the hundreds, tens and ones separately.
> 325 + 133?
> Think 300 + 100 plus 20 + 30 plus 5 + 3 equals 458.

a 42 + 35 = _____

b 31 + 54 = _____

c 62 − 32 = _____

d 23 + 45 = _____

e 42 + 54 = _____

f 48 + 26 = _____

g 66 − 34 = _____

h 57 + 28 = _____

i 23 + 35 = _____

j 24 + 67 = _____

k 68 − 47 = _____

l 75 + 36 = _____

m 325 + 133 = _____

n 372 + 125 = _____

o 427 + 132 = _____

p 534 + 354 = _____

q 627 + 252 = _____

r 309 + 490 = _____

s 378 − 267 = _____

t 784 + 141 = _____

u 356 + 277 = _____

2 Bridge to a decade to calculate the answers.

> 38 + 37?
> Think, 38 + 30 = 68, then add 2 and 5 more.

a 35 + 27 = _____

b 46 + 28 = _____

c 35 + 27 = _____

d 49 + 23 = _____

e 67 + 35 = _____

f 58 + 29 = _____

g 72 − 33 = _____

h 83 − 24 = _____

i 94 − 35 = _____

j 64 − 26 = _____

k 75 − 36 = _____

l 82 − 47 = _____

m 127 + 27 = _____

n 236 + 37 = _____

o 357 + 46 = _____

p 268 + 35 = _____

q 352 − 25 = _____

r 293 − 35 = _____

3 Estimate an answer to each of the additions and subtractions by rounding each number. The first one is done for you.

	Question	Estimate
a	297 + 509	800
b	687 − 217	
c	607 + 384	
d	717 + 279	
e	689 − 321	
f	773 + 228	
g	456 + 249	

	Question	Estimate
h	227 + 477	
i	408 + 179	
j	575 − 325	
k	297 + 313	
l	556 + 437	
m	717 + 477	
n	569 − 437	

	Question	Estimate
o	937 + 387	
p	878 − 427	
q	769 − 440	
r	435 + 867	
s	789 − 423	
t	827 + 579	
u	698 + 713	

4 Solve these problems using your mental arithmetic skills.

a Jim has 54 m of timber in one pile and 38 m of timber in another. How much timber does he have altogether? _____

b Sarah had $73 in her bank account but spent $48 on clothes. How much money does she have left in her bank account? _____

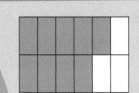
$$\frac{9}{12}$$

The **numerator** shows us how many parts out of the whole (the fractional part).

The **denominator** shows us how many parts are in the whole.

5 What fraction of each shape is shaded? The first one has been done for you.

a 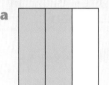 $\frac{2}{3}$

b 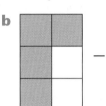 —

c 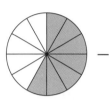 —

d  —

e 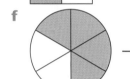 —

f  —

g —

h  —

6 Shade the fractions.

a  $\frac{2}{3}$

b 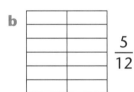 $\frac{5}{12}$

c  $\frac{5}{6}$

d 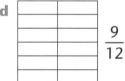 $\frac{9}{12}$

7 Shade the fraction of each group.

a $\frac{5}{6}$

b $\frac{2}{3}$

c $\frac{7}{12}$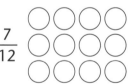

8 Label the fractions on the number line.

a

0 $\frac{\ }{3}$ $\frac{\ }{3}$ 1
Thirds

b
0 $\frac{\ }{6}$ $\frac{\ }{6}$ $\frac{\ }{6}$ $\frac{\ }{6}$ $\frac{\ }{6}$ 1
Sixths

c
0 $\frac{\ }{12}$ $\frac{\ }{12}$ $\frac{\ }{12}$ $\frac{\ }{12}$ $\frac{\ }{12}$ $\frac{\ }{12}$ $\frac{\ }{12}$ $\frac{\ }{12}$ $\frac{\ }{12}$ $\frac{\ }{12}$ $\frac{\ }{12}$ 1
Twelfths

9 Which fraction is larger $\frac{4}{6}$ or $\frac{7}{12}$? _____

Recognising angles

Angles are classified according to the amount of turn between two arms.

Right angle	Obtuse angle	Acute angle	Straight angle	Reflex angle
Square corner 90°	Larger than a right angle; greater than 90°	Smaller than a right angle; less than 90°	Can be made from two right angles 180°	Larger than a straight angle; greater than 180°

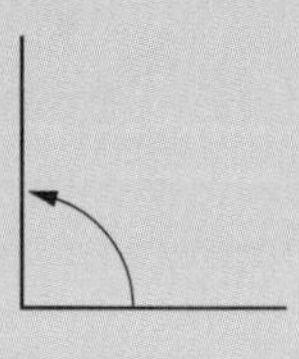

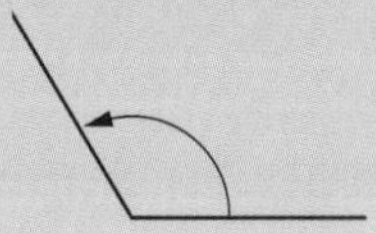

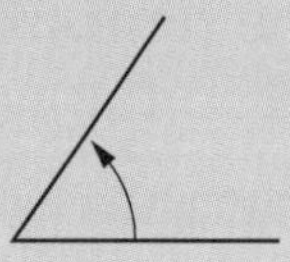

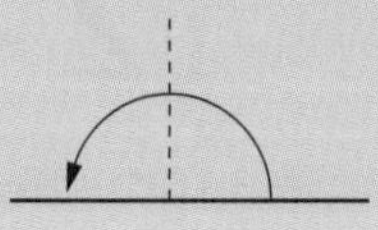

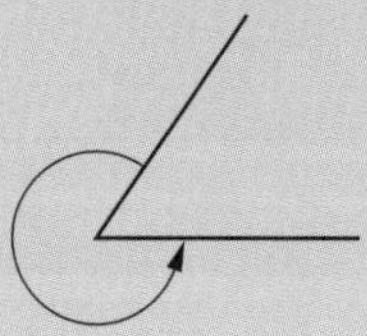

10 Label the angles either right angle, obtuse, acute, reflex or straight.

a   d   g   j

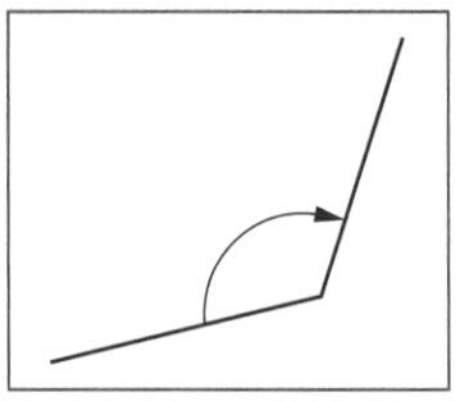

b   e   h   k

c   f   i   l

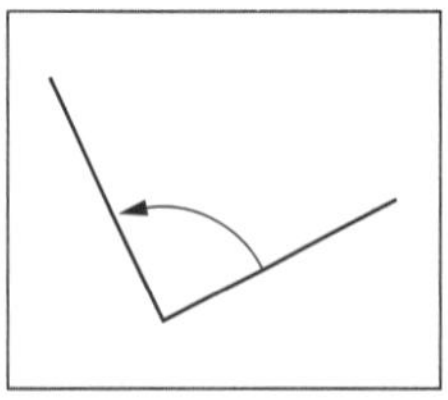

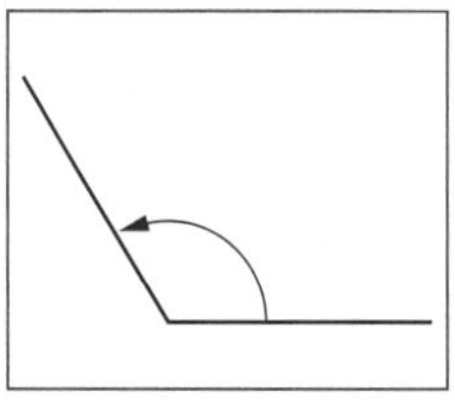

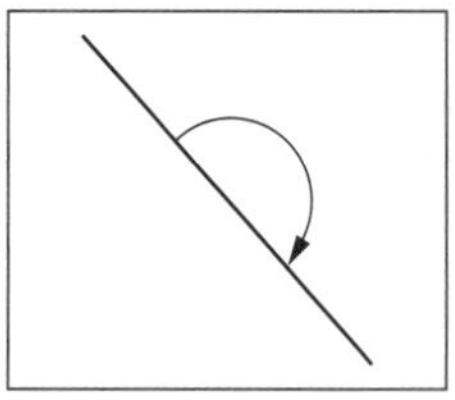

A   B 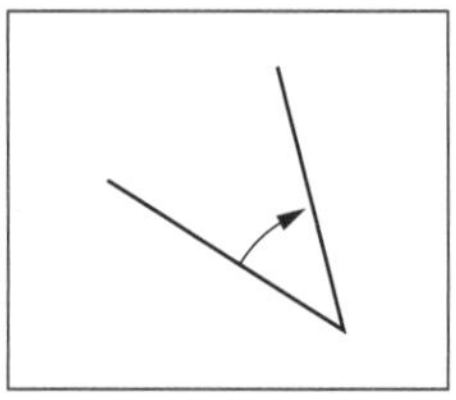   C 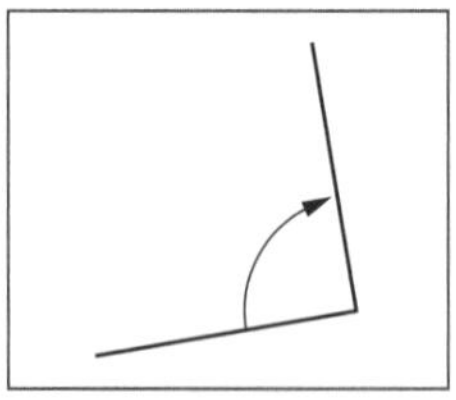   D 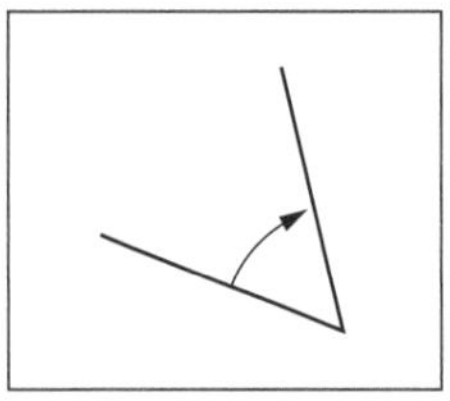   E

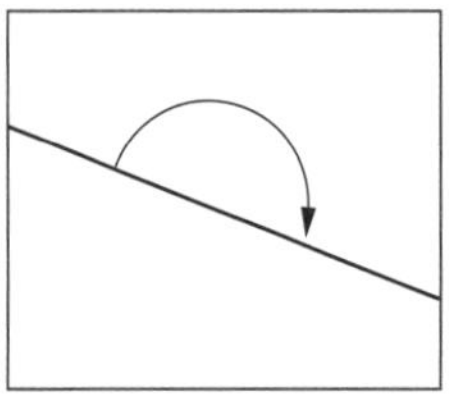

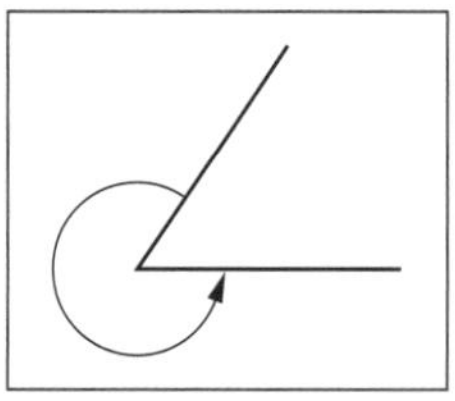

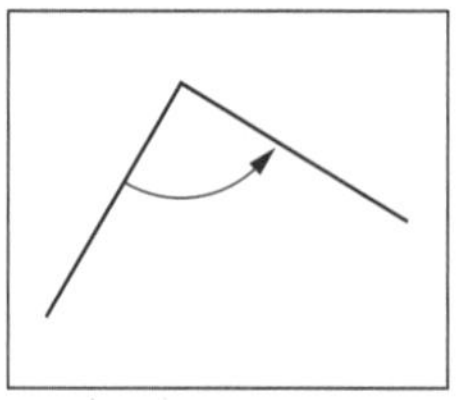

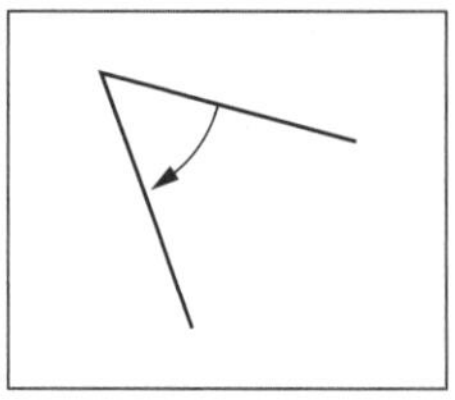

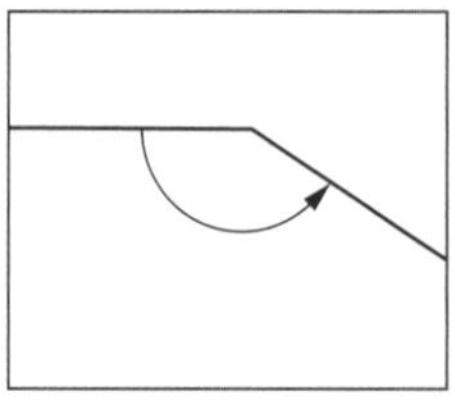

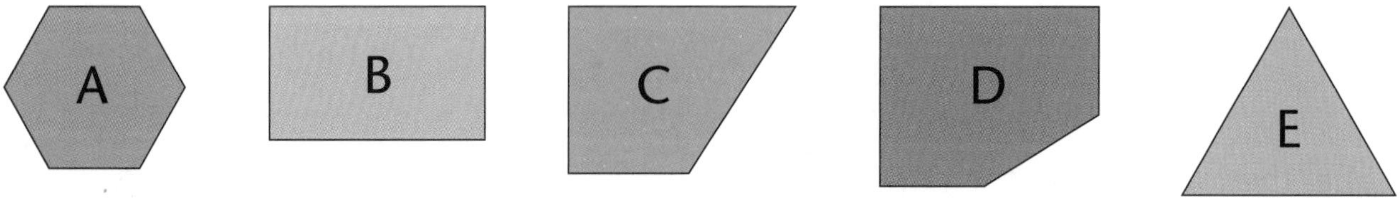

11 Identify which shape is being described.

a I have four right angles. _____

b I have one obtuse angle, one acute angle and two right angles. _____

c I have three acute angles. _____

d I have three right angles and two obtuse angles. _____

e I have six obtuse angles. _____

12 Find an acute angle and an obtuse angle in your classroom then write them below.

Acute [   ]   Obtuse [   ]

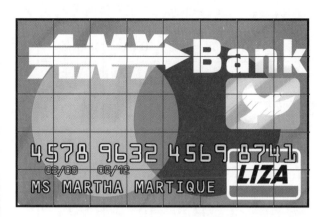

13 Martha wanted to know what the area of her credit card was, so she divided it exactly into square centimetres and counted them.

a Find a quicker way for finding the area using the square centimetres Martha drew on the card.

b Explain what it is.

_____

_____

_____

_____

The area of rectangles can be found by multiplying the length by the breadth.
Area = length × breadth
(This is known as the formula for area.)

14 Apply the formula: "Area = length × breadth" to find the area of these shapes.

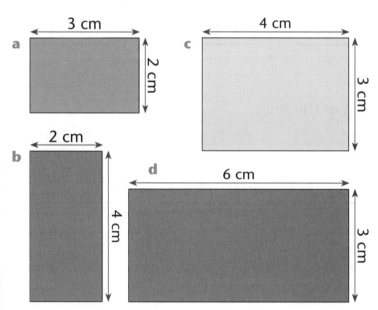

a 3 cm, 2 cm

b 2 cm, 4 cm

c 4 cm, 3 cm

d 6 cm, 3 cm

Area = length × breadth

	Length	Breadth	Area
a	cm	cm	cm²
b	cm	cm	cm²
c	cm	cm	cm²
d	cm	cm	cm²

15 Calculate the areas of the parts of this ticket.

a What is the area of the smaller section of the ticket? _____ cm²

b What is the area of the larger section of the ticket? _____ cm²

c What is the total area of the ticket? _____ cm²

STADIUM AUSTRALIA

B12

8:00 pm
30 NOV

STADIUM AUSTRALIA

B12

8:00 pm
30 NOV

WMS3.4, WMS3.2

MS3.2 Selects and uses the appropriate unit to calculate area, including the area of squares, rectangles and triangles.

9

Revising 3-digit subtraction

Trading in subtraction

Subtract 1 hundred from 2 hundreds to give 1 hundred.

Hund	Tens	Ones
2	^{3}4	^{1}3
− 1	1	9
1	2	4

Subtract 1 ten from 3 tens to give 2 tens.

Trade a 10 for 10 ones.

Process

9 ones from 3 ones can't be done. Trade a ten from the tens column to the ones column to make 13 ones. 4 tens becomes 3 tens. 9 ones from 13 ones equals 4 ones.

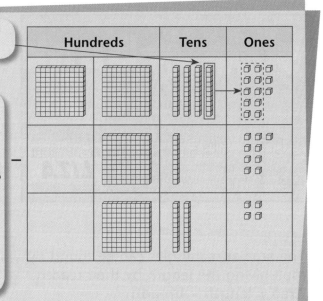

Hundreds		Tens	Ones

1 Complete these subtractions without trading.

a
Hund	Tens	Ones
8	7	9
− 2	5	7

b
Hund	Tens	Ones
9	8	3
− 3	4	2

c
Hund	Tens	Ones
7	5	4
− 2	3	3

d
Hund	Tens	Ones
8	7	9
− 4	3	4

e
Hund	Tens	Ones
3	5	8
− 1	2	3

2 Complete these subtractions with trading in the ones.

a
Hund	Tens	Ones
8	5	2
− 4	3	4

b
Hund	Tens	Ones
9	3	2
− 6	1	5

c
Hund	Tens	Ones
4	4	4
− 2	3	7

d
Hund	Tens	Ones
9	4	3
− 6	2	5

e
Hund	Tens	Ones
7	9	5
− 4	6	8

3 Complete these subtractions with trading in the tens.

a
Hund	Tens	Ones
6	4	8
− 2	6	3

b
Hund	Tens	Ones
8	2	8
− 2	6	3

c
Hund	Tens	Ones
7	4	9
− 2	5	6

d
Hund	Tens	Ones
7	6	8
−	8	3

e
Hund	Tens	Ones
6	3	7
−	5	2

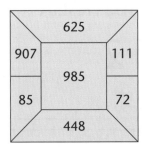

625
907   111
985
85   72
448

4 Crack this secret code by matching shapes with their numbers.

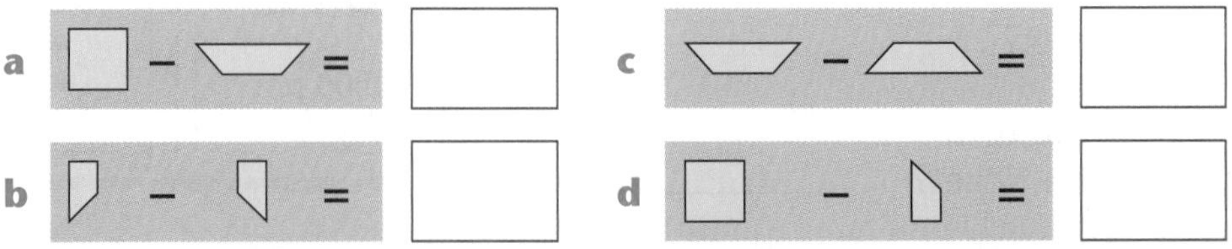

a ☐ − ▽ = ☐

c ▽ − △ = ☐

b ◺ − ◺ = ☐

d ☐ − � = ☐

Revising division facts

5 Answer the division facts.

	÷ 3
a 6	
12	
9	
18	
24	

	÷ 5
b 10	
20	
30	
45	
35	

	÷ 6
c 12	
24	
18	
30	
42	

	÷ 7
d 14	
28	
21	
35	
49	

	÷ 8
e 48	
72	
24	
56	
80	

6 Answer these division facts with remainders. The first one has been done for you.

a 25 ÷ 4 = 6 r 1

b 25 ÷ 6 = ___ r ___

c 15 ÷ 7 = ___ r ___

d 21 ÷ 4 = ___ r ___

e 30 ÷ 4 = ___ r ___

f 29 ÷ 5 = ___ r ___

g 32 ÷ 6 = ___ r ___

h 37 ÷ 7 = ___ r ___

i 45 ÷ 6 = ___ r ___

j 51 ÷ 7 = ___ r ___

k 65 ÷ 8 = ___ r ___

l 84 ÷ 9 = ___ r ___

7 Share the bag of 33 marbles.

a 33 ÷ 2 = ___ r ___

b 33 ÷ 4 = ___ r ___

c 33 ÷ 6 = ___ r ___

d 33 ÷ 5 = ___ r ___

e 33 ÷ 8 = ___ r ___

8 Make as many divisions as you can with an answer of 6.

18 ÷ 3 = 6

WMS3.3
NS3.3 Selects and applies appropriate
strategies for multiplicaiton and division
11

UNIT 3 Picture graphs

When using **picture graphs** a single symbol can represent more than one of the objects.

9 Use the key to the picture graph to answer the following questions about the animals on the farm.

Key

1 animal picture = 10 animals

a How many cows are there? _____

b How many sheep are there? _____

c How many horses and pigs are there altogether? _____

d How many goats are there? _____

e How many more horses are there than goats? _____

f Are there more than 450 animals on the farm? _____

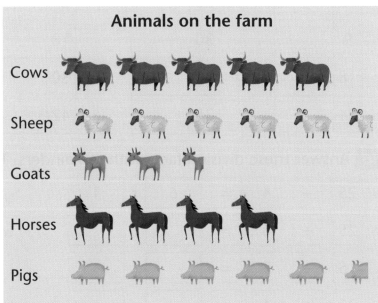

Animals on the farm

Cows

Sheep

Goats

Horses

Pigs

10 Examine the key carefully before attempting the questions.

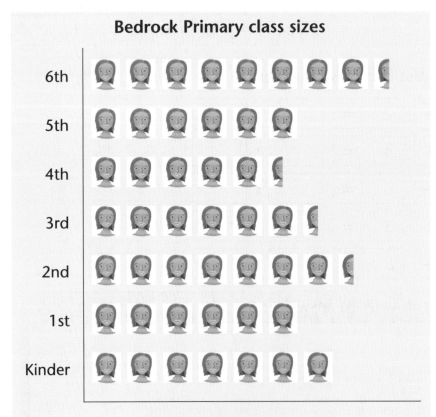

Bedrock Primary class sizes

6th
5th
4th
3rd
2nd
1st
Kinder

= 4 children

a How many children in 5th grade? _____

b How many children in kindergarten? _____

c How many children in 3rd grade? _____

d How many children in 6th grade? _____

e Which is the smallest class? _____

f Which is the largest class? _____

g Which class has 22 children? _____

h How many more children are in 2nd grade than in 5th grade? _____

i How many children in the school? _____

a   b   c   d   e   f   g

11 Which shapes above are most suitable for packing or stacking? _____

12 Explain why. _____

A base unit for measuring **volume** is the **cubic centimetre**. It is a cube measuring 1 cm long, 1 cm wide and 1 cm high. A centicube or Base 10 one are good examples of a cubic centimetre (**cm³**).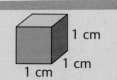

13 Use centicubes or Base 10 ones to build each prism, then record the volume of each.

a
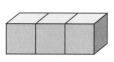
_____ cm³

b
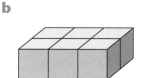
_____ cm³

c
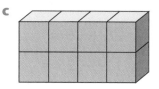
_____ cm³

d
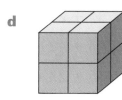
_____ cm³

e
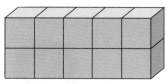
_____ cm³

f
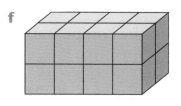
_____ cm³

g
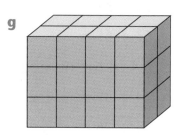
_____ cm³

h
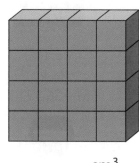
_____ cm³

i
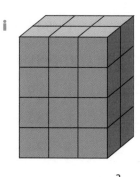
_____ cm³

j
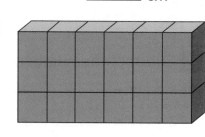
_____ cm³

14 Challenge! Linda has constructed a shape that has a volume of 24 cm³. Construct a shape of your own that has the same volume, then sketch it in the box.

MS3.3 Selects and uses the appropriate unit to estimate and measure volume and capacity, including the volume of rectangular prisms

Addition and subtraction strategies

Last year the following strategies were taught.
Use them to answer the questions on this page.

1 Use your knowledge of number facts to extend these additions and subtractions.

a 7 + 8 = _____

b 70 + 80 = _____

c 700 + 800 = _____

d 60 + 70 = _____

e 90 + 50 = _____

f 150 − 60 = _____

g 300 + 700 = _____

h 800 − 400 = _____

i 400 + 900 = _____

j 180 + 70 = _____

k 250 + 80 = _____

l 800 − 500 = _____

3 + 5 = 8,
so 30 + 50 = 80
and
300 + 500 = 800.

2 Use the jump strategy to add and subtract these numbers.

a 26 + 15 = _____

b 35 + 27 = _____

c 46 + 42 = _____

d 35 + 23 = _____

e 48 − 25 = _____

f 58 − 37 = _____

g 63 + 65 = _____

h 57 − 26 = _____

i 68 + 29 = _____

j 78 + 36 = _____

k 127 − 25 = _____

l 132 + 37 = _____

m 156 + 23 = _____

n 142 + 34 = _____

o 148 + 24 = _____

p 137 − 36 = _____

q 146 + 25 = _____

r 157 − 26 = _____

s 185 − 24 = _____

t 297 + 33 = _____

u 347 + 46 = _____

38 + 43?
Think
38 + 40 + 3 = 81.

3 Add the numbers mentally using the compensation strategy.

a 24 + 39 = _____

b 36 + 28 = _____

c 54 + 21 = _____

d 47 + 49 = _____

e 27 + 42 = _____

f 53 + 38 = _____

g 36 + 32 = _____

h 47 + 32 = _____

i 336 + 33 = _____

j 242 + 41 = _____

k 137 + 57 = _____

l 545 + 27 = _____

35 + 48?
Think
35 + 50 minus 2.

4 Subtract the numbers mentally using the compensation strategy.

a 65 − 29 = _____

b 72 − 39 = _____

c 85 − 38 = _____

d 73 − 49 = _____

e 83 − 49 = _____

f 92 − 78 = _____

g 64 − 37 = _____

h 72 − 37 = _____

i 196 − 37 = _____

j 285 − 57 = _____

k 174 − 36 = _____

l 283 − 58 = _____

64 − 29?
Think
64 − 30 + 1.

5 Use the strategies above to write addition and subtraction number sentences that have an answer of 54.

39 + 15 = 54

NS3.2 Selects and applies appropriate strategies for addition and subtraction with counting numbers of any size

WMS3.2, WMS3.1

Place value to five digits

6 Write the numbers on the place value chart. The first one has been done for you.

	Number	Ten thousands	Thousands	Hundreds	Tens	Ones
a	367			3	6	7
b	1 454					
c	25 309					
d	87 936					
e	90 235					
f	37 294					

7 Order the numbers from smallest to largest.

a	345	665	6 745	5 867	
b	3 576	567	9 453	6 987	
c	23 567	22 899	32 567	22 998	
d	45 678	54 876	45 876	49 887	
e	45 887	5 999	12 898	21 889	
f	12 335	12 553	21 335	21 553	

8 Arrange the cards to make the largest number then the smallest number using all five digits.

5 4 3 2 1 ?

	Cards	Largest number	Smallest number
a	3 7 4 5 9		
b	9 6 8 3 7		
c	1 3 2 9 8		

9 Write these numbers in words.

a 237 _____

b 1 379 _____

c 25 327 _____

d 36 000 _____

Coordinates

N
NW   NE
W   E
SW   SE
S

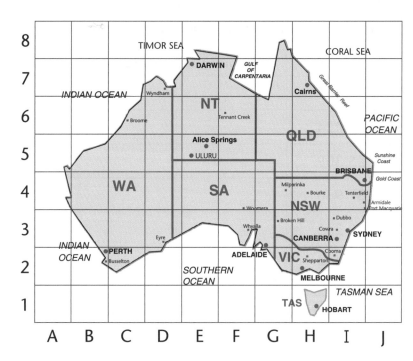

Remember! Read the
horizontal before the
vertical, for example
Broome = C6.

10 Give map coordinates for:

a Sydney _____

c Cairns _____

e Tasmania _____

b Alice Springs _____

d Whyalla _____

f Darwin _____

11 Give directions from the compass to complete these trips.

a Eyre (D3) to Wyndham (D7) _____

e Broome (C6) to Adelaide (G3) _____

b Brisbane (I4) to Port Macquarie (I3) _____

f Canberra (I3) to Milparinka (G4) _____

c Perth (B2) to Uluru (E5) _____

g Cairns (H7) to Eyre (D3) _____

d Uluru (E5) to Alice Springs (E5) _____

h Darwin (E7) to Bourke (H4) _____

Cricket Island

12 Follow the directions and
use the scale to find the
town.

Scale 1 cm = 12 km

a Start at Waugh and head
north 24 km.

b Head east 36 km before turning
north again and travelling
another 12 km.

c Head east 36 km then
north 36 km.

d What town did you find?

_____

13 Estimate the mass of each object in grams then measure them using standard masses.

	Object	Estimate	Mass
a	Pencil case		
b	Textbook		
c	Basketball		

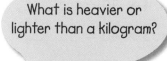
What is heavier or lighter than a kilogram?

14 Find four volunteers in your class that will allow you to measure their mass.

a Record their names, then estimate and measure their mass.

Name	Estimate	Mass

b Did your estimates improve as you worked through the exercise? _____

15 A cardboard box can hold a mass of 3 kg. How many of each item could be packed into a box of this type?

250 g   750 g   150 g   50 g

FRAGILE
Net Mass 3 kg

a ☐   b ☐   c ☐   d ☐

16 Colour code each object to match the most suitable measuring device.

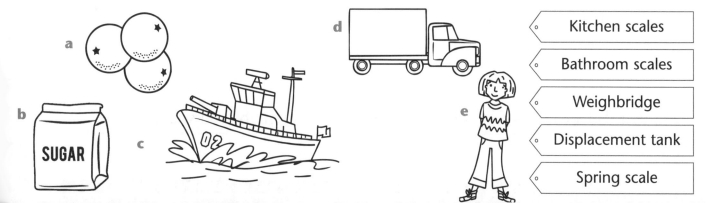

Kitchen scales

Bathroom scales

Weighbridge

Displacement tank

Spring scale

Multiplication strategies

1 Complete the multiplication facts using your knowledge of place value.

a $3 \times 30 =$ _____

b $4 \times 30 =$ _____

c $5 \times 40 =$ _____

d $6 \times 30 =$ _____

e $4 \times 60 =$ _____

f $5 \times 60 =$ _____

g $7 \times 30 =$ _____

h $4 \times 80 =$ _____

i $7 \times 40 =$ _____

j $8 \times 50 =$ _____

k $9 \times 60 =$ _____

l $7 \times 70 =$ _____

> $3 \times 5 = 15$
> So 3×5 tens $= 150$.

2 Use your knowledge of place value to multiply by tens.
For example 50×60 equals 5 tens $\times$ 6 tens which equals 30 hundreds (3 000).

a $20 \times 50 =$ _____

b $30 \times 40 =$ _____

c $40 \times 40 =$ _____

d $30 \times 50 =$ _____

e $40 \times 50 =$ _____

f $40 \times 60 =$ _____

g $60 \times 50 =$ _____

h $50 \times 50 =$ _____

i $70 \times 30 =$ _____

j $60 \times 60 =$ _____

k $40 \times 70 =$ _____

l $70 \times 70 =$ _____

m $70 \times 50 =$ _____

n $80 \times 80 =$ _____

o $80 \times 70 =$ _____

3 Mentally calculate the answers to these multiplications.

a $24 \times 4 =$ _____

b $23 \times 5 =$ _____

c $25 \times 6 =$ _____

d $13 \times 7 =$ _____

e $17 \times 8 =$ _____

f $19 \times 6 =$ _____

g $18 \times 7 =$ _____

h $34 \times 4 =$ _____

i $36 \times 4 =$ _____

j $34 \times 6 =$ _____

k $38 \times 4 =$ _____

l $43 \times 5 =$ _____

> 23×4?
> Think 4×20
> plus 4×3.

 $26

 $30

 $60

 $46

 $40

4 Use mental computation skills to solve the problems.

a Mary bought 6 CDs. How much did she spend? _____

b Thomas bought 3 telephones. How much did he spend? _____

c Sarah bought 5 shirts. How much did she spend? _____

d How much would 5 books cost? _____

e How much would 4 pairs of jeans cost? _____

5 If you had $150 to spend on the above items how might you spend it?

NS3.3 Selects and applies appropriate
strategies for multiplication and division   WMS3.3, WMS3.2

6 Discuss with a friend what strategies you would use to solve these problems. Solve them, then check your solutions with other groups in the class.

	Problem		Strategies	Answer
a	A farmer planted 78 trees in 6 paddocks. If the trees were shared equally, how many trees would there be in each paddock?			
b	A teacher shared 96 counters among 6 children. How many did each child receive?	96		
c	Mrs Cook bought 5 tins of beans for 79c per can and a can of dog food for 96c. How much did she spend on her purchases?			
d	Samuel saved $35 per week for 9 weeks from his weekly wages. How much did he save altogether?			
e	Mr Hill planted 100 flowers but only $\frac{3}{4}$ of them sprouted. How many flowers sprouted?			
f	A bicycle wheel has a circumference of 2 m. How many times will it need to turn to cover a distance of 528 m?			
g	The cake stall collected $296 at the fete. If $20 was spent hiring a tent and $70 was spent on ingredients, what was the cake stall profit?			
j	The cost of a camp was $40 per child plus $15 each for the bus. How much money did the teacher collect from 30 students?			

7 Think about the strategies you used to solve question 6g and write another method you could use in the future to solve a problem like it.

WMS3.2 Selects and applies appropriate problem solving strategies, including technological applications, in undertaking investigations

19

Chance experiments

8 **Dice rolling experiment**.

a If you rolled two dice and totalled the scores what do you think would be the most common score? _____

b Roll two dice 40 times, recording the total of each roll in the table below.

Total	Tally	Frequency	Total	Tally	Frequency
2			8		
3			9		
4			10		
5			11		
6			12		
7					

c Which total was most frequent? _____   d Which total was least frequent? _____

9 Use the data in the table above to order the scores from least to most.

_____

10 Do you think 7 would usually be rolled more than 12? _____

11 Explain why. _____

_____

12 Mr Craig put 30 of his favourite coloured rainbow ball lollies in a bag.

a How many of each lolly are there?

 R _____  Y _____ G _____ O _____

b Which is the most likely colour to be drawn out of the bag? _____

c How would you describe the chance of red being drawn out of the bag? _____

d Which is the least likely colour to be drawn out of the bag? _____

e Is it more likely that an orange lolly would be drawn than a green one? _____

f Is it more likely that a yellow lolly would be drawn than a green one? _____

Prisms have two bases that are the same shape and size. All other faces on a prism are rectangular. Prisms are named from the shape of their bases.

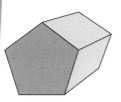

Pentagonal prism

Pyramids have only one base with all other faces being triangles. The triangular faces meet at a common apex. Pyramids are named from the shape of their bases.

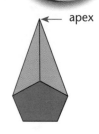

apex

Pentagonal pyramid

13 Draw a line to join each object to its name.

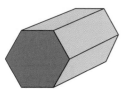

rectangular prism
rectangular pyramid
square pyramid
triangular pyramid
cube
hexagonal prism
triangular prism
pentagonal prism
pentagonal pyramid
octagonal prism
hexagonal pyramid
octagonal pyramid

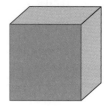

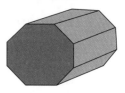

WMS3.3,
WMS3.2
SGS3.1 Identifies three-dimensional objects, including particular prisms and pyramids, on the basis of their properties, and visualises, sketches and constructs them given drawings of different views

21

Revising 2-digit division

Another way of recording division is by using the division symbol.   ÷

$$\frac{4}{3\overline{)12}} \text{ means } 12 ÷ 3 = 4$$

1 Complete these division facts.

a 3⟌15   b 4⟌20   c 5⟌25   d 6⟌24   e 7⟌49

f 4⟌12   g 3⟌18   h 6⟌30   i 7⟌42   j 8⟌64

k 5⟌15   l 4⟌28   m 5⟌45   n 8⟌40   o 9⟌72

An example of division that leaves a **remainder**:
Tina wanted to share 26 icy-pole sticks among 5 people. She knows that it will not work out equally and that there must be a remainder.

$$\frac{5 \text{ r}1}{5\overline{)26}}$$

26 shared among 5 people gives 5 to each person and 1 left over (remainder 1).

2 Solve these dvisions that have remainders. The first one is done for you.

a $\frac{5 \text{ r}1}{3\overline{)16}}$ b 3⟌22   c 7⟌45   d 8⟌45   e 6⟌44

f 4⟌18   g 4⟌34   h 6⟌45   i 9⟌47   j 7⟌52

k 5⟌22   l 5⟌33   m 7⟌50   n 8⟌43   o 8⟌50

3 There are 72 children in Year 6 who need to be transported to the Sports Carnival.

How many trips would each vehicle below make if it was the only vehicle available to transport the children? (Working paper needed.)

 a [trips]

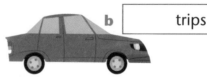 b [trips]

3 passengers

4 passengers

 c [trips]

 d [trips]

5 passengers

12 passengers

4 How many trips would the whole fleet of vehicles need to make if they transported the children together?   [trips]

5 Continue the number patterns.

a 15 20 25 30 ☐ ☐ ☐   e 536 532 528 524 ☐ ☐ ☐

b 12 16 20 24 ☐ ☐ ☐   f 213 227 241 255 ☐ ☐ ☐

c 4 7 10 13 ☐ ☐ ☐   g 3 6 12 24 ☐ ☐ ☐

d 5 12 19 26 ☐ ☐ ☐   h 198 191 184 177 ☐ ☐ ☐

6 Write a rule for each number pattern, then use it to predict the next two terms in the pattern.

You must look closely at the previous terms in the pattern.

	Rule	Pattern						
a		43	40	37	34	31		
b		53	57	61	65	69		
c		3.5	4	4.5	5	5.5		
d		1	2	4	8	16		
e		128	64	32	16	8		
f		1	3	9	27	81		
g		1	2	4	7	11		
h		1	1	2	3	5		

7 Continue to make the pattern of square numbers and record the numbers.

4   9   16   ☐   ☐   ☐

8 Look for a rule or a pattern in the square numbers then extend the table to the twelfth square number.

Square numbers 4 9 16 ☐ ☐ ☐ ☐ ☐ ☐ ☐ ☐ ☐

WMS3.4, WMS3.5

PAS3.1a Records, analyses and describes geometric and number patterns that involve one operation using tables and words

23

9 Make and interpret a column graph based on these monthly rainfall figures for a city.

January	47 mm	April	53 mm	July	49 mm	October	65 mm
February	46 mm	May	68 mm	August	57 mm	November	57 mm
March	44 mm	June	43 mm	September	53 mm	December	58 mm

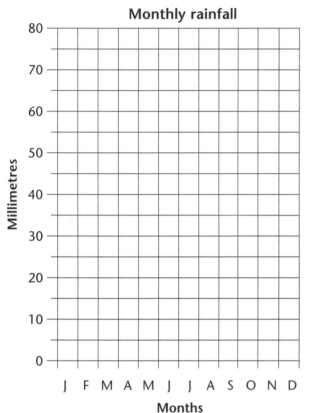

Monthly rainfall

Millimetres / Months

a Plot the information on the column graph.

b What is the difference between the highest and lowest rainfall? _____

c Which winter month has the lowest rainfall? _____

d Which summer month has the lowest rainfall? _____

e How much rain fell in October, November and December? _____

f How much rain fell in autumn? _____

g Which months would be good for overseas visitors to visit this destination? _____

10 This map shows the average maximum temperature in January for Australian capital cities (to the nearest 0.5°C). Record this information on the column graph.

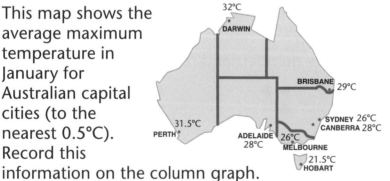

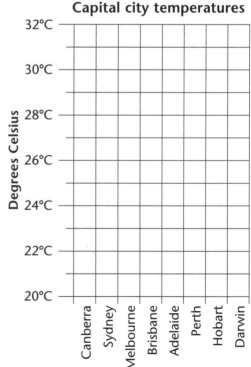

Capital city temperatures

Degrees Celsius

Canberra, Sydney, Melbourne, Brisbane, Adelaide, Perth, Hobart, Darwin

a Which city is the warmest? _____

b Which city is the coolest? _____

c What is the difference between the highest and the lowest temperatures shown? _____

d Which are the two hottest cities? _____

e Which cities share the same average temperatures?

_____

am and pm time

am is an abbreviation for *ante meridiem* which means "before midday".
pm is an abbreviation for *post meridiem* which means "after midday".

11 Write a digital label for each clock using "am and pm" notation.

a morning	b morning	c morning	d evening

1:30 am	:	:	:

e afternoon	f evening	g morning	h evening

:	:	:	:

i afternoon	j evening	k morning	l evening

:	:	:	:

12 Order these times from earliest to latest in the day.

a	3:00 pm	3:00 am	6:00 pm	
b	8:30 am	8:27 am	9:03 pm	
c	2:06 am	2:03 pm	1:15 am	
d	8:34 pm	7:36 pm	7:15 am	
e	7:51 am	7:52 pm	7:53 am	

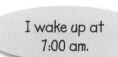

I wake up at 7:00 am.

13 Solve these problems.

a What time is 25 minutes after 3:10 am? _____

b What time is 23 minutes after 4:30 am? _____

c What time is 20 minutes after 11:50 am? _____

Two digits multiplied by one digit

Hund	Tens	Ones
	¹3	5
×		3
1	0	5

3 × 5 = 15 ones
Write 5 in the ones column and trade 10 ones for 1 ten and write the 1 in the tens column.
3 × 3 tens equals 9 tens plus 1 ten which equals 10 tens.
Write the 0 in the tens column and the 1 in the hundreds.

1 Solve each multiplication using the shortened form.

a
Hund	Tens	Ones
	2	7
×		3

b
Hund	Tens	Ones
	2	3
×		4

c
Hund	Tens	Ones
	2	9
×		3

d
Hund	Tens	Ones
	3	7
×		5

e
Hund	Tens	Ones
	4	6
×		4

f
Hund	Tens	Ones
	6	3
×		4

g
Hund	Tens	Ones
	4	8
×		5

h
Hund	Tens	Ones
	7	4
×		6

i
Hund	Tens	Ones
	2	9
×		7

j
Hund	Tens	Ones
	6	3
×		8

k
Hund	Tens	Ones
	5	6
×		6

l
Hund	Tens	Ones
	4	9
×		8

m
Hund	Tens	Ones
	2	8
×		7

n
Hund	Tens	Ones
	4	6
×		5

o
Hund	Tens	Ones
	6	4
×		4

2 Solve these problems.

a The pilot usually completes 29 flights each month. How many flights will she complete in 9 months?

b How many sultanas are there if there are 7 packs with 52 sultanas in each pack?

c The average mass of each netball player in the squad is 68 kg. What is the total mass of the 9 members of the team?

3 Multiply 45 by any number so that the product is a number between 120 and 370.

NS3.3 Selects and applies appropriate strategies for multiplication and division

WMS3.2

Fractions can name part of a group.

$\frac{1}{3}$ of 6 girls = 2 girls

4 Find the fraction of each group.

a $\frac{1}{3}$ of 12 = ____   e $\frac{1}{6}$ of 18 = ____   i $\frac{1}{3}$ of 27 = ____   m $\frac{1}{12}$ of 36 = ____   q $\frac{1}{6}$ of 60 = ____

b $\frac{1}{3}$ of 24 = ____   f $\frac{1}{3}$ of 21 = ____   j $\frac{1}{3}$ of 60 = ____   n $\frac{1}{6}$ of 24 = ____   r $\frac{1}{6}$ of 54 = ____

c $\frac{1}{3}$ of 18 = ____   g $\frac{1}{6}$ of 30 = ____   k $\frac{1}{3}$ of 15 = ____   o $\frac{1}{3}$ of 30 = ____   s $\frac{1}{12}$ of 72 = ____

d $\frac{1}{6}$ of 12 = ____   h $\frac{1}{12}$ of 24 = ____   l $\frac{1}{6}$ of 36 = ____   p $\frac{1}{12}$ of 60 = ____   t $\frac{1}{3}$ of 90 = ____

5 Use the array to find these fractions of the group of 48.

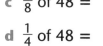

a $\frac{1}{3}$ of 48 =

b $\frac{1}{6}$ of 48 =

c $\frac{1}{8}$ of 48 =

d $\frac{1}{4}$ of 48 =

$\frac{1}{2}$ of 48 = 24

6 Solve these problems.

a There were 3 dozen cakes on a tray until Jana tripped on a loose tile and spilt $\frac{1}{4}$ of them. How many did she spill?

c $\frac{1}{12}$ of the 96 seats in the restaurant were reserved for Tim's birthday party. How many were reserved for Tim's party?

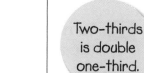

Two-thirds is double one-third.

b Jackson had 60 cents to spend. How much was the ice cream he bought if it was equal to $\frac{1}{3}$ of his money?

d Our family had 48 raffle tickets to sell. How many did Aunty Donna buy if she bought $\frac{1}{6}$ of them?

7 Can you solve these?

a If $\frac{1}{3}$ of a group is worth 5 what would $\frac{2}{3}$ of the group be worth?

b If $\frac{1}{6}$ of a group is worth 2 what would $\frac{3}{6}$ of the group be worth?

8 Answer these questions about the protractor.

a Complete the degrees on the protractor. You'll need to look closely at a protractor to do this.

b Why do you think the numbers go both ways?

_____

_____

_____

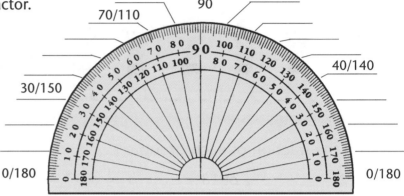

70/110   90

30/150

0/180   40/140

0/180

9 Name each angle and then write its size in degrees.

a
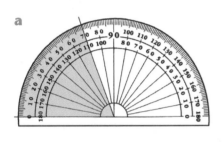

_____

b
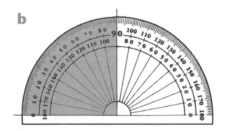

_____

c
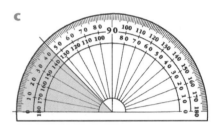

_____

d
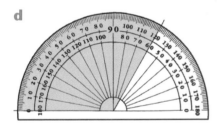

_____

e
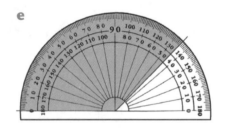

_____

f
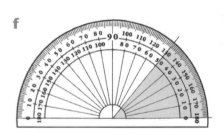

_____

10 To measure these angles, place the base-line of a protractor along the lower arm of the angle, and place the centre point of the protractor on the vertex of the angle.

a
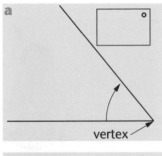
vertex

b
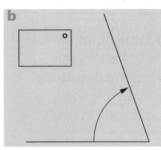

c
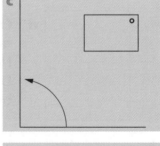

d
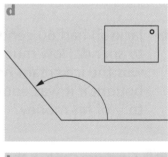

e
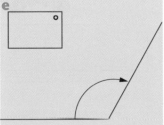

f
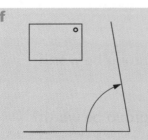

g
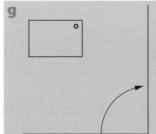

h
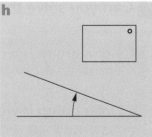

Metres to kilometres

> To convert **metres** to **kilometres** divide by 1 000.

To change
metres to
kilometres,
I divide by 1 000.

11 Use a calculator to convert the metres to kilometres. Your calculator will express some measurements as decimals. The first one is done for you.

Metres	1 525	2 399	3 514	4 786	2 905	4 567	2 063	2 560
Kilometres	1.525							

12 Which distance above is closest to 3 km? _____

> To convert **kilometres** to **metres** multiply by 1 000.

To change
kilometres into
metres, I multiply
by 1 000.

13 Convert these measurements from kilometres into metres without the use of a calculator. Then use a calculator to check.

Kilometres	3.505	2.459	8.355	7.684	9.502	6.349	82	35
Metres	3 505							

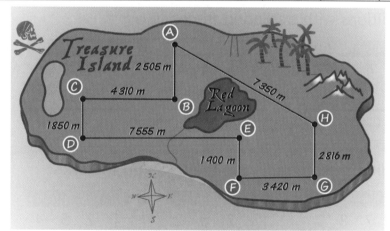

Treasure Island 2 505 m
4 310 m
7 350 m
Red Lagoon
1 850 m
7 555 m
1 900 m
2 816 m
3 420 m

14 Calculate the distances between towns in metres, then convert the metres into kilometres.

	Distance	Metres	Kilometres
a	A to B to C		
b	C to D to E		
c	E to F to G		

	Distance	Metres	Kilometres
d	H to G to F		
e	F to E to D		
f	D to C to B to A		

15 Name a journey longer than 13 km.

4-digit addition with trading

Learning to trade in an addition sum

Process

5 thousand plus 3 thousand plus 1 thousand equals 9 thousand.

Thou	Hund	Tens	Ones
¹3	4	¹3	3
+ 5	9	1	9
9	3	5	2

9 ones plus 3 ones equals 12 ones. Exchange 10 ones for 1 ten. Record 2 in the ones column.

Add 9 hundreds to 4 hundreds = 13 hundreds. Exchange 10 hundreds for 1 thousand. Record the 3 in the hundreds column.

Add 1 ten + 3 tens plus 1 ten equals 5 tens.

1 Complete these additions without trading.

a
Thou	Hund	Tens	Ones
3	2	4	2
+ 5	4	4	7

b
Thou	Hund	Tens	Ones
1	2	3	4
+ 3	4	5	4

c
Thou	Hund	Tens	Ones
5	6	7	8
+ 4	2	1	0

d
Thou	Hund	Tens	Ones
6	7	8	9
+	2	1	0

e
Thou	Hund	Tens	Ones
6	0	3	4
+ 1	5	5	5

2 Complete these additions with trading in the ones.

a
Thou	Hund	Tens	Ones
3	0	6	4
+ 2	3	0	6

b
Thou	Hund	Tens	Ones
4	4	4	8
+ 2	3	4	5

c
Thou	Hund	Tens	Ones
3	5	4	7
+ 2	3	3	6

d
Thou	Hund	Tens	Ones
3	0	0	6
+ 4	0	7	6

e
Thou	Hund	Tens	Ones
5	4	3	2
+ 3	5	4	9

3 Complete these additions with trading in the tens and the ones.

a
Thou	Hund	Tens	Ones
3	5	6	0
+ 2	0	7	4

b
Thou	Hund	Tens	Ones
3	7	8	2
+ 2	0	6	4

c
Thou	Hund	Tens	Ones
3	7	6	2
+ 5	0	6	8

d
Thou	Hund	Tens	Ones
1	2	5	4
+ 5	2	8	6

e
Thou	Hund	Tens	Ones
2	3	4	5
+ 6	3	9	8

Thou	Hund	Tens	Ones
5	5	4	4
+ 4	7	3	3
9	2	7	7

4 Mark did this question and got it wrong. Explain what he did wrong.

_____

_____

5 Write a problem to describe the number sentence: 2 357 + 1 329 =

NS3.2 Selects and applies appropriate strategies for addition and subtraction with counting numbers of any size

WMS3.1, WMS3.2, WMS3.4

6 Solve each number sentence by finding the missing numbers.

a 3 + ☐ = 11   f 3 × ☐ = 27   k 3 × 5 + ☐ = 19

b 20 − ☐ = 13   g 10 × ☐ = 30   l 6 × 3 + ☐ = 30

c 27 + ☐ = 40   h 16 ÷ ☐ = 4   m 5 × ☐ + 6 = 26

d 30 − ☐ = 15   i 42 ÷ ☐ = 7   n 6 × ☐ − 5 = 25

e 35 − ☐ = 20   j 6 × ☐ = 54   o 7 × ☐ + 9 = 58

7 Given the value of the triangle in each group, find the value of all the other shapes. Write their values on them, then complete the number sentences.

△ = 7   △ = 5

a  = 15

 = 17

△ + ☐ + ○ = _____

b   = 35

 = 42

37 − ☐ = _____

42 − ☐ = _____

(△ + ○) × ☐ = _____

Mmmmmm!

8 Solve these equations expressed in words.

a Seventeen oranges plus 8 oranges minus 6 oranges = _____ oranges

b Twenty dollars plus $27 plus $30 = $ _____

c Nine dollars times 6 plus $16 = $ _____

d Thirty-five books shared among five children = _____ books

9 Challenge! Use the numbers 4, 5 and 6 in each equation to obtain the answer.

a ☐ × ☐ + ☐ = 26   c ☐ × ☐ + ☐ = 29

b ☐ × ☐ + ☐ = 34   d ☐ × ☐ − ☐ = 19

10 Create and solve a long equation of your own.

☐ ☐ ☐ ☐ ☐ ☐ ☐ ☐ ☐ ☐ = ☐

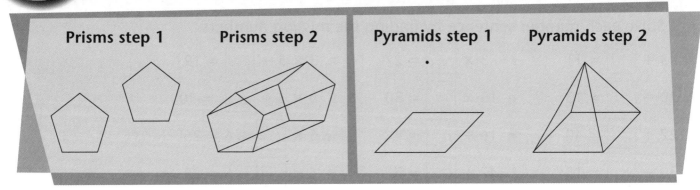

| Prisms step 1 | Prisms step 2 | Pyramids step 1 | Pyramids step 2 |

11 Trace the bases of the objects before joining their corners.

a

b
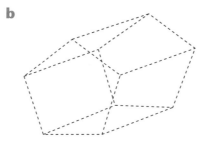

c
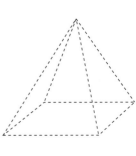

d
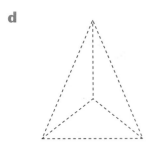

e
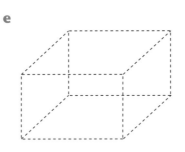

f
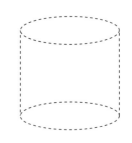

12 Put dotted lines in the following drawings to show the hidden detail (faces, edges and vertices). The first one has been done for you.

a
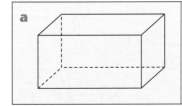

b
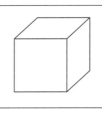

c
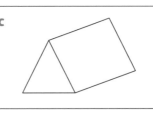

d
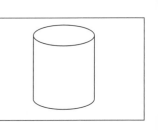

13 Study the objects, then use a ruler and a pencil to draw them. Always draw lightly first, then firmly later, so trial and error mistakes don't show.

a
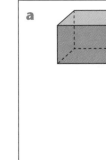

b

c
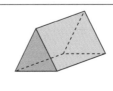

d
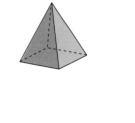

SGS3.1 Identifies three-dimensional objects, including particular prisms and pyramids, on the basis of their properties, and visualises, sketches and constructs them given drawings of different views
WMS3.3

14 The number of cars that used a major city car park during one week were recorded, then the information was graphed on a picture graph to analyse the results.

Cars in car park

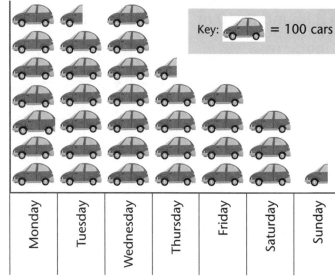

Key: 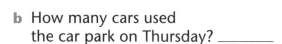 = 100 cars

a On which days was the car park used the most?

_____

b How many cars used the car park on Thursday? _____

c How many cars were in the car park on Tuesday? _____

d If the owners of the car park couldn't afford to open on 7 days, which day could they close?

_____

e How many more cars were in the car park on Wednesday than on Sunday? _____

f How many cars used the car park in the week? _____

Monday Tuesday Wednesday Thursday Friday Saturday Sunday

15 Name another scale that could be used for this data.

 = _____ cars

16 Design a picture graph to display the data presented in the column graph.

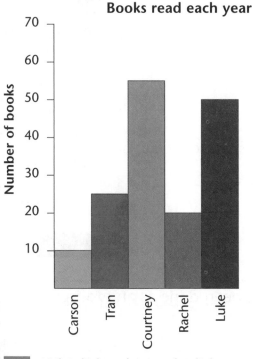

Books read each year

Number of books

70
60
50
40
30
20
10

Carson Tran Courtney Rachel Luke

Key: _____ = _____ books

17 Which book graph did you prefer? Why? _____

_____

Division strategies

We can use **rounding** to the nearest 10 or 100 to estimate division,
e.g. 492 ÷ 5:   492 is almost 500, so the answer is about 100.   (500 ÷ 5 = 100)

1 Round to 10 or 100 to estimate an answer to each division.

a 99 ÷ 10 ≈ _____	f 41 ÷ 8 ≈ _____	k 499 ÷ 10 ≈ _____
b 62 ÷ 6 ≈ _____	g 41 ÷ 5 ≈ _____	l 207 ÷ 4 ≈ _____
c 29 ÷ 6 ≈ _____	h 82 ÷ 8 ≈ _____	m 212 ÷ 5 ≈ _____
d 39 ÷ 5 ≈ _____	i 399 ÷ 4 ≈ _____	n 313 ÷ 6 ≈ _____
e 22 ÷ 4 ≈ _____	j 199 ÷ 2 ≈ _____	o 293 ÷ 5 ≈ _____

≈ means approximately equal to.

We know that 63 ÷ 7 = 9, so 630 ÷ 7 must equal 90.

150 ÷ 3 = ?
Think 15 ÷ 3 = 5
so 150 ÷ 3 = 50.

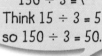

2 Extend these division facts.

a 9 ÷ 3 = _____	e 80 ÷ 4 = _____	i 240 ÷ 4 = _____
b 90 ÷ 3 = _____	f 800 ÷ 4 = _____	j 360 ÷ 6 = _____
c 900 ÷ 3 = _____	g 150 ÷ 5 = _____	k 420 ÷ 7 = _____
d 8 ÷ 4 = _____	h 160 ÷ 4 = _____	l 350 ÷ 5 = _____

36 ÷ 4 = ?
Think $\frac{1}{2}$ of 36 = 18.
$\frac{1}{2}$ of 18 = 9

3 Use the halve and halve again strategy to divide by 4.

a 24 ÷ 4 = _____	e 60 ÷ 4 = _____	i 200 ÷ 4 = _____
b 32 ÷ 4 = _____	f 80 ÷ 4 = _____	j 240 ÷ 4 = _____
c 40 ÷ 4 = _____	g 76 ÷ 4 = _____	k 180 ÷ 4 = _____
d 48 ÷ 4 = _____	h 120 ÷ 4 = _____	l 220 ÷ 4 = _____

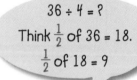

48 ÷ 8 = ?
Think $\frac{1}{2}$ of 48 = 24.
$\frac{1}{2}$ of 24 = 12
$\frac{1}{2}$ of 12 = 6

4 Use the halve, halve again and halve again strategy to divide by 8.

a 40 ÷ 8 = _____	d 80 ÷ 8 = _____	g 240 ÷ 8 = _____
b 32 ÷ 8 = _____	e 120 ÷ 8 = _____	h 320 ÷ 8 = _____
c 64 ÷ 8 = _____	f 200 ÷ 8 = _____	i 480 ÷ 8 = _____

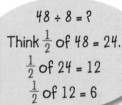

5 Create your own number sentences. The first one has been done as an example.

a 24 ÷ 4 = 12 ÷ 2	c 64 ÷ 4 = ⬚	e 80 ÷ 8 = ⬚
b 80 ÷ 4 = ⬚	d 160 ÷ 4 = ⬚	f 128 ÷ 8 = ⬚

 NS3.3 Selects and applies appropriate
strategies for multiplication and division

PAS3.1A, WMS3.3, WMS3.2

Equivalent thirds, sixths and twelfths

UNIT **9**

Equivalent fractions

1 Whole												Whole
					$\frac{1}{2}$						$\frac{2}{2}$	Halves
		$\frac{1}{4}$			$\frac{2}{4}$			$\frac{3}{4}$			$\frac{4}{4}$	Quarters
			$\frac{1}{3}$				$\frac{2}{3}$				$\frac{3}{3}$	Thirds
	$\frac{1}{6}$		$\frac{2}{6}$		$\frac{3}{6}$		$\frac{4}{6}$		$\frac{5}{6}$		$\frac{6}{6}$	Sixths
$\frac{1}{12}$	$\frac{2}{12}$	$\frac{3}{12}$	$\frac{4}{12}$	$\frac{5}{12}$	$\frac{6}{12}$	$\frac{7}{12}$	$\frac{8}{12}$	$\frac{9}{12}$	$\frac{10}{12}$	$\frac{11}{12}$	$\frac{12}{12}$	Twelfths

6 Use the fraction grid to write an equivalent fraction for each fraction given below. The first one is done for you.

a $\frac{1}{2} = \frac{3}{6}$ d $\frac{1}{4} = \frac{}{12}$ g $\frac{2}{3} = \frac{}{12}$ j $\frac{4}{6} = \frac{}{12}$ m $1 = \frac{}{6}$

b $\frac{1}{2} = \frac{}{12}$ e $\frac{1}{3} = \frac{}{12}$ h $\frac{4}{6} = \frac{}{3}$ k $\frac{3}{4} = \frac{}{12}$ n $1 = \frac{}{12}$

c $\frac{1}{3} = \frac{}{6}$ f $\frac{2}{3} = \frac{}{6}$ i $\frac{2}{6} = \frac{}{12}$ l $1 = \frac{}{3}$ o $\frac{12}{12} = \frac{}{4}$

7 Use the greater than, less than, or equals symbols to make each number sentence true.

The three symbols are:
> greater than,
< less than and
= equals.

a $\frac{1}{2}$ > $\frac{1}{3}$ e $\frac{1}{4}$ ☐ $\frac{1}{3}$ i $\frac{9}{12}$ ☐ $\frac{3}{4}$

b $\frac{1}{2}$ ☐ $\frac{1}{12}$ f $\frac{3}{4}$ ☐ $\frac{1}{2}$ j $\frac{5}{6}$ ☐ $\frac{9}{12}$

c $\frac{1}{3}$ ☐ $\frac{1}{6}$ g $\frac{3}{4}$ ☐ $\frac{2}{3}$ k $\frac{3}{12}$ ☐ $\frac{1}{4}$

d $\frac{1}{12}$ ☐ $\frac{1}{6}$ h $\frac{2}{3}$ ☐ $\frac{5}{6}$ l $\frac{2}{3}$ ☐ $\frac{11}{12}$

8 Grandad decided to share 36 of his old football cards with his four grandchildren. Tom received $\frac{1}{12}$ of the set, Millie received $\frac{1}{3}$ and Jessica received $\frac{1}{6}$. George received what was left.

a How many did Tom receive? _____

b How many did Millie receive? _____

c How many did Jessica receive? _____

d How many did George receive? _____

Classifying 3D objects

Faces are the surfaces that make up a 3D object. A cube has six faces.

An edge is where two faces meet or intersect. Edges can be straight or curved.

A vertex is where two or more lines meet to form an angle or a corner.

The plural of vertex is vertices.

9 Use the words "face", "edge" or "vertex" to label each set of arrows.

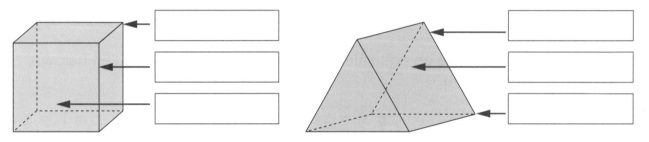

10 Give a clear description of each 3D shape by recording its properties. Remember pyramids are named from their bases.

	Shape	Name	Faces	Edges	Vertices
a					
b					
c					
d					
e					
f					
g					

A triangular pyramid has 4 faces, 6 edges and 4 vertices.

SGS3.1 Identifies three-dimensional objects, including particular prisms and pyramids, on the basis of their properties, and visualises, sketches and constructs them given drawings of different views

WMS3.2

11 What is the most common vowel?

a Choose any paragraph from something you can read and make a tally of the number of times each vowel appears in that paragraph.

Stop when one vowel reaches 30.

Vowel	Tally	Frequency
A		
E		
I		
O		
U		

b Which vowel occurred the least? _____

c Which vowel occurred the most? _____

d How many words did not contain a vowel? _____

e Construct a column graph of the data you have collected.

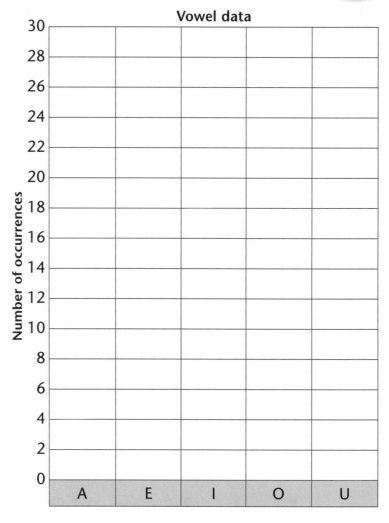

Vowel data

12 Making a column graph.

a Construct a column graph on the graph paper to record the number of people attending Dr Know's surgery for sports injuries.
The number of patients is recorded in the table below.

You will need to work out a scale for the vertical axis of the graph, before you can start.

Month	Dec	Jan	Feb	Mar	Apr
Patients	14	16	24	28	30

b Which month was the worst for sports injuries? _____

c Which month had the least number of sports injuries recorded? _____

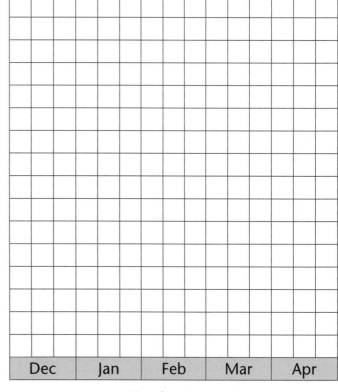

Sports injuries

Months

Diagnostic review 1

PART 1   NS3.1

a Make the largest number you can from the digits: 7, 2, 5, 6, 3

b Write 63 125 in words. _____

_____

c Arrange the following numbers in order of size, from the smallest to the largest.

167 412   617 412   716 241   617 241

PART 2   NS3.2

Answer these questions.

a
```
  2 3 4
+   5 4 8
_____
```

b
```
  2 7 3 7
+   4 6 8 4
_____
```

c
```
  5 4 . 9
-   3 6 . 5
_____
```

d
```
  3 5 2
-     5 1
_____
```

e
```
  6 8 5
-     7 4
_____
```

f
```
  7 4 3
-     4 0
_____
```

g 496 children belong to the softball club. If 324 are girls, how many are boys?

_____ boys

Use any strategy to solve these additions and subtractions.

h 94 − 35 = _____   **j** 89 − 42 = _____

i 125 + 47 = _____   **k** 181 − 39 = _____

PART 3   NS3.4

Shade the fractions.

a $\frac{1}{3}$

b $\frac{5}{6}$

c $\frac{3}{6}$

d $\frac{7}{12}$

Find the fraction of each collection.

e $\frac{1}{3}$ of 12 = _____   **h** $\frac{2}{3}$ of 9 = _____

f $\frac{1}{6}$ of 18 = _____   **i** $\frac{2}{3}$ of 15 = _____

g $\frac{1}{12}$ of 24 = _____   **j** $\frac{5}{6}$ of 12 = _____

PART 4   NS3.3

Complete the grid and questions.

×	2	3	5	7	6	8	9
a 5							
b 7							
c 8							

d 24 ÷ 4 = ☐   **h** 32 ÷ 5 = ☐

e 30 ÷ 5 = ☐   **i** 47 ÷ 5 = ☐

f 36 ÷ 6 = ☐   **j** 8 × 40 = ☐

g 42 ÷ 7 = ☐   **k** 30 × 20 = ☐

l $5\overline{)45}$ **m** $5\overline{)27}$ **n** $6\overline{)45}$

o
```
  6 4
×   4
_____
```

p
```
  7 5
×   5
_____
```

q
```
  3 6
×   6
_____
```

PART 5   PAS3.1b–1a

Find the missing numbers.

a 17 + ☐ = 40   **c** ☐ × 7 = 42

b 5 × ☐ = 45   **d** ☐ × 7 = 49

Complete the patterns.

e

27	30	33	36		

f

147	152	157	162		

g

1	2	4	8		

Diagnostic review 1

PART 6
SGS3.2b

Use the words "acute", "obtuse" and "right" to name the angles.

a **b** **c**

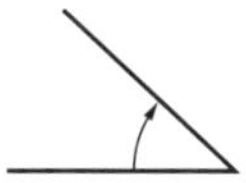

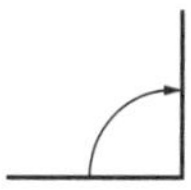

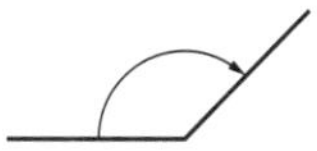

_____   _____   _____

PART 7
SGS3.2a

Draw a line to match each shape to its name.

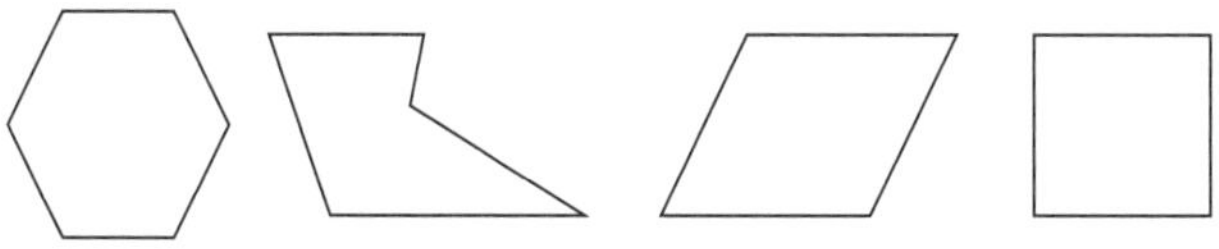

| pentagon | hexagon | square | parallelogram |

PART 8
SGS3.1

Answer these questions.

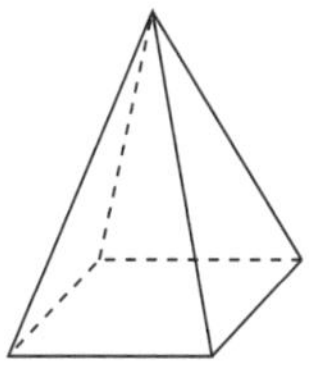

a How many edges does this object have? _____

b How many vertices does it have? _____

c How many faces does it have? _____

d Name this object. _____

PART 9
SGS3.3

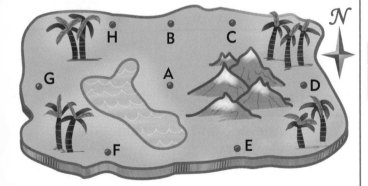

What direction are these letters from A?

a B _____   **d** F _____

b C _____   **e** G _____

c D _____   **f** E _____

PART 10
MS3.5

Write digital times in "am and pm" notation for these clocks.

morning   evening    morning

a   **b**   **c**

PART 11
MS3.2

Draw a rectangle with an area of 8 cm^2.

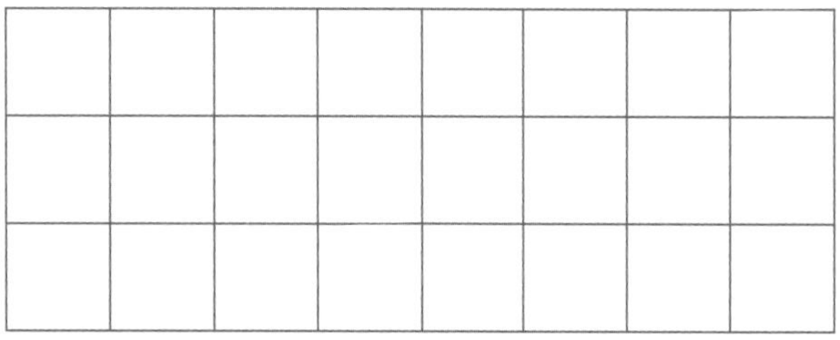

PART 12
MS3.3

Calculate the volume of each object made from 1 cm cubes.

b

a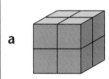

_____ cm^3 _____ cm^3

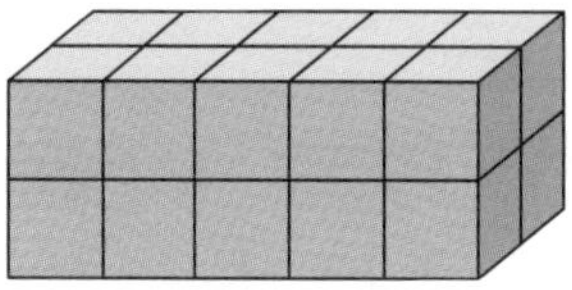

PART 13
DS3.1

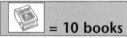 = 10 books

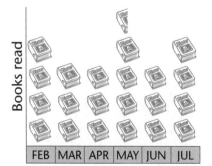

a How many books were read in March? _____

b How many books were read in May? _____

4-digit subtraction

Learning to trade in a subtraction

2 thousands from 5 thousands equals 3 thousands.

Thou	Hund	Tens	Ones
5 6	1 2	4 5	1 3
− 2	4	2	4
3	8	2	9

4 ones from 3 ones can't be done. Trade a ten from the tens column to the ones column to make 13 ones. 5 tens becomes 4 tens. 4 ones from 13 ones equals 9 ones.

4 hundreds from 2 hundreds can't be done, so trade a thousand from the thousands column to make 12 hundreds. 6 thousand becomes 5 thousand. 4 hundreds from 12 hundreds equals 8 hundreds.

Subtract 2 tens from 4 tens equals 2 tens.

1 Complete these subtractions with trading in the ones.

a
Thou	Hund	Tens	Ones
6	9	5	4
− 4	0	0	7

b
Thou	Hund	Tens	Ones
7	4	3	5
− 3	0	0	7

c
Thou	Hund	Tens	Ones
9	6	7	2
− 6	5	4	8

d
Thou	Hund	Tens	Ones
8	9	3	3
− 5	3	2	5

e
Thou	Hund	Tens	Ones
5	5	5	2
− 4	3	2	4

2 Complete these subtractions with trading in the tens or ones.

a
Thou	Hund	Tens	Ones
5	4	5	8
− 4	2	7	6

b
Thou	Hund	Tens	Ones
3	5	8	4
− 3	4	4	6

c
Thou	Hund	Tens	Ones
7	8	3	7
− 6	5	5	6

d
Thou	Hund	Tens	Ones
8	5	6	4
− 7	2	8	6

e
Thou	Hund	Tens	Ones
4	4	8	3
− 2	1	2	8

f
Thou	Hund	Tens	Ones
6	4	2	3
− 2	1	6	6

g
Thou	Hund	Tens	Ones
7	5	3	4
− 2	3	8	6

h
Thou	Hund	Tens	Ones
8	6	2	3
− 3	4	6	4

i
Thou	Hund	Tens	Ones
7	5	5	2
−	3	6	6

j
Thou	Hund	Tens	Ones
6	6	4	4
−	2	2	6

From Sydney

CANBERRA 284 km
MELBOURNE 869 km
ADELAIDE 1422 km
KALGOORLIE 3440 km
PERTH 3967 km
BROOME 5280 km

3 Calculate the distances between:

a Melbourne and Canberra	b Adelaide and Canberra	c Kalgoorlie and Adelaide
d Perth and Melbourne	e Perth and Canberra	f Broome and Perth

NS3.2 Selects and applies appropriate strategies for addition and subtraction with counting numbers of any size

WMS3.2

Prime and composite numbers

Prime numbers are numbers that have only themselves and 1 as factors. For example: 2, 3, 5 and 7 are prime numbers but 4, 8 and 9 are not.
Composite numbers are numbers with more than two factors, e.g. 24 has factors of 1, 2, 3, 4, 6, 8, 12 and 24.

4 Write all the factors of these numbers then write whether they are prime or composite.

	Number	Factors	Prime or composite
a	8		
b	7		
c	9		
d	11		

	Number	Factors	Prime or composite
e	18		
f	16		
g	23		
h	17		

5 Write prime or composite after each number.

a 5 _____   e 29 _____   i 32 _____

b 20 _____   f 42 _____   j 37 _____

c 19 _____   g 31 _____   k 40 _____

d 24 _____   h 60 _____   l 45 _____

Prime numbers have only themselves and 1 as factors.

6 Explain why you agree or disagree with these statements.

a All odd numbers are prime numbers. _____

_____

b There are more composite numbers than prime numbers. _____

_____

7 Square and oblong numbers

9 is a "square" number.

8 is an "oblong" number.

Write the numbers under 101 that are both square and oblong.

A **triangle** is a three-sided shape with three angles. The total of all angles is always 180°. There are three main types of triangles: **equilateral**, **isosceles** and **scalene**.

8 Study the three types of triangles pictured, then answer the questions.

Equilateral triangle

Scalene triangle

Isosceles triangle

a Which triangle has all sides of equal length? _____

b Which triangle has only two sides of equal length? _____

c Which triangle has all angles the same size? _____

d Which triangle has only two angles the same size? _____

e Which triangle has no sides the same length? _____

f Which triangle has no angles the same size? _____

A right-angled triangle is a triangle in which one angle is a right angle.

9 Colour the right-angled triangles.

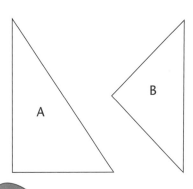

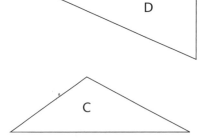

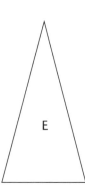

Did you find three right-angled triangles?

10 Sketch examples of each triangle. The dot paper may help you.

11 Use the formula "length × breadth = area" to calculate the area of each shape in square centimetres.

a
A = _____ cm²

b
A = _____ cm²

c
A = _____ cm²

d
A = _____ cm²

e
A = _____ cm²

f
A = _____ cm²

12 Use the formula "length × breadth = area" to create two rectangles, each with an area of 24 cm².

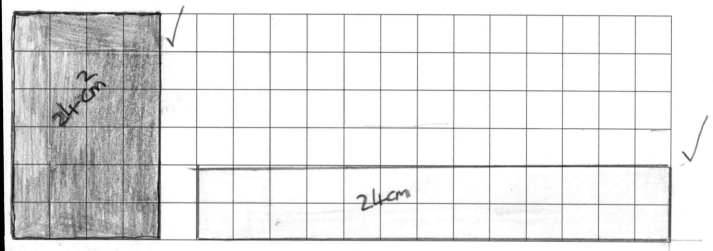

13 Kate drew this 12 cm² shape and told her friend that all shapes with a 12 cm² area have a perimeter of 16 cm. Draw two more shapes of 12 cm² to find out if Kate is right.

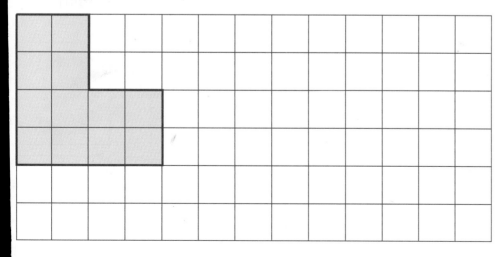

Are area and perimeter related?

WMS3.3, WMS3.2, WMS3.4

MS3.2 Selects and uses the appropriate unit to calculate area, including the area of squares, rectangles and triangles

43

2-digit division

Mr Cook had 75 stamps to share among his five children. This is what he did.

75 shared among 5

5) 7 5

Share out the tens, with each person getting 1.

1
5) 7 5

Trade the 2 tens left for 20 ones. Now share the 25 ones among 5.

1 5
5) 7²5

1 Solve these divisions.

a 3) 4 5

b 4) 5 2

c 5) 6 5

d 6) 7 2

e 4) 5 6

f 2) 3 6

g 3) 4 8

h 5) 7 0

i 2) 3 2

j 3) 4 2

k 2) 5 2

l 4) 9 6

m 2) 3 8

n 3) 5 1

o 4) 9 2

p 6) 8 4

65 lollies shared among 5 people?

1 3
5) 6¹5

That's 13 lollies each.

2 Write a division fact from each multiplication fact.

a	6	×	4	=	24		24	÷	6	=	
b	7	×	5	=				÷		=	
c	8	×	6	=				÷		=	
d	9	×	7	=				÷		=	

3 Solve these problems and discuss with your classmates what you might do with any remainder.

a Jon had 27 football cards to share among himself and another two boys. How many cards did each child receive?

b There were 42 stickers to be shared among 8 children. How many did each child receive?

c Fatima had a bag of 34 lollies which she shared among herself and 3 other friends. How many did each child get?

d Jody scored 28 home runs in 7 softball matches. What was her average score of home runs per match?

NS3.3 Selects and applies appropriate strategies for multiplication and division

WMS3.2

4 Describe the shaded section of the hundreds grids as a two-place decimal. The first one is done for you.

	Ones	Tenths	Hundredths
a	0	. 4	8
b		.	
c		.	

	Ones	Tenths	Hundredths
d		.	
e		.	
f		.	

5 Place these decimals in ascending order.

0.43, 2.57, 0.28, 4.35, 2.50, 8.22, 4.45.

_____

6 Use a decimal point to separate whole metres from fractions of a metre. The first one has been done for you.

a 127 cm __1.27__ m

b 352 cm _ . ____ m

c 427 cm _ . ____ m

d 563 cm _ . ____ m

e 742 cm _ . ____ m

f 890 cm _ . ____ m

g 842 cm _ . ____ m

h 906 cm _ . ____ m

i 1423 cm ____ . ____ m

7 The six people in the following group were measured and their heights recorded.

Kimberly	1.53 m	Scott	1.47 m	Sarah	1.09 m
James	1.35 m	Trent	1.90 m	Catherine	1.49 m

a Who was the tallest person? _____

b Who was the shortest person? _____

c Who is 2 cm taller than Scott? _____

d Explain why 1.90 m is taller than 1.09 m

_____

193 cm means 1 m and 93 cm.

8 Write true or false to answer these questions.

a 0.6 > 0.75 _____

b 1.6 < 6.1 _____

c 0.23 > 0.04 _____

d 1.5 > 5.1 _____

e 0.69 > 0.96 _____

f 0.07 > 0.03 _____

g 1.45 < 1.54 _____

h 7.98 > 8.97 _____

i 1.06 > 1.60 _____

Chance can be recorded on a scale of 0 to 1.
  0 describes an event that is impossible to happen.
  1 describes an event that is certain to happen.
  0.5 describes events with an equal chance of happening.
  All other points on the scale are given a numerical value between 0 and 1.

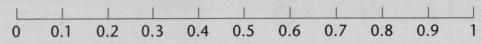

| 0 | 0.1 | 0.2 | 0.3 | 0.4 | 0.5 | 0.6 | 0.7 | 0.8 | 0.9 | 1 |

9 Draw a line to match each word to a place on the number line.

a Impossible   b Unlikely   c Even chance   d Likely   e Certain

| 0 | 0.1 | 0.2 | 0.3 | 0.4 | 0.5 | 0.6 | 0.7 | 0.8 | 0.9 | 1 |

Unlikely events fall between 0 and 0.5 and likely events fall between 0.5 and 1.
Some events are more or less likely than others.

10 Rate the likelihood of these events happening using the range of 0–1.

	Event	Probability
a	I'll clean my teeth tonight.	
b	A tossed coin lands on heads.	
c	Everyone will be at school tomorrow.	
d	A chocolate wheel numbered 1 to 10 lands on 6.	
e	I'll be invited to a birthday party next month.	
f	I'll go to high school next year.	
g	I'll have the same teacher next year.	
h	It will rain tonight.	
i	I'll watch television tonight.	
j	A spinner divided equally into red, blue, yellow, black and green lands on red.	

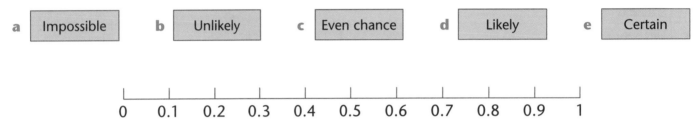

I'll probably clean my teeth tonight. 0.9

11 List two events which could happen tomorrow, and rate their probability.

a _____ . __

b _____ . __

NS3.5 Orders the likelihood of simple
events on a number line from zero to one

WMS3.3

12 Scale.

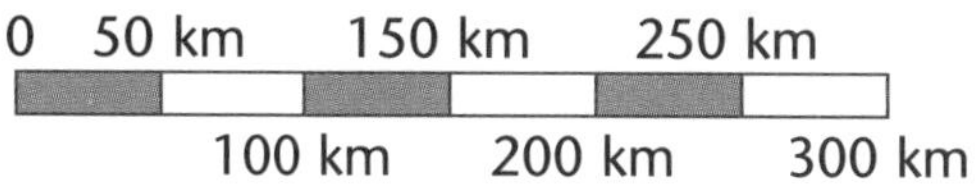

The scale shown is used to represent long distances.
Each 1 cm length represents a distance of 50 km. Use the
scale to determine the length represented by each line.

0	50 km	150 km	250 km
	100 km	200 km	300 km

a _____ _____ km

b _____ _____ km

c _____ _____ km

d _____ _____ km

e _____ _____ km

f _____ _____ km

13 Using scale on a map.

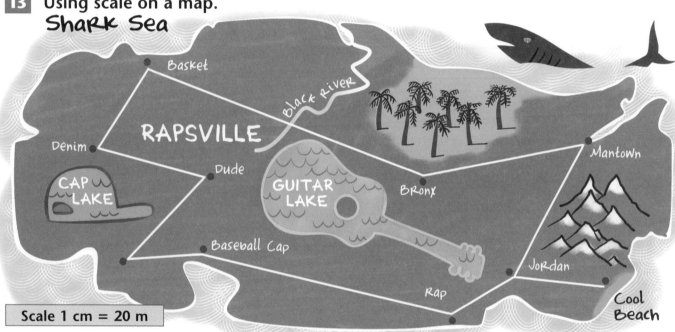

Shark Sea

Basket

Black River

RAPSVILLE

Denim

CAP LAKE

Dude

GUITAR LAKE

Bronx

Mantown

Baseball Cap

Jordan

Rap

Cool Beach

Scale 1 cm = 20 m

Use the scale to determine the shortest distances between:

a Baseball Cap and Rap

b Mantown and Bronx

c Denim and Mantown

d Baseball Cap and Denim

e Bronx and Baseball Cap
   via Mantown

f Dude and Jordan

g Basket and Cool Beach
   via Mantown

14 Use the scale to find:

a the length of Rapsville

b the width of Rapsville

4-digit addition with trading

1 Complete these additions with trading in the tens and ones.

a 3 4 2 9   b 2 4 7 4   c 3 6 7 3   d 3 5 5 5   e 3 8 4 7
+ 4 0 5 6   + 3 2 9 9   + 5 2 7 5   + 2 0 7 6   + 2 0 7 7
_____   _____   _____   _____   _____

2 Complete these additions with trading in the hundreds.

a 3 6 5 4   b 5 7 6 4   c 5 8 3 4   d 2 5 7 4   e 5 9 6 5
+ 2 7 3 2   + 2 7 3 1   + 1 7 6 5   + 3 6 1 5   + 2 9 1 3
_____   _____   _____   _____   _____

3 Complete these additions with trading in the hundreds, tens or ones.

a 3 5 6 7   b 5 6 9 4   c 6 3 6 8   d 7 7 5 4   e 5 5 7 8
+ 2 2 7 7   + 1 7 6 2   + 2 3 8 8   + 1 8 8 8   + 3 9 6 3
_____   _____   _____   _____   _____

4 Calculate the distance travelled by each family.

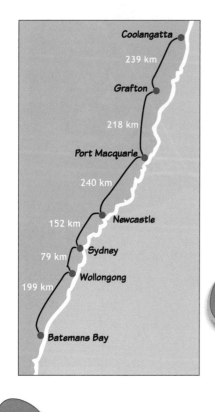

a Batemans Bay to Sydney.	**b** Wollongong to Port Macquarie.	**c** Batemans Bay to Port Macquarie.
d Sydney to Grafton.	**e** Sydney to Coolangatta.	**f** Coolangatta to Newcastle.

5 Calculate a return journey that is between 450 km and 600 km.

6 From one destination on the map to another, calculate a return journey that is between 1 100 km and 1 300 km.

NS3.2 Selects and applies appropriate strategies for addition and subtraction with counting numbers of any size

WMS3.2

Roman numerals were invented by the people of early Roman times. They were used for many years and had their own place value system. Roman numerals can still be seen today on books, clocks or buildings. Let's look at the Roman numerals below.

Roman numerals	Hindu–Arabic	How they work	Roman numerals	Hindu–Arabic	How they work
I	1	1 stroke	XII	12	2 more than 10
II	2	2 strokes	XX	20	2 tens
III	3	3 strokes	XXX	30	3 tens
IV	4	1 less than V	XL	40	10 less than 50
V	5	V is the symbol for 5	L	50	L is the symbol for 50
VI	6	1 more than V	LX	60	10 more than 50
VII	7	2 more than V	LXX	70	20 more than 50
VIII	8	3 more than V	LXXX	80	30 more than 50
IX	9	1 less than X	XC	90	10 less than 100
X	10	X is the symbol for 10	C	100	C is the symbol for 100
XI	11	1 more than 10			

7 Use the table above to help you write Roman numerals for each number. You will need to combine Roman numerals for hundreds, tens and ones (e.g. 23 = XX + III = XXIII). You may not group more than three Roman numerals together (e.g. XXX or III).

a 33 __XXXIII__

b 20 _____

c 28 _____

d 6 _____

e 36 _____

f 46 _____

g 19 _____

h 23 _____

i 56 _____

j 74 _____

k 69 _____

l 47 _____

m 66 _____

n 86 _____

o 120 _____

p 150 _____

q 172 _____

r 227 _____

s 223 _____

t 334 _____

u 365 _____

237 equals CCXXXVII.

8 Complete the Roman numeral magic squares.

a

X		
V	VII	
	IV	

b

IV		
	V	
VIII		VI

c

VIII		IV
	V	
VI		

Data can be recorded on a **line graph** by using a line to join plotted points. Meaning can be attached to any point along the line.

9 An average Australian car uses 12 litres of petrol for every 100 km travelled.

a Complete the table to show how far the car could travel on the litres supplied.

Litres	6	12	18	24	30	36	46
Kilometres	50	100	150				

b Record this information on the line graph.

c How far did the car travel on 24 L of petrol? _____

d How far did the car travel on 36 L of petrol? _____

e How far would the car travel on 9 L of petrol? _____

f How many litres would the car use for a 250 km trip? _____

g How many litres would the car use for a 350 km trip? _____

h How many litres would the car use for a 400 km trip? _____

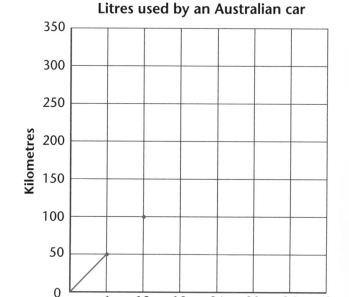

Litres used by an Australian car

10 **Drawing a line graph.**

Jane's athletic coach made a table of the distance she walked in 6 minutes.

Minutes	1	2	3	4	5	6
Metres	200	400	600	800	1 000	1 200

a Create a line graph to represent this data. You will need to work out a scale for the vertical axis before you start.

b If Jane walked for 10 minutes, how far would she walk? _____

c How far would she walk in $2\frac{1}{2}$ minutes? _____

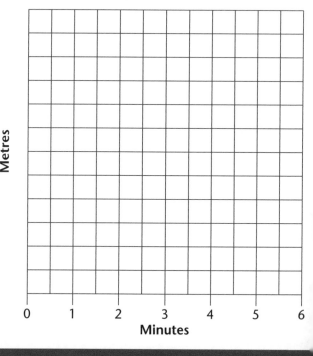

Jane's Walk

11 Sarah, John and Alisha built three rectangular prisms out of centicubes. In groups of three make the three prisms. Complete the grid for length, breadth and height. Record the volume for each prism by counting the centicubes.

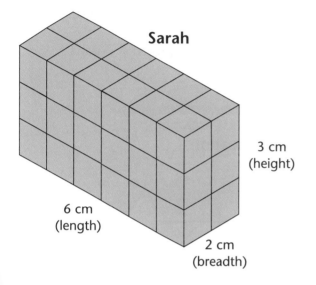

Sarah

3 cm
(height)

6 cm
(length)

2 cm
(breadth)

Prism	Length	Breadth	Height	Volume
Sarah				cm³
John				cm³
Alisha				cm³

Alisha

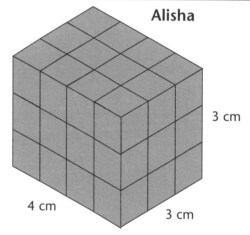

3 cm

4 cm

3 cm

John

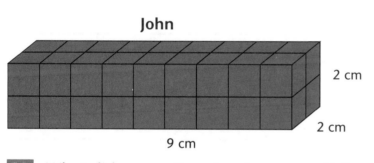

2 cm

2 cm

9 cm

12 What did you notice about your results? _____

_____

_____

13 Use centicubes to make models having these dimensions. Record the number of cubes used in the tally column of the grid, then record the volume of each model.

Did any prisms have the same volume?

	Length	Breadth	Height	Tally	Volume (cm³)
a	4 cm	2 cm	2 cm	ⅢⅢ ⅢⅢ ⅢⅢ Ⅰ	
b	4 cm	3 cm	3 cm		
c	6 cm	2 cm	3 cm		
d	6 cm	1 cm	4 cm		
e	4 cm	2 cm	4 cm		
f	8 cm	1 cm	4 cm		

WMS3.3, WMS3.4

MS3.3 Selects and uses the appropriate unit to estimate and measure volume and capacity, including the volume of rectangular prisms

51

Three digits multiplied by one digit

Hund	Tens	Ones	
¹2	¹4	5	
×		3	
7	3	5	

3 × 5 = 15 ones
Write 5 in the ones column and trade the 10 ones for 1 ten, then write the 1 at the top of the tens column.
3 × 4 tens = 12 tens plus the 1 traded ten equals 13 tens.
Write 3 in the tens column and trade the 10 tens for 1 hundred, then place a 1 at the top of the hundreds column.
3 × 2 hundreds = 6 hundreds plus the 1 traded hundred equals 7 hundreds.
Write 7 in the hundreds column.

1 Solve each example using the shortened form of multiplication.

a   2   3   5   b   8   4   7   c   9   0   0   d   7   6   0   e   8   5   7
×   3   ×   4   ×   5   ×   6   ×   7
_____   _____   _____   _____   _____

f   3   6   3   g   2   4   8   h   4   7   4   i   3   2   9   j   2   6   3
×   5   ×   6   ×   7   ×   8   ×   9
_____   _____   _____   _____   _____

k   2   5   6   l   3   4   9   m   4   2   8   n   5   4   6   o   6   6   4
×   5   ×   7   ×   6   ×   4   ×   5
_____   _____   _____   _____   _____

2 Problems to solve.

a   The Earth takes about 365 days to orbit the Sun. How many days would it take to complete 5 orbits?

b   A plane flew at 505 km per hour on a 4-hour flight. How long was the flight?

c   How much mineral water did Hans drink if he drank all 3 of his 375 mL cans?

3 What numbers could 124 be multiplied by to give an answer of between 600 and 1 000?

Constructing number sentences

UNIT **13**

4 Supply the missing number to make each number sentence equal.

a 6 + ☐ = 18 − 5

b 9 + 6 = ☐ − 17

c 4 × 7 = ☐ − 22

d 4 × 6 = ☐ + 6

e ☐ + 7 = 20 − 8

f 5 × ☐ = 20 + 10

g ☐ × 5 = 36 + 9

h 100 ÷ 5 = 32 − ☐

i 9 + 8 = ☐ − 7

j 3 × 4 = 100 − ☐

k ☐ ÷ 5 = 25 × 2

l 56 ÷ ☐ = 94 − 86

5 **Celebrity heads.**

Read the number sentences and carry out the operations to find the missing numbers.

a If you multiply me by 2 and add 4 the answer is 10.

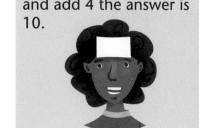

b If you halve me and halve me again the answer is 6.

c If you add 2 and multiply by 4 the answer is 36.

6 Write a number sentence to solve the problems. The first one is done for you.

a Double the number and add 6 to get 14.

b Multiply the number by 3 and subtract 7 to get 5.

c Subtract 5 from the number and add 8 to get 10.

d Divide the number by 5 and add 3 to get 7.

e Multiply the number by 4 and divide by 3 to give 8.

f Add 5 to the number and multiply by 7 to get 56.

g Subtract 15 from the number and divide by 5 to get 3.

4 × 2 + 6 = 14

7 Think of a secret number and write some clues so that a friend can work out your secret number.

8 Follow the instructions to draw a rectangle.

a Place a protractor exactly on the line AB, with the centre point exactly on the end of the line where A is.

b Put a pencil dot at 90° then draw a faint line from A to the dot.

c Repeat exactly for the B end of the line.

d Measure 4 cm on each vertical line you have drawn and put a dot.

e Join the dots to form a rectangle.

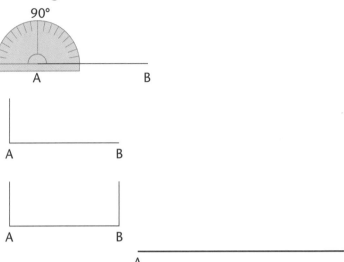

9 Now construct a congruent copy of the square below by following the same procedure as above. All the angles and sides are given on the shape.

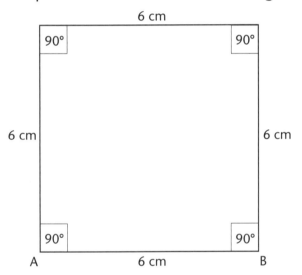

10 Play the robot game on the 5 mm grid paper.

Rules: Forward **FD**   Right **RT**   Left **LT**

Start at the dot then follow the instructions.
Note: a and **b** have been done for you and turns are always made from the direction you are coming from.

a FD 60 mm

b RT 90°   FD 60 mm

c RT 90°   FD 20 mm

d RT 90°   FD 30 mm

e LT 90°   FD 20 mm

f LT 90°   FD 30 mm

g RT 90°   FD 20 mm

h RT 90°   FD 60 mm

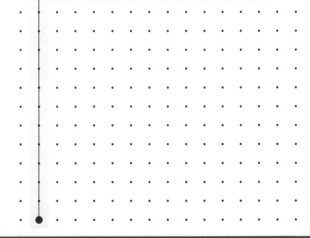

SGS3.2a Manipulates, classifies and draws two-dimensional shapes and describes side and angle properties

WMS3.3

A day has 24 hours. Time can be expressed in 12-hour am/pm form or 24-hour time. Note that, when writing 24-hour time, neither punctuation nor a space is used, e.g. 0745 = 7:45 am; 2318 = 11:18 pm.

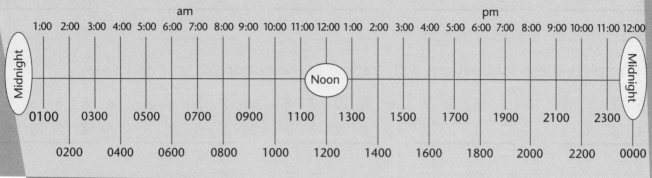

11 Convert these from 12-hour "am and pm" time to 24-hour time. The first is done for you.

a 3:00 am __0300__   d 6:00 pm _____   g 10:00 pm _____   j 7:30 pm _____

b 8:00 am _____   e 2:00 pm _____   h 6:00 am _____   k 7:30 am _____

c 4:00 pm _____   f 11:00 pm _____   i 8:00 pm _____   l 9:15 pm _____

12 Complete this grid showing time expressed in analog, digital and 24-hour forms.

Analog	(clock)	(clock)	(clock)	(clock)	(clock)	(clock)	(clock)
Digital	3:00 am		5:40 pm		9:35 pm	10:05 am	12:45 am
24-hour	0300	1815		1145			

Channel 6

6:00	Sunshine News
7:00	Cartoon Connection
8:00	Play School
9:00	Home Shopping
10:00	Lifeline
10:30	News
11:00	Entertainment Tonight
12:00	Movie: Tarzan
2:00	Days of the Young
3:30	Disney Adventures
4:00	Bewitched
5:00	Growing Up
6:00	News
6:30	Tonight Today
7:30	Home and Away
8:00	Enemies
8:30	Water Snakes
9:30	Susan's Closet
10:30	Sportstime
12:00	Close

13 Read the program guide then answer the questions to set the video using 24-hour time.

a Jim set his video to tape Channel 6 at 0900 for one hour. What show did he tape? _____

b Maria wanted to tape *Home and Away*. Complete the information she would need.

   Channel _____   Time _____   Duration _____

c Mohammed set his video to tape Channel 6 at 1600 for one hour. What show did he tape? _____

d Sylvester wanted to tape *Water Snakes* so he set his video for Channel 6 at 1830 for one hour. Was he successful? _____

e Ronald wanted to tape *Sportstime*. Complete the information he would need.

   Channel _____   Time _____   Duration _____

4-digit subtraction

1 Complete these subtractions with trading in the hundreds.

a	6 6 5 7	b	7 2 9 8	c	8 4 7 8	d	3 3 4 7	e	8 2 6 5
−	3 8 4 3	−	3 5 7 6	−	6 8 4 7	−	2 6 3 4	−	3 7 3 3

2 Complete these subtractions with trading in the hundreds, tens and ones.

a	6 2 8 8	b	7 6 5 9	c	8 0 7 5	d	7 1 3 4	e	8 8 5 5
−	4 6 5 4	−	3 4 8 7	−	6 2 3 7	−	5 3 8 3	−	4 3 8 4

f	7 4 3 4	g	6 3 8 0	h	7 2 2 1	i	9 9 2 4	j	7 3 5 0
−	4 1 5 6	−	3 5 1 3	−	4 6	−	2 6 6	−	2 6 6 6

3 **Sports car production.**

Calculate the difference in car production between the months.

Month	Number
January	932
February	3 945
March	2 130
April	2 506
May	2 904

a January and February	b February and March	c March and April
d April and May	e April and January	f May and March

4 Round to estimate an answer, then solve the problem.

		Estimate	Answer
a	The school dance received $2 856 in ticket money. How much profit was made if $976 was spent on expenses?		
b	The Town Hall has room for 5 070 people. How many more people can fit in if there are 3 667 already in the Town Hall?		
c	6 537 eggs were taken from the farms to the packaging factory. How many were broken if 6 238 were placed into cartons?		
d	Eve has paid a deposit of $972 for the car she wants to buy. How much does she owe if the car is $9 720?		

2-digit division

Sometimes divisions don't work out equally and have **remainders**. Let's see how Mrs King shared 83 cakes among 5 groups.

83 shared among 5	Share out the tens, with each getting 1.	Trade the 3 tens left for 30 ones. Now share the 33 ones among 5.
$5\overline{)83}$	$\dfrac{1}{5\overline{)83}}$	$\dfrac{1\,6\;r\,3}{5\overline{)8^33}}$

Answer: 16 remainder 3

5 Solve the divisions.

a $\dfrac{\qquad r}{3\overline{)43}}$
b $\dfrac{\qquad r}{4\overline{)53}}$
c $\dfrac{\qquad r}{4\overline{)65}}$
d $\dfrac{\qquad r}{5\overline{)78}}$

e $\dfrac{\qquad r}{4\overline{)57}}$
f $\dfrac{\qquad r}{3\overline{)47}}$
g $\dfrac{\qquad r}{6\overline{)83}}$
h $\dfrac{\qquad r}{6\overline{)92}}$

i $\dfrac{\qquad r}{5\overline{)67}}$
j $\dfrac{\qquad r}{5\overline{)72}}$
k $\dfrac{\qquad r}{6\overline{)85}}$
l $\dfrac{\qquad r}{7\overline{)99}}$

m $\dfrac{\qquad r}{6\overline{)73}}$
n $\dfrac{\qquad r}{6\overline{)79}}$
o $\dfrac{\qquad r}{5\overline{)92}}$
p $\dfrac{\qquad r}{4\overline{)97}}$

68 lollies shared among 5 people?

$\dfrac{1\;3\,r3}{5\overline{)6^18}}$

That's 13 lollies each, with three left over.

6 Find the winning bingo card by crossing off the numbers on both cards as you calculate the answers.

a $3\overline{)36}$
b $8\overline{)80}$
c $6\overline{)88}$

d $5\overline{)61}$
e $9\overline{)63}$
f $6\overline{)48}$

g $9\overline{)45}$
h $7\overline{)91}$
i $4\overline{)85}$

j $9\overline{)36}$
k $6\overline{)76}$
l $6\overline{)90}$

Bingo

	12		7				21r1
14r4		12r1		5		13		10
	8		4		12r4		15

5		7			4		21r1
	12		13			12r1	
14r4		8		17r1		10		6

7 Write as many divisions as you can with a remainder of 2.

23 ÷ 7 = 3 r2

8 Draw lines to match each piece of information with a skeletal model and a prism name.

Name	Information	Skeletal model

Cube

I have 8 vertices and 12 edges. Each one of my 6 faces is a square.

Rectangular prism

I have 6 rectangular faces, 12 edges and 8 vertices. A shoe box is a good example of me.

Triangular prism

I have 9 edges and 6 vertices. I have 5 faces of which 2 are triangular and 3 are rectangular.

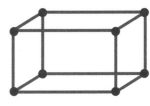

Hexagonal prism

I have 5 rectangular sides, 10 vertices and 15 edges. My other 2 faces are pentagons.

Pentagonal prism

I have 12 vertices and 18 edges. Two of my 8 faces are hexagonal while the others are rectangular.

9 Study real examples of these shapes then list their similarities and differences.

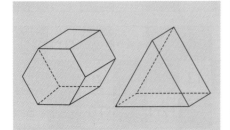

Hexagonal prism and triangular prism.

Similarities _____

Differences _____

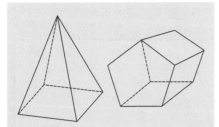

Pentagonal prism and square pyramid.

Similarities _____

Differences _____

10 Measure the length of each side to calculate the perimeter of each shape.

a

P = ____ cm

b

P = ____ cm

> The perimeter is the distance around the outside of a shape.

c

P = ____ cm

d

P = ____ cm

e

P = ____

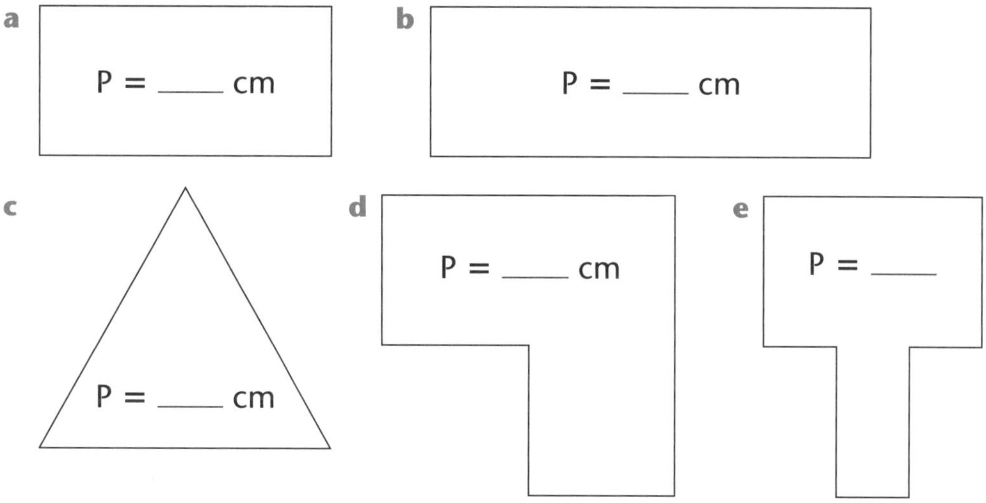

11 Estimate and then measure the perimeter of each shape, in centimetres.

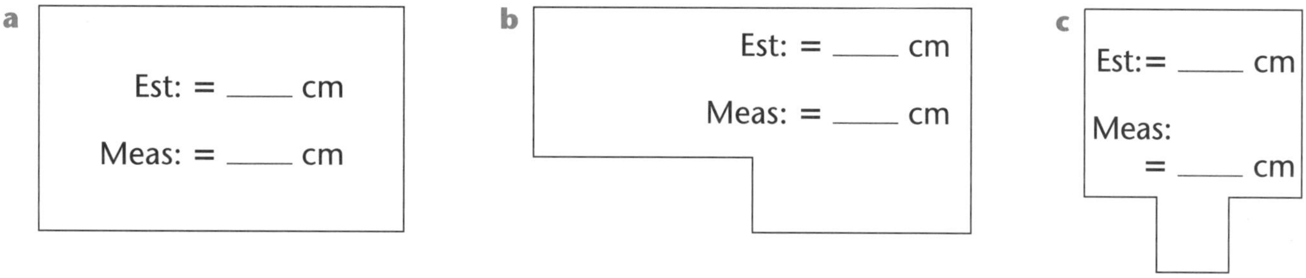

a

Est: = ____ cm

Meas: = ____ cm

b

Est: = ____ cm

Meas: = ____ cm

c

Est:= ____ cm

Meas:
= ____ cm

12 Use the dot paper to make two staircase shapes, one with a perimeter of 12 cm and another with a perimeter of 16 cm.

a 12 cm perimeter

b 16 cm perimeter

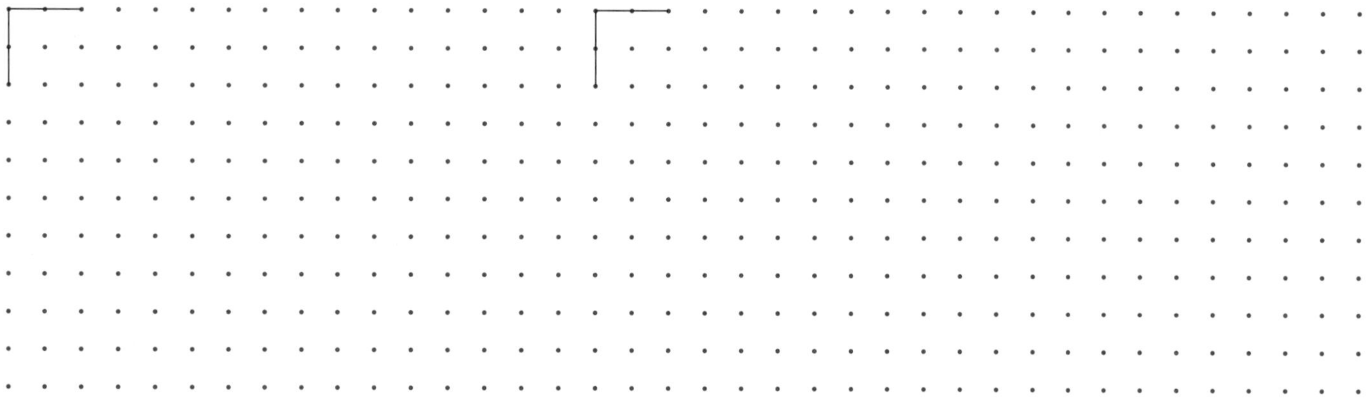

13 State the perimeters of these gardens.

a Peter made a rectangular garden with sides 7 m and 3 m. _____ m

b Jenny made a triangular garden bed with sides measuring 4 m, 3 m and 5 m. _____ m

c Tony made a hexagonal garden bed with each side measuring 4 m. _____ m

Multiplication

1 Solve each multiplication.

a	Hund	Tens	Ones
	3	2	6
×			4

b	Hund	Tens	Ones
	4	8	2
×			5

c	Hund	Tens	Ones
	3	9	5
×			3

d	Hund	Tens	Ones
	7	0	8
×			8

e	Hund	Tens	Ones
	6	1	2
×			7

f	Hund	Tens	Ones
	4	3	7
×			4

g	Hund	Tens	Ones
	8	0	5
×			6

h	Hund	Tens	Ones
	7	3	0
×			5

i	Hund	Tens	Ones
	6	0	7
×			6

j	Hund	Tens	Ones
	3	4	5
×			9

k	Hund	Tens	Ones
	8	6	0
×			7

l	Hund	Tens	Ones
	4	5	6
×			8

m	Hund	Tens	Ones
	3	5	7
×			6

n	Hund	Tens	Ones
	6	7	4
×			5

o	Hund	Tens	Ones
	8	7	4
×			4

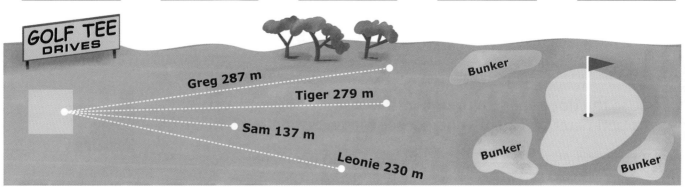

GOLF TEE DRIVES

Greg 287 m

Tiger 279 m

Sam 137 m

Leonie 230 m

Bunker

Bunker

Bunker

2 Four golfers of various abilities worked out their average drives over a year of golf.

a Using the average drive information, calculate how far Greg could hit the ball in 6 drives.

☐ m

b How far would Sam hit the ball in 8 drives?

☐ m

3 Create your own problem to suit the algorithm. Solve it. Illustrate your problem.

Problem	Illustration	Working
		1 2 5 × 5

Adding and subtracting fractions

4 Colour each fraction addition in a different colour to find the answer. The first one is done for you.

a $\frac{2}{6} + \frac{2}{6} = \frac{\square}{6}$

c $\frac{2}{12} + \frac{5}{12} = \frac{\square}{12}$

e $\frac{3}{6} + \frac{2}{6} = \frac{\square}{6}$

g $\frac{5}{12} + \frac{4}{12} = \frac{\square}{12}$

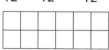

b $\frac{3}{10} + \frac{4}{10} = \frac{\square}{10}$

d $\frac{2}{4} + \frac{1}{4} = \frac{\square}{4}$

f $\frac{3}{8} + \frac{3}{8} = \frac{\square}{8}$

h $\frac{3}{10} + \frac{5}{10} = \frac{\square}{10}$

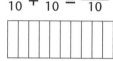

5 Complete these addition sentences.

a $\frac{3}{12} + \frac{4}{12} = $ —

d $\frac{5}{8} + \frac{1}{8} = $ —

g $\frac{4}{6} + \frac{1}{6} = $ —

j $\frac{2}{6} + \frac{2}{6} = $ —

b $\frac{2}{4} + \frac{1}{4} = $ —

e $\frac{2}{5} + \frac{2}{5} = $ —

h $\frac{6}{8} + \frac{1}{8} = $ —

k $\frac{3}{6} + \frac{2}{6} = $ —

c $\frac{3}{10} + \frac{4}{10} = $ —

f $\frac{1}{6} + \frac{2}{6} = $ —

i $\frac{1}{6} + \frac{1}{6} + \frac{1}{6} = $ —

l $\frac{2}{12} + \frac{2}{12} + \frac{2}{12} = $ —

6 Complete these operations.

a $\frac{7}{10} - \frac{4}{10} = $

f $\frac{4}{6} - \frac{1}{6} = $

k $\frac{2}{3} - \frac{1}{3} = $

b $\frac{7}{12} - \frac{5}{12} = $

g $\frac{4}{5} - \frac{3}{5} = $

l $\frac{5}{6} - \frac{2}{6} = $

c $\frac{9}{12} - \frac{5}{12} = $

h $\frac{5}{12} - \frac{3}{12} = $

m $\frac{5}{6} - \frac{3}{6} = $

d $\frac{7}{12} - \frac{3}{12} = $

i $\frac{6}{8} - \frac{3}{8} = $

n $\frac{4}{6} - \frac{1}{6} = $

e $\frac{8}{10} - \frac{5}{10} = $

j $\frac{3}{4} - \frac{1}{4} = $

o $\frac{4}{6} - \frac{3}{6} = $

Subtracting like fractions is easy.
$\frac{7}{10} - \frac{2}{10} = \frac{5}{10}$

7 Find pairs of fractions that could be added or subtracted to give the answer $\frac{9}{12}$.

$\frac{5}{12}$ $\frac{6}{12}$ $\frac{8}{12}$ $\frac{2}{12}$ $\frac{10}{12}$ $\frac{4}{12}$

$\frac{7}{12}$ $\frac{12}{12}$ $\frac{1}{12}$ $\frac{3}{12}$ $\frac{11}{12}$

Answers

Databases

Databases are often used to store and organise data. Mailing lists, inventories and large amounts of data, such as historical records, can be kept on databases.

Gillian Walters wants to create a telephone list of all her friends. She also wants to list their birth dates to remind her when to buy birthday presents. To do this she will make five fields on her database: first names, surnames, suburbs, telephone numbers and dates of birth.

		First name	Surname	Date of birth	Suburb	Telephone
☐	1	Jessica	Field	21/8/94	Botany	964 4711
☐	2	Helen	Smith	4/10/93	Botany	964 3773
☐	3	Julia	Shepherd	15/6/92	Rosebery	953 6789
☐	4	Jason	Hobbs	21/9/92	Brighton	953 3456
☐	5	John	Hardy	10/3/95	Rosebery	953 9201
☐	6	Tom	Kouris	21/9/91	Mascot	969 1356
☐	7	Zena	Roberts	18/2/93	Kensington	948 4596
☐	8	Stephen	Clark	13/1/95	Randwick	938 4667
☐	9	Taryn	Walters	31/12/95	Coogee	942 3546
☐	10	Mark	Walters	16/4/92	Rosebery	953 6001
☐	11	Samantha	Wood	27/11/92	Brighton	953 3466
☐	12	Merryn	Cook	1/12/95	Malabar	986 3899
☐	13					
☐	14					
☐	15					

Table title: **Telephone list**

8 Gillian needs to enter three more people, whose details she has scribbled on a scrap of paper, to complete her database. Enter the data on the database for her.

Brett Sattler, 21/9/94, Kensington, 948 6098
Lauren Lockett, Kensington, 2/9/93, 948 4788
Catherine Laws, 5/6/94, Maroubra, 941 5671

Databases can be used to print out various lists of information.

9 Complete the lists of information from the database. The first one is done for you.

a

Friends that live in Kensington
Zena
Brett
Lauren

b

Friends that live in Rosebery

c

Friends born in 1993

d

Friends born in 1994

e

Friends with a telephone number beginning with 964

f

Friends with the surname of Walters

DS3.1 Displays and interprets data in graphs with scales of many-to-one correspondence

WMS3.2, WMS3.5

Square metres

The formula for area is Area = length × breadth.

10 Use the formula A = L × B to calculate the area of these billboards by the highway.

Length 9 m

Breadth 6 m

Breadth 6 m

Length 8 m

	Poster	A = L × B	Area	
a	Arctic Cola	9×6	54 m²	✓
b	Lunar Planet	8×6	48 m²	✓

11 Calculate the area of these shapes in square metres if they are drawn so that 1 cm represents 1 metre.

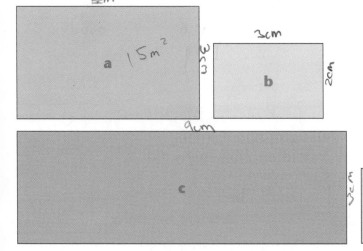

Shape	A = L × B	Area	
a	3×5	15 m²	✓
b	2×3	6 m²	✓
c	9×3	27 m²	✓
d	6×2	12 m²	✓

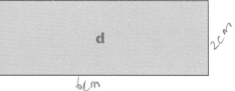

12 Solve these problems.

a Alison's room is 4 metres long and 3 metres in breadth. How much will it cost to carpet her room if carpet is $20 a square metre?

b What would be the perimeter and area of a court 30 metres long and 15 metres in breadth?

3-digit division

There are many ways of doing division. Here is one method.

Share out the hundreds with each paddock getting 1.

$$
\begin{array}{r}
1 \\
3\overline{)4\,2\,6}
\end{array}
$$

Trade the 1 hundred left over for 10 tens. Now share the 12 tens. Each paddock gets 4.

$$
\begin{array}{r}
1\;4 \\
3\overline{)4^{1}2\,6}
\end{array}
$$

Share out the 6 ones with each paddock getting 2.

$$
\begin{array}{r}
1\;4\;2 \\
3\overline{)4^{1}2\,6}
\end{array}
$$

426 sheep shared among 3 paddocks?

1 Complete these division algorithms. You may need to work them through on paper before recording your answers.

a 2)268   b 2)864   c 3)693   d 3)396   e 4)484

f 3)697   g 2)865   h 4)849   i 3)695   j 4)487

2 Complete the divisions with trading.

a 3)426   b 4)568   c 2)328   d 3)456   e 4)528

f 4)648   g 8)968   h 4)684   i 3)516   j 7)847

k 5)655   l 6)726   m 7)917   n 6)846   o 6)966

3 Solve these problems.

a Mia shared 698 football cards among 3 friends and herself. How many did they each receive?
   ☐ cards

c A bag of 755 centicubes was distributed among 5 children. How many did each receive?
   ☐ centicubes

b A box of 729 lollies was shared among Tim and 6 friends. How many did Tim get?
   ☐ lollies

d Mr Drummond had a 964 L water tank. How many 4 L containers could he fill from his tank?
   ☐ containers

4 Write three divisions that have an answer between 150 and 200.

NS3.3 Selects and applies appropriate strategies for multiplication and division

WMS3.2, WMS3.3

5 Write the numbers.

a Twenty-six thousand, two hundred and thirty-seven.

b Forty-two thousand, seven hundred and thirteen.

c Sixty-seven thousand, three hundred and sixty.

d Thirty-five thousand and nine.

e Fifty thousand, two hundred and four.

6 State the place value of each bold digit.

a 23**4** _____

b 2 **3**45 _____

c **3**4 _____

d **6** 778 _____

e 7 **7**77 _____

f 6 6**5**6 _____

g 3**2** 345 _____

h **3**4 898 _____

i 56 **8**73 _____

j **9**9 564 _____

k **3**67 234 _____

l 33**3** 444 _____

7 Expand the following numbers. The first one is done for you.

a 235 247 | 200 000 | + | 30 000 | + | 5 000 | + | 200 | + | 40 | + | 7

b 364 382 | ☐ + ☐ + ☐ + ☐ + ☐ + ☐

c 491 456 | ☐ + ☐ + ☐ + ☐ + ☐ + ☐

d 670 291 | ☐ + ☐ + ☐ + ☐ + ☐

e 782 008 | ☐ + ☐ + ☐ + ☐

f 899 099 | ☐ + ☐ + ☐ + ☐ + ☐

8 What number am I?

I am an odd number between 5 000 and 5 999. The number in the thousands place is odd and is between 3 and 7, and the number in the tens place is a multiple of 4 which is greater than 4. The number in the hundreds place is equal to 3 squared and the number in the ones place is 23 less than 30.

I am ☐

9 **a** Build the geometric pattern of triangles with matches, then sketch the next set of triangles in the sequence.

b Complete and extend the table to record the number of matches needed to make the pattern of triangles.

Triangles	1	2	3	4	5	6	7
Matches	3	6					

c In small groups discuss a rule to describe the number pattern formed by the triangles, then write it.

_____

d Use the rule to state how many matches would be needed for 15 triangles. _____

10 **a** Build the pattern of pentagons with matches, then sketch the next set of pentagons.

b Complete and extend the table to record the number of sides needed to make the pattern of pentagons.

Pentagons	1	2	3	4	5	6	7
Sides	5						

c Write a rule to describe the pattern.

_____

d How many sides would there be on 10 pentagons? _____

11 **a** Build the pattern of squares with matches, then sketch the next set of squares.

b Complete and extend the table to record the number of sides needed to make the pattern of squares.

Squares	1	2	3	4	5	6	7
Sides	4						

c Write a rule to describe the pattern.

_____

d How many sides would there be on 12 squares? _____

66 PAS3.1a Records, analyses and describes geometric and number patterns that involve one operation using tables and words

WMS3.4, WMS3.5

A shape has **rotational symmetry** if, after the shape is turned around its centre point, it matches the original shape more than once through a full turn.

12 Colour all the shapes that have rotational symmetry. You may need to trace the shapes and rotate them on a pin to discover the answers.

a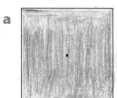

b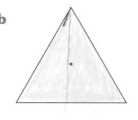

c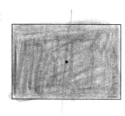

d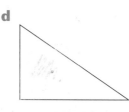

e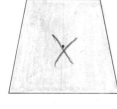

f

g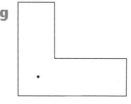

h

i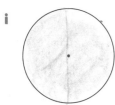

j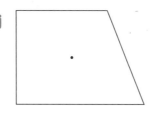

k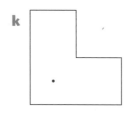

l

13 Giovanni is laying some pavers in his backyard. He lays them in a square pattern using four rectangular pavers and one square paver.

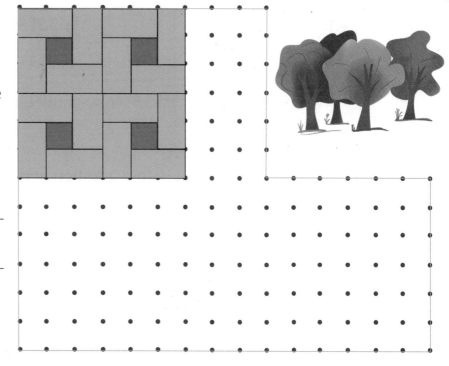

a Continue the pattern to finish the paving.

b How many rectangular pavers did he use? _____

c How many square pavers did he use? _____

14 Find a capital letter that has turning symmetry. _____

Order of operations

Rules for order of operations
- Always do the work in the grouping symbols (brackets) first.　　$(3 \times 6) \times 7 = 126$
- Do operations with division and multiplication from left to right.　　$3 \times 8 \div 2 = 12$
- Do operations with addition and subtraction from left to right.　　$5 + 8 - 6 = 7$
- Do multiplication and division before addition and subtraction.　　$6 + 8 \times 3 = 30$

1 Do the brackets first.

a $6 + (3 \times 7) =$

b $(6 + 3) \times 7 =$

c $7 + (3 \times 6) =$

d $3 + (7 \times 9) =$

e $40 + (6 \times 8) =$

f $63 - (9 \times 4) =$

g $8 + (5 \times 9) - 6 =$

h $50 + (7 \times 4) + 8 =$

i $100 - (27 \div 3) + 6 =$

2 Left to right.

a $8 \times 7 \div 2 =$

b $5 \times 8 \div 4 =$

c $6 \times 9 \div 3 =$

d $24 \div 6 \times 9 =$

e $36 \div 6 \times 10 =$

f $54 \div 9 \times 9 =$

g $9 \times 8 \div 2 =$

h $8 \times 8 \div 4 =$

i $3 \times 4 \times 3 \div 3 =$

3 Left to right.

a $3 + 8 + 24 - 20 =$

b $60 - 40 + 6 - 2 =$

c $8 + 18 - 10 + 32 =$

d $40 + 60 + 23 - 30 =$

e $70 + 18 + 9 - 22 =$

f $127 + 56 - 34 + 19 =$

g $121 + 67 + 34 - 6 =$

h $219 - 8 + 7 - 16 =$

i $400 - 250 + 750 =$

4 Do multiplication and division before addition and subtraction.

a $3 + 7 \times 2 =$

b $6 \times 3 - 8 =$

c $7 \div 7 \times 4 =$

d $7 + 64 \div 8 =$

e $3 + 99 \div 3 =$

f $230 - 5 \times 6 =$

g $80 - 5 \times 8 =$

h $60 + 65 \div 5 =$

i $130 + 9 \times 7 =$

j $3 \times 9 + 7 - 30 =$

k $126 + 36 \div 6 - 2 =$

l $3 \times 6 \div 6 + 47 =$

5 Write some operations and answers yourself.

NS3.3 Selects and applies appropriate strategies for multiplication and division　　**WMS3.1, WMS3.3**

Subtracting fractions from wholes

Fractions can be subtracted from whole numbers, e.g. Tom had a chocolate bar and gave away $\frac{1}{3}$ of it.

$1 - \frac{1}{3} = \frac{2}{3}$

6 Use the diagrams to help you subtract the fractions from one whole.

a $1 - \frac{1}{5} = $ _____

b $1 - \frac{1}{4} = $ _____

c $1 - \frac{1}{8} = $ _____

d $1 - \frac{1}{6} = $ _____

e $1 - \frac{1}{10} = $ _____

What would $1 - \frac{2}{3}$ equal?

Fractions can be subtracted from more than one whole number, e.g. Alexis had 2 pizzas and gave away $\frac{1}{4}$ of one.

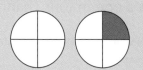

$2 - \frac{1}{4} = 1\frac{3}{4}$

7 Subtract the fractions of pizza.

a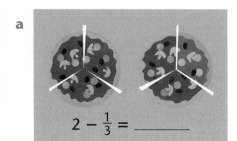

$2 - \frac{1}{3} = $ _____

b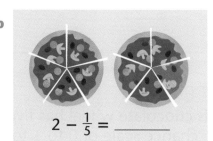

$2 - \frac{1}{5} = $ _____

c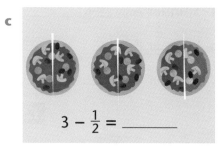

$3 - \frac{1}{2} = $ _____

8 Use the number lines to solve the subtractions.

0 $\frac{1}{4}$ $\frac{2}{4}$ $\frac{3}{4}$ 1 $1\frac{1}{4}$ $1\frac{2}{4}$ $1\frac{3}{4}$ 2 $2\frac{1}{4}$ $2\frac{2}{4}$ $2\frac{3}{4}$ 3 $3\frac{1}{4}$ $3\frac{2}{4}$ $3\frac{3}{4}$ 4

0 $\frac{1}{3}$ $\frac{2}{3}$ 1 $1\frac{1}{3}$ $1\frac{2}{3}$ 2 $2\frac{1}{3}$ $2\frac{2}{3}$ 3 $3\frac{1}{3}$ $3\frac{2}{3}$ 4 $4\frac{1}{3}$ $4\frac{2}{3}$ 5 $5\frac{1}{3}$

a $1 - \frac{1}{4} = $ _____

b $1 - \frac{1}{3} = $ _____

c $2 - \frac{1}{4} = $ _____

d $2 - \frac{1}{3} = $ _____

e $3 - \frac{1}{4} = $ _____

f $3 - \frac{1}{3} = $ _____

g $4 - \frac{1}{4} = $ _____

h $4 - \frac{1}{3} = $ _____

i $5 - \frac{1}{3} = $ _____

NS3.4 Compares, orders and calculates with decimals, simple fractions and simple percentages

Spinner A
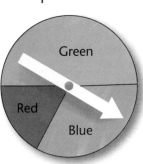

Spinner B
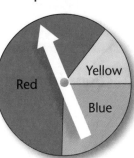

Spinner C
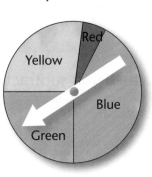

Spinner D
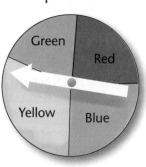

9 Which spinner has the most chance of landing on:

a red? _____   b green? _____   c yellow? _____   d blue? _____

10

a Is it true that Spinner A has a 50% chance of spinning green?   _____

b Which spinner has a better than 50% chance of spinning red?   _____

c Which spinner has a one-in-four chance of spinning green?   _____

d Which two spinners have a one-in-four chance of spinning blue?   _____

e Which spinner has slightly more than a one-in-four chance of spinning yellow?_____

11 Order the chance of the spinners landing on the colours, from least likely to most likely.

a Spinner A ___red,_____

b Spinner B _____

c Spinner C _____

12 This chocolate wheel has five colours and 10 sections. Use the chance scale of 0 to 1 to match the chance each colour has of being spun.

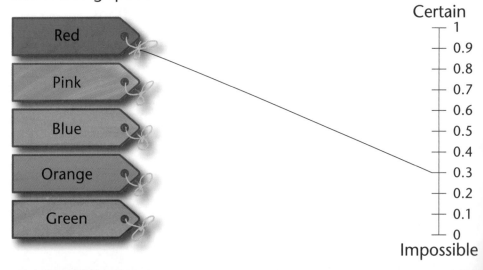

Red

Pink

Blue

Orange

Green

Certain
— 1
+ 0.9
+ 0.8
+ 0.7
+ 0.6
+ 0.5
+ 0.4
+ 0.3
+ 0.2
+ 0.1
— 0
Impossible

3D objects can be represented by drawings of their views from the top, front and side.

13 Find objects similar to these, then draw the top, front and side view of each.

a	b	c	d
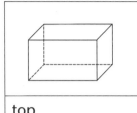	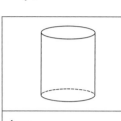	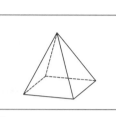	
top	top	top	top
front	front	front	front
side	side	side	side

14 Draw the top, front and side views of each object.

	Top view	Front view	Side view
a 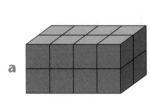			
b 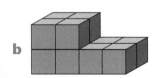			
c 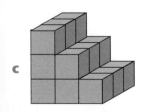			

WMS3.3   **SGS3.1**   Identifies three-dimensional objects, including particular prisms and pyramids, on the basis
of their properties, and visualises, sketches and constructs them given drawings of different views

71

5-digit addition

1 Complete these additions.

a 3 5 6 3 3
 +4 2 3 5 6
_____

b 3 4 3 5 7
 +4 4 1 0 8
_____

c 4 2 4 5 6
 +1 3 2 8 8
_____

d 5 2 6 4 0
 +3 1 8 7 5
_____

e 4 1 3 2 5
 +4 3 9 0 8
_____

f 6 6 3 2 8
 +2 1 7 6 6
_____

g 5 8 4 3 2
 +3 6 2 3 8
_____

h 2 4 2 3 5
 +4 2 9 6 8
_____

i 8 0 3 6 7
 +3 9 0 8 5
_____

j 7 5 2 8 6
 +4 8 1 4 6
_____

k 3 4 5 6 7
  3 9 8 7 8
 +2 0 0 3 6
_____

l 2 6 5 4 3
   3 4 7 4
 + 2 6 0 3
_____

m 3 5 9 7 4
  2 0 6 0 7
 +3 0 7 0 8
_____

n 3 8 3 0 9
  3 0 6 0 3
 +1 0 4 7 2
_____

o 3 5 7 0 4
   8 5 0 6
 +   7 5
_____

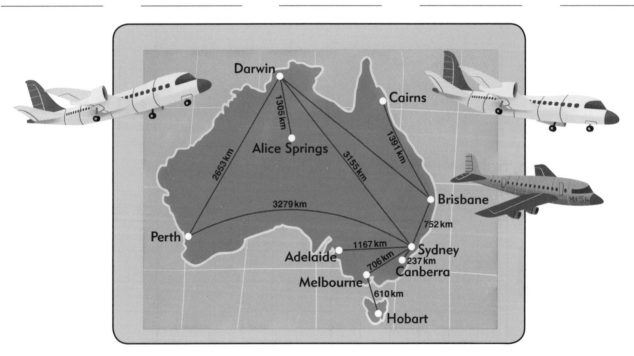

2 Calculate the length of each journey (working paper needed).

a Hobart to Sydney via Melbourne.   [ ] km

b Cairns to Melbourne via Brisbane and Sydney.   [ ] km

c Perth to Brisbane via Sydney.   [ ] km

d Alice Springs to Melbourne via Darwin and Sydney.   [ ] km

e Adelaide to Cairns via Sydney and Brisbane.   [ ] km

f Cairns to Hobart via Brisbane, Sydney and Melbourne   [ ] km

NS3.2 Selects and applies appropriate strategies for
addition and subtraction with counting numbers of any size   **WMS3.2**

Roman numerals

UNIT
18

3 Use the grid to assist you in providing Roman numerals for each number. You will need to combine Roman numerals for tens and ones. For example, 36 = XXXVI.

Roman numerals			
1	I	20	XX
2	II	30	XXX
3	III	40	XL
4	IV	50	L
5	V	60	LX
6	VI	70	LXX
7	VII	80	LXXX
8	VIII	90	XC
9	IX	100	C
10	X	500	D

a 27 _____   h 78 _____   o 252_____

b 34 _____   i 74 _____   p 263_____

c 26 _____   j 59 _____   q 364_____

d 38 _____   k 37 _____   r 464_____

e 42 _____   l 126_____   s 521_____

f 53 _____   m 115_____   t 632_____

g 64 _____   n 135_____   u 724_____

4 Supply the next Roman numeral in each sequence.

a | V | VI | VII | |

b | XV | XVI | XVII | |

c | XXI | XXII | XXIII | |

d | XV | XX | XXV | |

e | XXIV | XXIII | XXII | |

f | LIII | LIV | LV | |

g | LXI | LXII | LXIII | |

h | LXXV | LXXX | LXXXV | |

5 Calculate the distances between towns. The first step is to convert the Roman numerals into Hindu-Arabic. The first one is done for you.

Distance from Sydney

BLACKHEATH CXXX km
OBERON CC km
ORANGE CCLXXV km
DUBBO CDX km
IVANHOE DCL km

a
Oberon	200 km
Blackheath	130 km
	70 km

b
Dubbo	km
Blackheath	km
	km

c
Ivanhoe	km
Dubbo	km
	km

d
Orange	km
Oberon	km
	km

6 Write five numbers between 100 and 300 in Roman numerals.

WMS3.2, WMS3.5   NS3.1 Orders, reads and writes numbers of any size   73

7 Study the line graph carefully before attempting the questions.

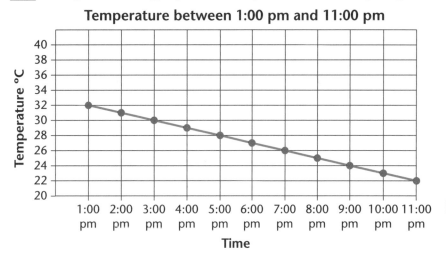

a What was the temperature
at 1:00 pm? _____°C

b What was the temperature
at 4:00 pm? _____°C

c What was the temperature
at 10:00 pm? _____°C

d Estimate the temperature
at 1:30 pm. _____°C

e Estimate the temperature
at 6:30 pm. _____°C

f What was the difference
in temperature between
1:00 pm and 7:00 pm? _____°C

g Estimate what the temperature
may have been at 12:00 noon. _____°C

8 A hose uses 2 L of water every 10 seconds.

a Use this information to complete the table, then record the information on a line graph.

Seconds	10	20	30	40	50	60	70	80	90	100	110	120	130	140	150	160
Litres	2	4	6	8	10											

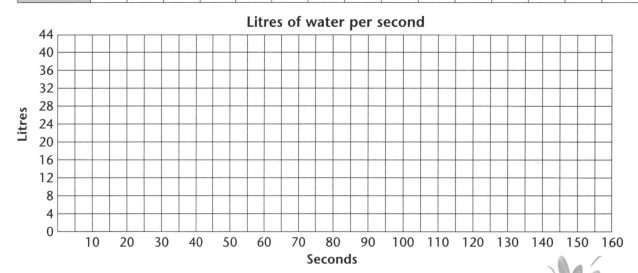

b How many litres of water were used in 70 seconds? _____

c How many litres of water were used in 85 seconds? _____

d How long would it take the hose to use 40 L? _____

Cubic centimetres and millilitres

A small unit for measuring capacity is the **millilitre**.   **1000 mL = 1 L**

9 Estimate and measure the capacity of each of these small vessels in millilitres (mL).
(You may need a medicine glass or a 1 mL eye dropper.)

a teaspoon   **b** tea cup   **c** screwcap   **d** mug

Estimate: _____   Estimate: _____   Estimate: _____   Estimate: _____

Capacity: _____   Capacity: _____   Capacity: _____   Capacity: _____

10 Does 1 cubic centimetre displace one millilitre of water?
Conduct this experiment to see.

Use a measuring glass filled to 30 mL to measure the water displaced by cubic
centimetres (centicubes). Colour the new water levels on each measuring glass below.

a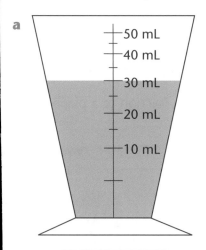

50 mL
40 mL
30 mL
20 mL
10 mL

5 cm³
(5 centicubes)

b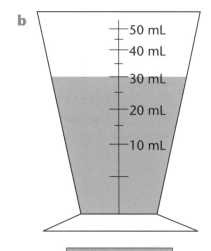

50 mL
40 mL
30 mL
20 mL
10 mL

10 cm³
(10 centicubes)

c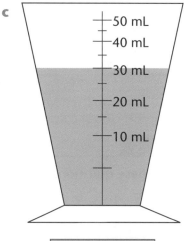

50 mL
40 mL
30 mL
20 mL
10 mL

15 cm³
(15 centicubes)

d Did you notice any relationship between the cubic centimetres and the water
displaced by them? _____

e What is it? _____

_____

_____

11 How many centicubes (cm³) would be needed to displace 100 mL? _____

Diagnostic review 2

L = 50 V = 5

PART 1 NS3.1

Give the place value of each bold number.

a 35 7**4**9   4 tens ✓

b 23 **5**21   5 hundreds ✓

c 12**3** 456   3 thousands ✓

d **3**57 296   300, thousands ✓

What is the value of each Roman numeral?

e X =   10 ✓   h XX =   20 ✓

f XVIII =   18 ✓   i XXXVI =   36 ✓

g LXXI =   171 ✓   j XLIV =   66 ✗

PART 2 NS3.2

Answer these questions.

a
```
    3 5 6
    2 0 7
  +   3 4
  ───────
    5 9 7 ✓
```

b
```
    3 2 0 6
  + 4 0 6 8
  ─────────
    7 2 7 4 ✓
```

c
```
   $ 3 0 . 5 7
 + $ 2 9 . 6 8
 ─────────────
   $ 6 0 . 2 5 ✓
```

d
```
    7 4 ³ 3 6
  -   2 4 3
  ──────────
    7 1 9 3 ✓
```

e
```
    3 5 ⁴ ⁹ 0 0
  -     2 3 5
  ────────────
    3 2 6 5 ✓
```

f
```
    2 6 ¹ 5 ¹² 3 ¹ 4
  -   1 4 3 5
  ──────────────
    1 1 9 9 ✓
```

PART 3 NS3.3

Answer these questions.

a
```
    2 5 4
  ×     3
  ───────
    7 6 2 ✓
```

b
```
    3 5 0
  ×     7
  ───────
  2 4 5 0 ✓
```

c
```
    2 6 7
  ×     8
  ───────
  2 1 3 6 ✓
```

d 8
6)48 ✓

e 3 r¹ ... 3
7)21 ✓

f 7 r⁵⁵ ... 7
7)49 ✓

g 9 r5
8)77 ✓

h 4 r3
9)39 ✓

i 9 r4
9)85 ✓

j 121
7)847 ✓

k 172
3)516 ✓

l 121
8)968 ✓

m (3 + 7) × 5 = 50 ✓   n 3 + (7 × 5) = 38 ✓

o 16 ÷ 4 × 3 = 12 ✓   p 16 ÷ 4 + 7 = 11 ✓

B/x O/✓ D/✓ M/✓ A S

X = 10

Write prime or composite after each number.

q 25 composite ✓   r 13 prime ✓

s 7 prime ✓   t 12 composite ✓

PART 4 NS3.4

Write the fraction and decimal as modelled in the shading on each hundredth grid.

	Fraction	Decimal
a	$\frac{23}{100}$	0.23 ✓
b	$\frac{46}{100}$	0.46 ✓
c	$\frac{37}{100}$	0.37 ✓

Add or subtract the fractions.

d $\frac{2}{6} + \frac{3}{6} = \frac{5}{6}$ ✓   e $\frac{5}{12} - \frac{3}{12} = \frac{2}{12}$ ✓

f $\frac{5}{6} - \frac{2}{6} = \frac{3}{6}$ ✓   g $\frac{3}{12} + \frac{8}{12} = \frac{11}{12}$ ✓

Draw a line to match each fraction to a place on the number line.

h $0 \quad \frac{1}{8} \quad \frac{1}{4} \quad \frac{1}{2} \quad \frac{3}{4} \quad 1\frac{1}{4} \quad 2\frac{1}{4}$

$\frac{1}{8}$ $1\frac{1}{4}$ $2\frac{1}{4}$

PART 5 NS3.5

Draw a line to the scale of 0 to 1 to show the chance of the spinner landing on red.

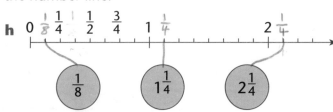

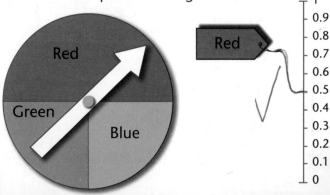

Diagnostic review 2

PART 6 — SGS3.2a

Draw a line to match each triangle with its name.

| Isosceles | Equilateral | Scalene |

PART 7 — SGS3.1

Draw this object on the isometric dot paper.

 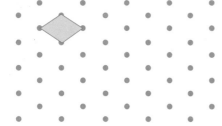

PART 8 — SGS3.2a

Tick the shapes that have rotational symmetry.

a 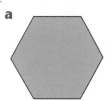 b 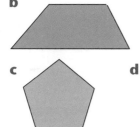 d

c

PART 9 — SGS3.3

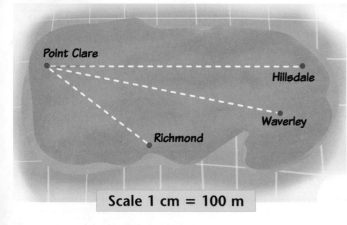

Scale 1 cm = 100 m

Use the scale to calculate the distance:

a from Point Clare to Hillsdale _____

b from Point Clare to Waverley _____

PART 10 — MS3.1, MS3.2

a Draw a square with a perimeter of 20 cm on the 1 cm grid paper.

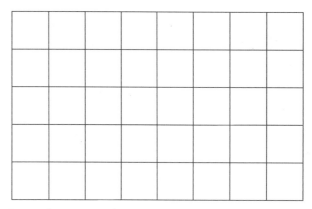

b Does the square have an area of 20 cm²? _____

PART 11 — MS3.3

Tick the object with the larger volume.

a 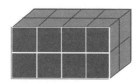 b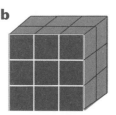

PART 12 — MS3.5

Write these times in 24-hour time.

a 9:36 am _____

b 3:35 pm _____

c 8:25 pm _____

PART 13 — DS3.1

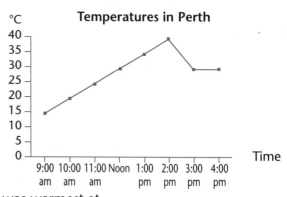

a It was warmest at _____

b The coolest temperature shown is _____

c The temperature at 11:00 am was _____

3-digit division

573 paint brushes were shared among 4 schools . . .

Share out the hundreds, with each school getting 1. One hundred is left over.

$$\begin{array}{r} 1 \\ 4)\overline{5\ 7\ 3} \end{array}$$

Trade the 1 hundred left over for 10 tens. Now share the 17 tens. Each school gets 4.

$$\begin{array}{r} 1\ 4 \\ 4)\overline{5\ ^17\ 3} \end{array}$$

Trade the 1 ten left over for 10 ones. Now share out the 13 ones. Each school gets 3. That leaves a remainder of 1.

$$\begin{array}{r} 1\ 4\ 3\ r1 \\ 4)\overline{5\ ^17\ ^13} \end{array}$$

1 Complete these divisions.

a $5)\overline{7\ 6\ 5}$ b $6)\overline{8\ 6\ 4}$ c $4)\overline{6\ 5\ 2}$ d $7)\overline{9\ 4\ 5}$ e $4)\overline{7\ 5\ 2}$

f $3)\overline{5\ 5\ 5}$ g $4)\overline{7\ 0\ 8}$ h $6)\overline{7\ 5\ 0}$ i $5)\overline{9\ 2\ 0}$ j $8)\overline{9\ 9\ 2}$

k $3)\overline{4\ 4\ 5}$ l $4)\overline{7\ 7\ 7}$ m $5)\overline{8\ 4\ 1}$ n $6)\overline{7\ 3\ 9}$ o $7)\overline{9\ 1\ 7}$

p $8)\overline{9\ 5\ 1}$ q $4)\overline{6\ 6\ 7}$ r $6)\overline{9\ 7\ 7}$ s $8)\overline{9\ 4\ 6}$ t $7)\overline{9\ 7\ 9}$

2 Calculate the solutions to these.

a $3)\overline{2\ 2\ 2}$ b $5)\overline{3\ 7\ 5}$ c $4)\overline{3\ 0\ 8}$ d $6)\overline{3\ 9\ 6}$ e $7)\overline{4\ 4\ 1}$

f $8)\overline{6\ 7\ 5}$ g $9)\overline{7\ 6\ 3}$ h $7)\overline{3\ 9\ 7}$ i $8)\overline{3\ 6\ 6}$ j $6)\overline{2\ 9\ 1}$

k $4)\overline{3\ 7\ 5}$ l $6)\overline{4\ 5\ 5}$ m $5)\overline{4\ 9\ 3}$ n $3)\overline{3\ 2\ 2}$ o $7)\overline{5\ 9\ 9}$

p $3)\overline{3\ 0\ 7}$ q $4)\overline{4\ 0\ 4}$ r $7)\overline{7\ 0\ 6}$ s $5)\overline{5\ 0\ 2}$ t $6)\overline{6\ 0\ 7}$

u $3)\overline{6\ 0\ 9}$ v $4)\overline{5\ 2\ 8}$ w $5)\overline{7\ 7\ 7}$ x $6)\overline{3\ 6\ 7}$ y $7)\overline{8\ 9\ 7}$

3 Write a problem to reflect this division $3)\overline{693}$.

NS3.3 Selects and applies appropriate strategies for multiplication and division   **WMS3.1, WMS3.3**

Percentage equivalences

A **percentage** is another way of recording a fraction with a denominator of 100 (out of 100). A percentage sign **%** is used to display percentages, for example $\frac{85}{100}$ can be written as 85%.

4 Shade the grids to display the percentages.

| a 52% | b 94% | c 63% | d 88% | e 5% |

5 Complete the equivalence tables.

	Visual	Fraction	Hundredths	Decimal	Percentage
a		$\frac{1}{10}$	$\frac{10}{100}$	0.10	10%
b		$\frac{2}{10}$	$\frac{}{100}$	0.	%
c		$\frac{1}{4}$	$\frac{}{100}$	0.	%
d		$\frac{3}{10}$	$\frac{}{100}$	0.	%
e		$\frac{4}{10}$	$\frac{}{100}$	0.	%
f		$\frac{1}{2}$	$\frac{}{100}$	0.	%

	Visual	Fraction	Hundredths	Decimal	Percentage
g		$\frac{6}{10}$	$\frac{}{100}$	0.	%
h		$\frac{7}{10}$	$\frac{}{100}$	0.	%
i		$\frac{3}{4}$	$\frac{}{100}$	0.	%
j		$\frac{8}{10}$	$\frac{}{100}$	0.	%
k		$\frac{9}{10}$	$\frac{}{100}$	0.	%
l		1	$\frac{}{100}$		%

6 Write a percentage for each fraction or decimal.

a $\frac{23}{100}$ = _____%　b $\frac{1}{4}$ = _____%　c $\frac{1}{2}$ = _____%　d $\frac{7}{10}$ = _____%　e $\frac{3}{4}$ = _____%

7 Mr Snodgrass is thinking about buying a one-bedroom city apartment. He has been given this plan and a scale to work from.
Use the scale to help Mr Snodgrass work out the sizes of his rooms.

Scale 1 cm = 1 m

	Room	Length	Breadth
a	Bathroom		
b	Lounge		
c	Kitchen		
d	Bedroom		

Bedroom   Kitchen   Bathroom   Lounge

8 Lauren has a new bedroom and some new furniture. Use the scale and follow the instructions to draw a plan view of her room as you would like it. (Plan views are views from above.)

a Use the scale to draw the boundary of the room first.

b Place her bed in an appropriate position.

c Put her new desk against a wall.

d Put her mat on the floor.

e Put her shelves against a wall.

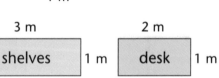

Scale 2 cm = 1 m

1 tonne = 1 000 kilograms. The tonne is used to measure large masses such as cars. The symbol for tonne is **t**.

9 Explain some situations when it would be more convenient to measure mass in tonnes rather than in kilograms.

_____

_____

10 Place the ships and vehicles in order of mass, from lightest to heaviest.

Destroyer 4 788 t

4-wheel drive 2 t

Submarine 2 456 t

Frigate 3 921 t

Truck 14 t

Semi-trailer 36 t

	a	b	c	d	e	f
Name						
Mass						

11 Complete these problems.

a What is the difference in mass between a destroyer and a submarine?

c What is the difference in mass between a semi-trailer and the truck

b What is the total mass of all three ships?

d What is the difference in mass between a frigate and a 4-wheel drive car?

12 How many kilograms are in each of these masses?

a 1 t = _____ kg   **d** $\frac{1}{2}$ t = _____ kg   **g** 2.5 t = _____ kg

b 2 t = _____ kg   **e** $\frac{1}{4}$ t = _____ kg   **h** 3.5 t = _____ kg

c 3 t = _____ kg   **f** $\frac{3}{4}$ t = _____ kg   **i** 1.25 t = _____ kg

$3\frac{3}{4}$ t equals 3 750 kg.

Addition and estimation

1 Calculate the answer to each addition.

a	b	c	d
2 5 3 4 7 + 2 4 8	1 0 3 5 6 4 4 2 4 + 3 0 3	2 3 4 5 7 2 6 6 2 + 3 3 0 7	3 5 7 6 4 2 6 8 5 + 3 0 7

2 Kim has written her estimates for the questions in the table below. Use your estimation skills, such as rounding to the nearest ten, to write your own estimates and decide whether her estimates are reasonable or unreasonable.

	Question	Kim's estimate	My estimate	Reasonable	Unreasonable
a	39 + 43	80			
b	149 + 52	250			
c	212 + 68	380			
d	331 + 71	400			
e	309 + 78	500			
f	1 111 + 83	1 900			
g	2 127 + 43	2 170			

To estimate 137 + 42, think 140 + 40. Estimate = 180.

3 Calculate the cost of a return trip to London for a family of four people.

JUZ FLIGHTS	JET TRAVEL	WHISPER TRAVEL	FLY HIGH TRAVEL
Sydney to London	Sydney to London	Sydney to London	Sydney to London
$2 080 return Children $1 020	$1 247 one way Children $654	$3 170 return Children FREE	$1 457 return Children $1 457

	Travel agent	Father	Mother	Son	Daughter	Total
a	Juz Flights					$
b	Jet Travel					$
c	Whisper Travel					$
d	Fly High Travel					$

e Which is the most expensive travel agent? _____

f Which is the most economical travel agent? _____

Averages

	Question:	How do you find the average?
	Answer:	**Averages** are found by totalling the scores then dividing by the number of scores.

The average age of children in our family is 10. $(8 + 10 + 12) \div 3 = 10$.

4 Find the averages of these numbers.

	Numbers	Total of scores	Number of scores	Average
a	4, 5, 6, 7, 8	30	5	6
b	8, 10, 12, 14, 16			
c	7, 9, 13, 11, 5			
d	18, 6, 9, 15, 12			
e	30, 10, 15, 25			
f	40, 36, 32			
g	12, 15, 18, 21, 24, 27, 30			

5 Find the averages.

a What was the average time taken to run a race if Ryan took 11 seconds, Brooke took 9 seconds, Conrad took 10 seconds and Marcel 14 seconds?

b Four types of gifts were for sale at the Mother's Day stall, for $4, $6, $10 and $12. What was the average price of the gifts?

c There are five children in the Wong family. Work out the average age of the children if they are 15, 13, 13, 9 and 5.

d The temperature in our classroom at 10:00 am, Monday to Friday, last week, was 21°C, 22°C, 23°C, 20°C and 24°C. Work out the average daily temperature for that week.

e What was the average amount of time Jo spent on her homework last week if her times were 10 minutes, 50 minutes, 20 minutes, 40 minutes and 30 minutes?

6 Write as many groups of numbers as you can that have an average of 10.

7 Enlarge these shapes by doubling their dimensions (sides).

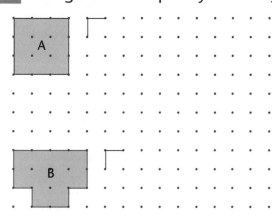
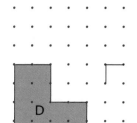
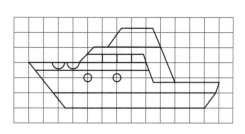
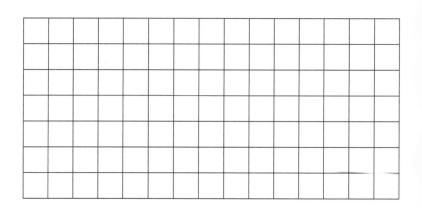

8 Enlarge the boat on the grid.

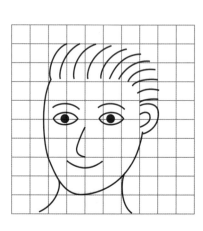

9 Enlarge the boy on the large grid, then reduce him on the smaller one.

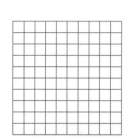
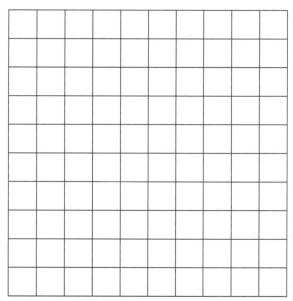

Sector graphs are used to show how a total is divided.

10 This sector graph represents the flavours of ice cream preferred by 96 customers at an ice-cream parlour.

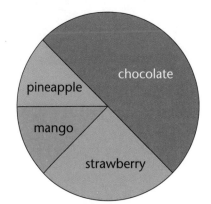

a About how many people chose chocolate? _____

b About how many people chose mango? _____

c About how many people chose strawberry? _____

d Which two flavours, when added, equal the popularity of strawberry?

_____

e According to the sector graph, is it true that chocolate is about 4 times as popular as pineapple? _____

11 This graph represents the number of hours Phillip spent doing these activities during his day. It has been broken up into units of 1 hour.

a How many hours did Phillip spend sleeping? _____

b How many hours did he watch television? _____

c Did he spend less time on sport than playing? _____

d What three activities does he spend the same amount of time on?

_____

12 How does your day differ from Phillip's?

a In the table, record the time you spend on various activities. Make sure they total 24 hours.

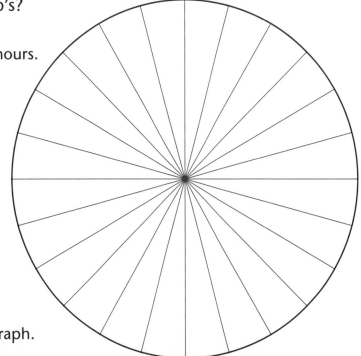

Activity	Hours
Sleeping	

b Transfer this information onto the sector graph.

3-digit mental multiplication

Mental strategies can be used to complete 3-digit × 1-digit multiplications.

543 × 6?

543 × 6

Think:

500 × 6 =	3 0 0 0
40 × 6 =	2 4 0
3 × 6 =	1 8

That's: **3 2 5 8**

1 Use mental and written strategies to complete these multiplications.

a   254 × 5 =

b   467 × 6 =

c   493 × 3 =

d   365 × 7 =

e   284 × 4 =

f   326 × 8 =

g   707 × 4 =

h   854 × 6 =

i   732 × 9 =

2 Calculate how much each person earned while working at the Royal Easter Show.
Check your answers with a calculator.

	Name	Days	Pay rate per day	Total	Calculator
a	Erica	5	$125		
b	Rebecca	6	$216		
c	Jayde	9	$362		
d	Kylie	4	$237		
e	Mika	7	$364		

3 Here is the working out Stella used to solve a problem.
Write a problem to suit her working out.

| 300 × 5 = 1 500 |
| 60 × 5 =   300 |
| 5 × 5 =   25 |

When we read numbers, we read them in groups of hundreds, tens and ones. The following chart best illustrates this concept.

Examples	Millions			Thousands			Ones		
	Hund	Tens	Ones	Hund	Tens	Ones	Hund	Tens	Ones
765 364				7	6	5	3	6	4
32 305 706		3	2	3	0	5	7	0	6

Note: A space separates the millions from the thousands, and the thousands from the hundreds.

```
                   H  T  O            H  T  O
Example 1 reads:   7  6  5  thousand  3  6  4  ones

                   H  T  O            H  T  O                  H  T  O
Example 2 reads:      3  2  million   3  0  5  thousand  7  0  6  ones
```

4 Write these numbers in numerals. The first one is done for you.

a Two hundred and sixteen thousand, four hundred and twenty-six. 216 426

b Three hundred and twenty-one thousand, two hundred and sixteen. _____

c Four hundred and thirty-five thousand, five hundred and sixty. _____

d One million, five hundred and eighteen thousand, six hundred and twenty. _____

e Twelve million, two hundred and seventy thousand, four hundred and eighty. _____

f Twenty-eight million, three hundred and seventy-eight thousand, nine hundred and ninety-nine. _____

5 Answer the questions below.

NSW	Vic	ACT	Qld	WA	SA	NT	Tas
802 000 km²	228 000 km²	2 000 km²	1 727 000 km²	2 562 000 km²	984 000 km²	1 346 000 km²	68 000 km²

a List the states and territories in order of their areas.

ACT, _____

b Which state has an area closest to 1 000 000 km²? _____

c Which state has an area closest to 3 000 000 km²? _____

d Which states are more than double the area of NSW? _____

e Which state is more than double the area of SA? _____

f Which state is closest to the area of NSW? _____

Divided bar graphs

Divided bar graphs are used to show how a total is divided.

Favourite food of 100 children

Hamburgers	Pizza	Chips	Other

6 Study the divided bar graph and answer the questions.

a Do more children like pizza than like chips? _____

b Do more children like hamburgers than like pizza? _____

c Do more children like chips than like "other" foods? _____

d Estimate how many children like hamburgers. _____

e Do more children like hamburgers than like pizza and chips combined? _____

Thirty children were surveyed as to their favourite coloured caps and the results were recorded using tally marks.

black	blue	red	green	white
ⅢⅠ I	ⅢⅠ ⅢⅠ	ⅢⅠ II	IIII	III

7 Make a divided bar graph of the caps by allocating 1 space for every cap.

BLACK																				

8 Answer the questions.

a Which was the most popular cap colour? _____

b Was red more popular than green? _____

c Was green more popular than black? _____

I need a cap with my team colours.

9 Complete a survey of the hair colour of the children in your class and make a divided bar graph. You may not need to use all the sections of the graph provided for you.

Black	Brown	Fair	Blonde	Red

Our class hair colours

Bus timetable

Brisbane	Dep.	0900
Mount Ommaney		0920
Ipswich		0950
Gatton		1025
Toowoomba		1110
Pittsworth		1140
Goondiwindi		1345
Moree		1600
Narrabri		1715
Gilgrandra		1955
Dubbo	Arr.	2045
	Dep.	2130
Peak Hill		2220
Parkes		2300
Forbes		2325
Wyalong		0035
Griffith	Arr.	0230
	Dep.	0330
Deniliquin		0615
Echuca		0715
Bendigo	Arr.	0835
	Dep.	0910
Tullamarine		1055
Melbourne		1115

10 Refer to the bus timetable and write how long each section of the trip takes.

	Section	Time
a	Brisbane–Toowoomba	
b	Moree–Dubbo	
c	Peak Hill–Forbes	
d	Griffith–Deniliquin	
e	Deniliquin–Bendigo	
f	Bendigo–Tullamarine	
g	Tullamarine–Melbourne	

11 Answer these questions

	Section	Time
a	How long is the rest stop at Dubbo?	
b	How long is the rest stop at Griffith?	
c	How long is the rest stop at Bendigo?	
d	How long is the entire trip from Brisbane to Melbourne?	

12 Prepare a timetable for the events in your day.

Time	Activity
0700 to 0800	
0800 to 0900	
0900 to 1000	
1000 to 1100	
1100 to 1200	
1200 to 1300	
1300 to 1400	
1400 to 1500	
1500 to 1600	
1600 to 1700	
1700 to 1800	

1 Complete these algorithms.

a   9 5 6 2 3
  − 3 2 1 5 2
  _____

b   7 8 3 3 1
  − 4 4 1 0 9
  _____

c   2 9 4 5 3
  − 1 4 2 2 8
  _____

d   8 2 8 4 6
  − 3 1 6 7 5
  _____

e   9 6 3 2 5
  − 4 3 8 1 6
  _____

f   6 9 3 2 8
  − 2 1 7 1 3
  _____

g   5 9 4 3 2
  − 3 6 2 7 0
  _____

h   6 8 2 3 5
  − 4 2 9 2 1
  _____

i   9 4 2 9 9
  − 3 9 0 8 8
  _____

j   8 5 2 9 6
  − 4 8 1 4 9
  _____

k   8 3 4 4 6
  − 6 8 2 3 1
  _____

l   6 7 4 4 5
  − 2 5 7 3 3
  _____

m   8 9 4 8 0
  − 3 2 9 1 7
  _____

n   5 4 5 4 5
  − 2 3 8 0 9
  _____

o   7 5 4 8 7
  − 5 9 3 6 9
  _____

2 As part of Paula and Francis' job at the mail centre they need to know the population of the major towns in NSW and the differences in size between them. Help them calculate the difference in population between these towns.

Town	Population	Town	Population
Armidale	21 330	Forster	15 943
Ballina	14 554	Griffith	14 209
Broken Hill	20 963	Parkes	10 094
Byron Bay	5 001	Shellharbour	46 294
Coffs Harbour	22 177	Taree	16 702
Dubbo	30 102	Wagga Wagga	42 848

a
Broken Hill	
Byron Bay	
Difference	

c
Shellharbour	
Coffs Harbour	
Difference	

e
Armidale	
Ballina	
Difference	

b
Forster	
Griffith	
Difference	

d
Wagga Wagga	
Taree	
Difference	

f
Shellharbour	
Broken Hill	
Difference	

3 Which town has a population 16 192 less than Shellharbour? _____

Finding percentages

Percentages can be used to find fractions of a collection.

4 Use your calculator to find the percentage of each quantity.

a 10% of 40 sheep = _____
b 20% of 40 sheep = _____
c 10% of 50 sheep = _____
d 10% of 80 goats = _____
e 50% of 80 goats = _____
f 25% of 80 goats = _____
g 50% of 70 horses = _____
h 20% of 90 horses = _____

i 10% of 100 ducks = _____
j 50% of 180 ducks = _____
k 25% of 160 geese = _____
l 75% of 120 geese = _____
m 10% of 200 cows = _____
n 10% of 220 cows = _____
o 20% of 250 pigs = _____
p 50% of 240 pigs = _____

10% of 40?
Press these buttons
on your calculator:
4 0 x 1 0 % =

5 Find these percentages by converting the percentage to a common fraction.
(The chart on page 79 may help you.)

a 10% of 20 pencils = _____
b 50% of 20 rulers = _____
c 25% of 60 erasers = _____
d 10% of 40 desks = _____
e 25% of 80 mugs = _____
f 50% of 70 cups = _____

g 10% of 60 books = _____
h 20% of 60 pencils = _____
i 25% of 60 pens = _____
j 20% of 80 rulers = _____
k 10% of 30 matches = _____
l 20% of 120 rulers = _____

50% of 20?
Think $\frac{1}{2}$ of 20 = 10.

6 Calculate how much is being saved on each item.

a shirt $_____   b jeans $_____   c coat $_____   d dress $_____

7 Rainman sunglasses cost $160. Write as many percentages of $160 as you can?

8 **Making a pattern of hexagons.**

a Complete and extend the table to record the number of sides needed to make the pattern of hexagons.

Hexagons	1	2	3	4	5	6	7
Sides							

b Write a rule to describe the pattern.

_____

c How many sides would there be on 9 hexagons? _____

9 **Making a pattern of octagons.**

a Complete and extend the table to record the number of sides needed to make the pattern of octagons.

Octagons	1	2	3	4	5	6	7
Sides							

b Write a rule to describe the pattern.

_____

c How many sides would there be on 11 octagons? _____

10 **Making a pattern of decagons.**

a Complete and extend the table to record the number of sides needed to make the pattern of decagons.

Decagons	1	2	3	4	5	6	7
Sides							

b Write a rule to describe the pattern.

_____

c How many sides would there be on 15 decagons? _____

11 **Making a pattern of dodecagons.**

a Complete and extend the table to record the number of sides needed to make the pattern of dodecagons.

Dodectagons	1	2	3	4	5	6	7
Sides							

b Write a rule to describe the pattern.

_____

c How many sides would there be on 10 dodecagons? _____

12 Make up a table of your own based on any shape below.

heptagon   pentagon   nonagon

Shape	1	2	3	4	5	6	7
Sides							

92 PAS3.1a Records, analyses and describes geometric and number patterns that involve one operation using tables and words

WMS3.3, WMS3.4

13 Draw a line to match each object to its set of views.

	Top	Front	Side
a			
b			
c			
d			

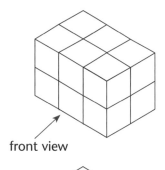

front view

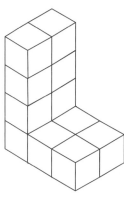

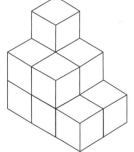

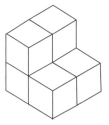

14 Construct the objects from their views then sketch them in the space provided. Useful materials may be centicubes, Base 10 ones or blocks.

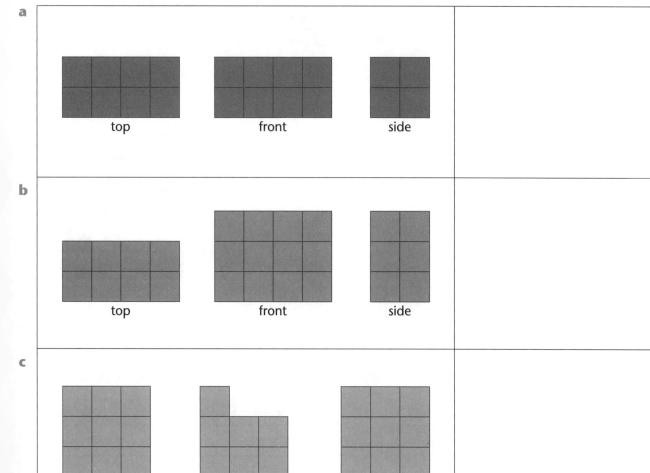

a

top   front   side

b

top   front   side

c

top   front   side

1 Complete these algorithms.

a
```
  3 9 1
×     4
_____

_____
```

b
```
  4 2 5
×     6
_____

_____
```

c
```
  2 3 6
×     5
_____

_____
```

d
```
  3 4 8
×     8
_____

_____
```

e
```
  2 7 0
×     6
_____

_____
```

f
```
  3 8 9
×     4
_____

_____
```

g
```
  2 5 3
×     9
_____

_____
```

h
```
  7 2 0
×     7
_____

_____
```

i
```
  8 0 5
×     4
_____

_____
```

j
```
  6 0 8
×     6
_____

_____
```

k
```
  3 2 3
×     5
_____

_____
```

l
```
  2 8 0
×     8
_____

_____
```

m
```
  4 0 7
×     9
_____

_____
```

n
```
  2 0 6
×     3
_____

_____
```

o
```
  4 0 3
×     6
_____

_____
```

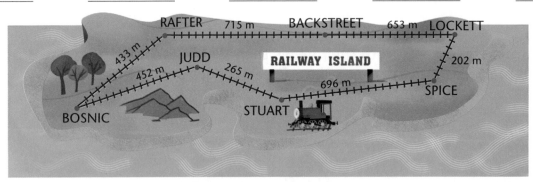

2 The only form of transport on Railway Island is by train. Calculate the distance of these train trips. You will need some scrap paper to do your working on.

a A return trip from Rafter to Backstreet. _____

b 6 journeys between Backstreet and Lockett. _____

c 5 trips between Judd and Stuart. _____

d 8 trips between Bosnic and Judd. _____

3 Name a trip that Linda completed 6 times if her total distance travelled was between 2 500 and 2 800 kilometres?

4 Use your knowledge of rounding to estimate before calculating the correct product.

	Calculation	Estimate	Product
a	3 × 29	3 × 30 = 90	87
b	4 × 48		
c	6 × 97		

	Calculation	Estimate	Product
d	6 × 213		
e	7 × 817		
f	9 × 482		

Improper fractions

Improper fractions have a numerator larger than the denominator, e.g. $\frac{5}{4}$, $\frac{7}{5}$, $\frac{8}{6}$. This means that the fraction has a value greater than 1.

Example | Jessica played all 4 quarters of her netball game and then played 1 quarter in her older sister's team. |  | This can be written like this: $\frac{5}{4}$

5 Write an improper fraction to describe the fraction of the shapes that have been shaded. Remember the numerator is larger than the denominator.

	Shapes	Improper fraction
a		$\frac{}{4}$
b		
c		
d		
e		

	Shapes	Improper fraction
f		
g		
h		
i		
j		

6 Name the improper fractions appearing on the number lines below each letter.

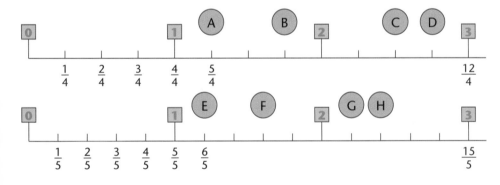

A	B	C	D
$\frac{5}{4}$			

E	F	G	H

7 Write the answer to these problems as improper fractions.

	Shapes	Improper fraction
a	How many quarters did Jasmine eat if she ate all of her orange and $\frac{1}{4}$ of her brother's orange?	
b	How many halves did Alex play if he played half a game in the first match and all of the second match?	
c	How many tenths of the pizza did Tim eat if he ate 1 whole pizza and $\frac{3}{10}$ of another?	
d	How many fifths did Julia eat if she ate one whole chocolate bar and $\frac{2}{5}$ of another bar?	

I played $\frac{6}{4}$ of netball last Saturday.

Chance

Tree diagrams are used to display all possible outcomes from a simple chance experiment.

Ms Smith wanted to order a new sports car. Her choices were as follows:

Red or black	Automatic or manual
Convertible or hard top	V6 engine or 4-cylinder

8 Complete the tree diagram to find all possible combinations of sports car.

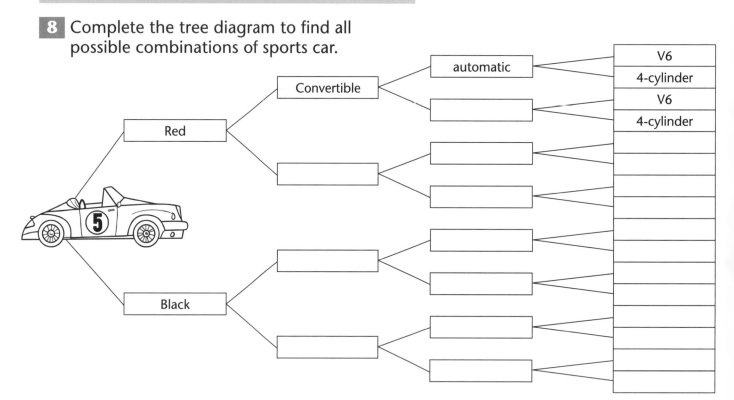

Mrs Wills made her daughter a sandwich. Her choices were chicken or salad, on white or brown bread, with or without margarine.

9 Draw a tree diagram to display all possible combinations of the sandwich.

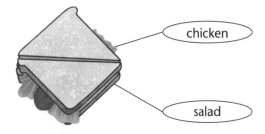

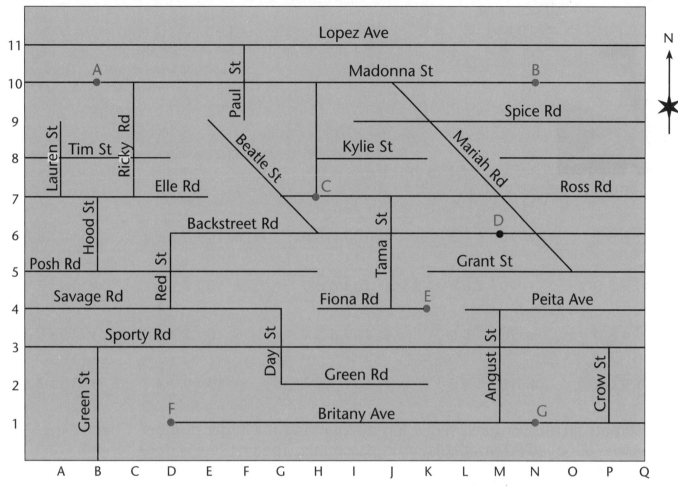

10 Name the streets found at these coordinate points.

Scale 1 cm = 100 m

a (A3) _____   c (C9) _____   e (F8) _____

b (E4) _____   d (N1) _____   f (L8) _____

11 Give one set of coordinate points for each location.

a Point B _____   b Point A _____   c Point E _____

12 Use the scale and direction to find the destination.

a Start at B and travel west 600 m. Turn south and travel another 300 m before turning east and travelling another 200 m. Head south again 300 m and east 100 m.
What letter did you find? _____

b Start at D and go west 900 m before turning south and going 200 m. Head east 300 m then south 100 m. Now go east 600 m, south 200 m then west 900 m.
What letter did you find? _____

13 Use the scale to calculate the shortest distance between the following points.

a A and B _____   c C and D _____   e A and E _____

b B and C _____   d F and G _____   f D and F _____

Division by ten

575 nails were shared among 10 carpenters.

Divide 57 tens by 10. Each carpenter gets 5.

$$\begin{array}{r} 5 \\ 10\overline{)5\ 7\ 5} \end{array}$$

Trade the 7 tens for 70 ones. Now share the 75 ones. Each carpenter gets 7. That leaves a remainder of 5.

$$\begin{array}{r} 5\ 7\ r5 \\ 10\overline{)5\ 7^7 5} \end{array}$$

1 Complete these divisions.

a $10\overline{)8\ 6\ 0}$ e $10\overline{)8\ 1\ 0}$ i $10\overline{)7\ 8\ 0}$ m $10\overline{)3\ 2\ 5}$ q $10\overline{)6\ 8\ 5}$

b $10\overline{)7\ 5\ 0}$ f $10\overline{)7\ 0\ 0}$ j $10\overline{)8\ 6\ 0}$ n $10\overline{)7\ 7\ 7}$ r $10\overline{)7\ 9\ 7}$

c $10\overline{)4\ 8\ 0}$ g $10\overline{)9\ 8\ 0}$ k $10\overline{)6\ 5\ 4}$ o $10\overline{)5\ 1\ 1}$ s $10\overline{)8\ 7\ 4}$

d $10\overline{)9\ 0\ 0}$ h $10\overline{)3\ 9\ 0}$ l $10\overline{)3\ 5\ 7}$ p $10\overline{)9\ 7\ 4}$ t $10\overline{)7\ 8\ 9}$

2 Estimate an answer to each division by rounding the larger number. Check if the answer supplied is reasonable or unreasonable. The first one is done for you.

	Question	Answer	Estimate	Reasonable	Unreasonable
a	388 ÷ 4	97	100	✓	
b	318 ÷ 6	53			
c	776 ÷ 4	94			
d	1 590 ÷ 8	198 r6			
e	2 417 ÷ 4	404 r1			

3 Find the averages.

Averages are found by totalling the scores, then dividing by the number of scores.

a John has 7 cards, Jill 6, Leanne 5, Toula 7 and Jim 30. What is the average number of cards per child? _____

b Jacqui scored 17 runs, 6 runs, 10 runs and 11 runs in 4 innings. What was her average? _____

c Sam is 127 cm high, Jilly 140 cm, Tom 153 cm, Soula 133 cm and Tim 147 cm. What is the average height of the group? _____

4 Mr Smith said that the average amount of money saved was $8. If there were between 5 and 10 children, how much money could have been saved?

Mixed numerals

A **mixed numeral** is a number that consists of a whole number and a fraction, e.g. $1\frac{1}{2}$, $2\frac{3}{4}$, $5\frac{1}{2}$

Improper fractions can be changed to mixed numbers, e.g. $\frac{5}{4} = 1\frac{1}{4}$

5 Write an improper fraction and a mixed numeral to describe each set of shapes. The first one is done for you.

Five quarters of an orange = $\frac{5}{4}$ which is the same as $1\frac{1}{4}$.

	Shapes	Improper fraction	Mixed number
a		$\frac{5}{3}$	$1\frac{2}{3}$
b			
c			
d			
e			
f			
g			
h			
i			
j			

Gina labelled her number line using mixed numerals and improper fractions.

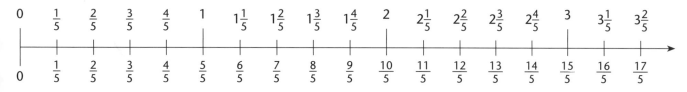

6 Use the number line to write an improper fraction for each mixed numeral.

a $1\frac{1}{5}$ = _____   b $1\frac{3}{5}$ = _____   c $2\frac{2}{5}$ = _____   d $2\frac{4}{5}$ = _____   e $3\frac{1}{5}$ = _____

7 Use the number line to write a mixed numeral for each improper fraction.

a $\frac{7}{5}$ = _____   b $\frac{9}{5}$ = _____   c $\frac{11}{5}$ = _____   d $\frac{13}{5}$ = _____   e $\frac{17}{5}$ = _____

8 Measure the angles in these triangles.

a Equilateral triangle

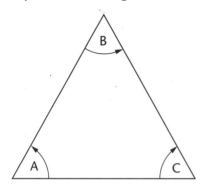

Angle A _____°

Angle B _____°

Angle C __62__°

b Scalene triangle

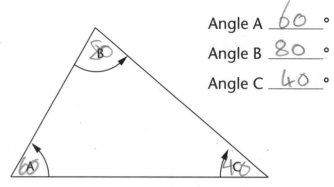

Angle A __60__°

Angle B __80__°

Angle C __40__°

c Isosceles triangle

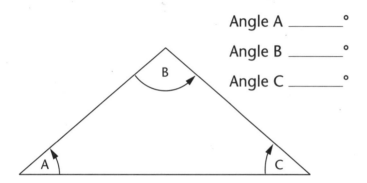

Angle A _____°

Angle B _____°

Angle C _____°

d Right-angled triangle

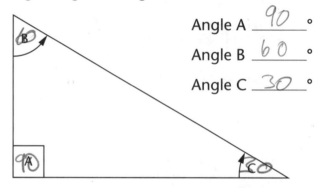

Angle A __90__°

Angle B __60__°

Angle C __30__°

9 What can you say about the size of the angles in an equilateral triangle? _____

10 What can you say about the size of the angles in a scalene triangle? _____

11 Follow the directions to draw an isosceles triangle using compasses.

a Set your compasses to 7 cm.

b Place the point of the compasses at A on the line drawn for you, then draw an arc softly.

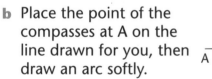

c Place the point of the compasses at B on the line, then draw an arc softly until it crosses the first arc you drew.

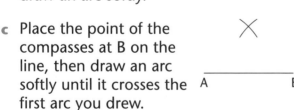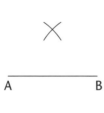

d Join the ends of the line to the point where the arcs cross.

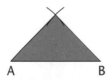

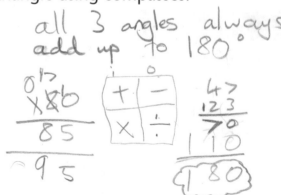

all 3 angles always add up to 180°

12 Measure then calculate the perimeter of each shape in millimetres.

a
P = _____ mm

b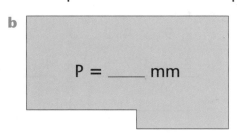
P = _____ mm

c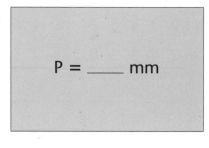
P = _____ mm

13 Explain how you could use a short cut to find the perimeters of these shapes.

a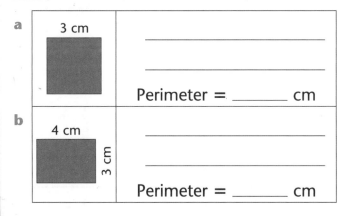
3 cm
_____
_____
Perimeter = _____ cm

b
4 cm
3 cm
_____
_____
Perimeter = _____ cm

c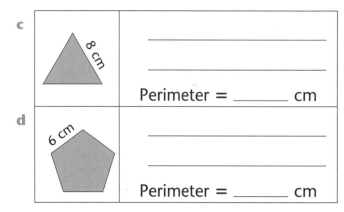
8 cm
_____
_____
Perimeter = _____ cm

d
6 cm
_____
_____
Perimeter = _____ cm

14 Calculate the perimeter of each room.

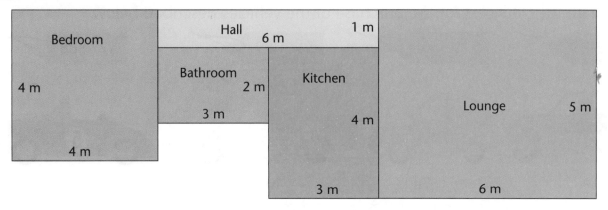

Bedroom
Hall 6 m 1 m
4 m
4 m
Bathroom 2 m
3 m
Kitchen
4 m
3 m
Lounge 5 m
6 m

a Bedroom _____ m   **c** Bathroom _____ m

b Lounge _____ m   **d** Kitchen _____ m

15 Calculate the perimeter of these shapes, using decimal notation.

a
3.5 m
3.3 m
P = _____

b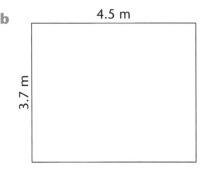
4.5 m
3.7 m
P = _____

c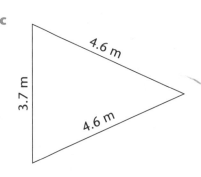
4.6 m
3.7 m
4.6 m
P = _____

5-digit addition

1 Complete these algorithms.

```
a   2 3 4 5 7     b   4 6 3 6 8     c   2 9 5 4 2     d   3 8 4 9 8     e   3 4 7 2 8
  + 2 4 3 3 8       + 2 3 4 2 9       + 2 0 3 7 5       + 4 1 2 8 1       + 4 3 3 6 5
  _____         _____         _____         _____         _____


f   3 4 7 5 4     g   2 5 8 4 3     h   3 3 7 7 7     i   4 2 8 7 8     j   5 4 3 6 8
  + 2 4 8 3 2       + 3 1 2 0 8       + 2 4 1 9 2       + 3 5 2 0 8       + 2 7 8 5 4
  _____         _____         _____         _____         _____
```

2 Supply the missing numbers to complete the additions.

```
a   5 2 □ 3 4     b   2 4 0 2 3     c   □ 3 1 □ 3     d   2 7 2 9 4     e   3 3 4 □ 6
    2 □ 7 2 4       2 □ 1 3 □         3 0 2 1 4         4 0 3 2 □         2 7 1 2 3
  + 1 4 0 2 5     + 3 4 4 7 1       + 2 8 1 3 2       + 2 □ 2 2 1       + 3 1 □ 2 7
    8 7 8 8 □       7 9 □ 2 6         7 □ 4 7 9       □ 4 8 □ 8         □ 2 4 0 6
```

3 Calculate the total cost for the purchase of the vehicles described below.

 $35 299

 $19 555

 $56 999

 $27 888

4WD   Bug   Mini-bus   Sportz

	Vehicles purchased	Working
a	Goode Real Estate bought the Mini-bus and the 4WD to transport their customers to look at houses for sale.	
b	Pete's Pizza bought the Bug and the Sportz cars because they thought customers wanted their pizzas delivered in new cars.	
c	Ocean Tours bought the 4WD and the Mini-bus to take tourists on trips, and the Bug for the Office Manager.	
d	Helen's Hire Cars bought the 4WD, the Bug and the Sportz because they are the most popular cars that people hire.	

We spent $47 443.

4 Complete these charts which involve multiplication by 10, 100 and 1 000.

	×	10	100	1 000
a	3	30	300	3 000
b	5			
c	6			
d	7			
e	9			
f	10			10 000

	×	10	100	1 000
g	18		1 800	
h	25			
i	31			31 000
j	44			
k	56			
l	78	780		

5 Estimate the following by rounding each number to the nearest 10 or 100 before multiplying them.

a 99 × 7 = _____

b 48 × 6 = _____

c 19 × 5 = _____

d 53 × 6 = _____

e 197 × 2 = _____

f 49 × 4 = _____

g 207 × 6 = _____

h 246 × 5 = _____

i 199 × 7 = _____

j 307 × 6 = _____

k 407 × 5 = _____

l 813 × 8 = _____

Always write the 0 first.

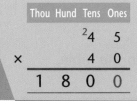

Thou	Hund	Tens	Ones
		^{2}4	5
×		4	0
1	8	0	0

Step 1: Write the 0 because you are multiplying by a ten.

Step 2: Multiply by 4 using the shortened method.

6 Complete these multiplications.

a
```
    2 4
×   2 0
───────

```

b
```
    2 6
×   4 0
───────

```

c
```
    3 5
×   3 0
───────

```

d
```
    2 7
×   4 0
───────

```

e
```
    1 8
×   5 0
───────

```

f
```
  1 2 7
×   2 0
───────

```

g
```
  1 3 5
×   5 0
───────

```

h
```
  1 2 8
×   4 0
───────

```

i
```
  2 3 6
×   3 0
───────

```

j
```
  2 4 8
×   5 0
───────

```

k
```
  3 4 5
×   4 0
───────

```

l
```
  4 6 3
×   6 0
───────

```

m
```
  2 7 5
×   7 0
───────

```

n
```
  2 3 8
×   8 0
───────

```

o
```
  4 4 7
×   9 0
───────

```

Number patterns

7 Identify the number pattern in each table then answer the questions.

a Complete the table.

First number	1	2	3	4	5	6	7
Second number	9	10	11	12			

b Describe the pattern in the table.

_____

c What would be the 10th term in the pattern? _____

d Complete the table.

First number	1	2	3	4	5	6	7
Second number	3	6	9				

e Describe the pattern in the table.

_____

f What would be the 10th term in the pattern? _____

g Complete the table.

First number	1	2	3	4	5	6	7
Second number	9	18	27				

h Describe the pattern in the table.

_____

i What would be the 10th term in the pattern? _____

j Complete the table.

First number	1	2	3	4	5	6	7
Second number	18			21			24

k Describe the pattern in the table.

_____

l What would be the 10th term in the pattern? _____

m Complete the table.

First number	11	10	9	8	7	6	5
Second number	99			72			45

n Describe the pattern in the table.

_____

o What would be the 10th term in the pattern? _____

p Complete the table.

First number	27	37	47	57	67	77	87
Second number	14			44			74

q Describe the pattern in the table.

_____

r What would be the 10th term in the pattern? _____

104 PAS3.1a Records, analyses and describes geometric and number patterns that involve one operation using tables and words

WMS3.3

8 Mr King has made a graph to represent how much money he spends in a week. Study the divided bar graph then answer the questions.

Weekly spending

Food	Entertainment	Clothes	Bills

Divided bar graphs are used to show how a total is

a On what does Mr King spend most of his money? _____

b On what does he spend the least? _____

c Does he spend more on entertainment than on bills? _____

d Does he spend more on clothes than on bills? _____

9 Mr King spends $200 on food each week. Shade the amount below that you think he would spend on entertainment.

$90 $300 $400 $160 $110 $500

10 We conducted a survey of 60 high school students to see which elective subjects were the most popular at high school. We presented our data as a divided bar graph.

Most popular elective subjects at high school

Pottery	Woodwork	Cooking	Metalwork	Art

Use the data from the graph to answer the questions.

a Which subject was the most popular? _____

b Which subject was the least popular? _____

c Which was more popular, metalwork or woodwork? _____

d If five people chose art, which estimate is closest to the number who did metalwork: 10, 15 or 50? _____

11 45 children in Class 5Y at our school tallied their shoe sizes.

 Size 4

 Size 5

 Size 6

 Size 7

|||| |||| |||| |||| |||| |||| | |||| |||| ||||

Colour the sections of the graph to represent the shoe sizes then label them. It has been started for you.

Shoe sizes of children

SIZE 4																								

Two digits multiplied by two digits

Long multiplication by 2 digits.

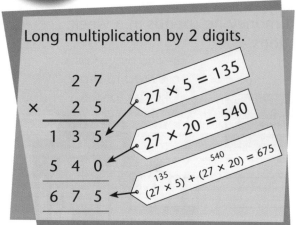

```
    2 7
×   2 5
───────
  1 3 5
  5 4 0
───────
  6 7 5
───────
```

27 × 5 = 135

27 × 20 = 540

                540
    135
(27 × 5) + (27 × 20) = 675

1 Complete these multiplications.

a
```
    2 5
×   2 3
───────
```

b
```
    3 6
×   3 4
───────
```

c
```
    4 5
×   2 5
───────
```

d
```
    3 6
×   3 5
───────
```

e
```
    2 9
×   4 6
───────
```

f
```
    2 7
×   3 7
───────
```

g
```
    5 6
×   4 5
───────
```

h
```
    3 9
×   5 6
───────
```

i
```
    2 7
×   2 8
───────
```

j
```
    3 5
×   3 9
───────
```

k
```
    5 7
×   4 7
───────
```

l
```
    2 7
×   5 6
───────
```

m
```
    8 6
×   2 9
───────
```

2 Each carton of tomato soup has 32 cans in it.
How many cans of soup are held on this pallet?

3 **Bill's party**
Bill spent between $400 and $600 on his party. How many people may have
attended the party if the average cost per person was $32?

Measurements are frequently recorded in thousandths (3-place decimals), e.g. 1.256 kg meaning 1 kg and 256 g, or 1 kilogram and 256 thousandths of a kilogram.

Decimal place value

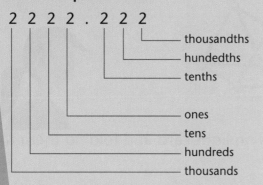

2 2 2 2 . 2 2 2

- thousandths
- hundedths
- tenths
- ones
- tens
- hundreds
- thousands

4 Record the place of each **bold** digit.

a 36.6**2** _____   f 666.9**8** _____

b 256.**7**3 _____   g 3.75**6** _____

c **4**5.35 _____   h 765.**3**5 _____

d **2**6.29 _____   i 23.**7**5 _____

e 13.45**6** _____   j 123.37**9**_____

5 Express these measurements as decimals.

	Measurement	Decimal
a	1 kg and 256 g	. kg
b	1 m and 378 mm	. m
c	2 L and 372 mL	. L
d	5 kg and 109 g	. kg

	Measurement	Decimal
e	3 m and 499 mm	. m
f	4 L and 649 mL	. L
g	6 kg and 296 g	. kg
h	7 m and 759 mm	. m

1 m and 273 mm is equal to 1.273 m.

6 Write a decimal for each fraction.

Zero can be used as a place holder for thousandths that are less than 100, e.g. $\frac{23}{1000}$ = 0.023.

$2\frac{274}{1000}$ is equal to 2.274.

a $\frac{236}{1000}$ = 0.☐   e $\frac{279}{1000}$ = 0.☐   i $\frac{74}{1000}$ = 0.☐

b $\frac{475}{1000}$ = 0.☐   f $\frac{352}{1000}$ = 0.☐   j $\frac{23}{1000}$ = 0.☐

c $\frac{259}{1000}$ = 0.☐   g $\frac{834}{1000}$ = 0.☐   k $\frac{88}{1000}$ = 0.☐

d $\frac{678}{1000}$ = 0.☐   h $\frac{994}{1000}$ = 0.☐   l $\frac{96}{1000}$ = 0.☐

7 Order the decimals, from the smallest to the largest.

a	0.123	0.456	0.111	0.423	
b	0.765	0.657	0.567	0.756	
c	2.234	1.999	1.459	0.978	
d	3.555	4.098	4.077	5.006	

8 Make copies of these 3D objects using straws and modelling clay or other construction materials. (For example, matches, toothpicks, playdough or commercial materials.)

Triangles help make objects rigid.

a
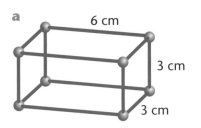
6 cm
3 cm
3 cm

b
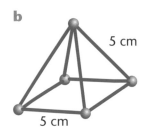
5 cm
5 cm

c
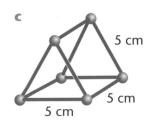
5 cm
5 cm
5 cm

9 Make a copy of these shapes by making their nets on light card and folding them to make the shapes. All dimensions are given.

a
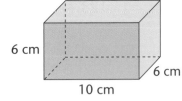
6 cm
6 cm
10 cm

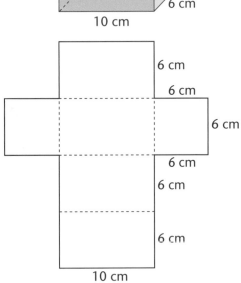
6 cm
6 cm
6 cm
6 cm
6 cm
6 cm
10 cm

b
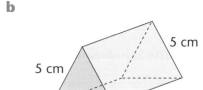
5 cm
5 cm
8 cm

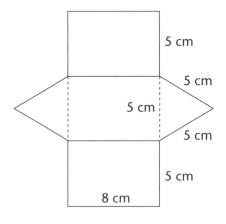
5 cm
5 cm
5 cm
5 cm
5 cm
8 cm

10 Mr Knox the jeweller wants to make a new box in which to sell his jewellery. He has drawn the box but can't draw the net. Design a net for Mr Knox's box on the 5 mm grid paper. It has been started for you.

3 cm
2 cm
2 cm
2 cm
2 cm
3 cm

Home of fine Jewellery

HANDLE WITH CARE

SGS3.1 Identifies three-dimensional objects, including particular prisms and pyramids, on the basis of their properties, and visualises, sketches and constructs them given drawings of different views

WMS3.2, WMS3.5

11 A recent newspaper article said that children spend too much time playing computer games. Gina spoke to her teacher and said that the article was not correct and that children do other things on the computer besides play games.

> Games are only a small part of what kids can do on

a Write some questions you could use in a survey to find out what other things children may do on a computer, to find out if Gina is correct.

(i) _____

(ii) _____

(iii) _____

b Who should you interview for this survey? _____

c Make your own prediction about how children use computers. _____

12 Conduct your survey and record your data in the table to find out how children use computers.

Games	Email					

13 Comment on your prediction after you have the survey results. _____
_____

14 Construct a column graph to record your data.

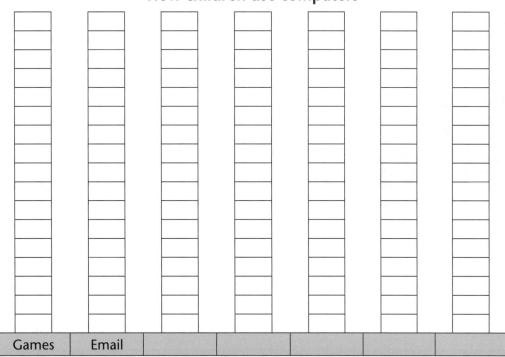

How children use computers

| Games | Email | | | | | |

Division with zeros

Five girls shared 515 lollies. How many lollies did each girl receive?

Divide the hundreds by five girls with each girl getting 1.

$$\begin{array}{r} 1 \\ 5\overline{)5\,1\,5} \end{array}$$

You cannot divide 5 into 1 so put a **zero**.

$$\begin{array}{r} 1\,0 \\ 5\overline{)5\,1\,5} \end{array}$$

Trade the 1 ten for 10 ones. Now divide the 15 ones by 5.

$$\begin{array}{r} 1\,0\,3 \\ 5\overline{)5\,1\,{}^15} \end{array}$$

1 Complete these divisions.

a $5\overline{)5\,1\,5}$ b $6\overline{)6\,1\,2}$ c $4\overline{)4\,1\,6}$ d $7\overline{)7\,1\,4}$ e $4\overline{)4\,1\,2}$

f $3\overline{)3\,1\,5}$ g $4\overline{)4\,2\,0}$ h $6\overline{)6\,1\,8}$ i $5\overline{)5\,2\,0}$ j $8\overline{)8\,1\,6}$

k $3\overline{)3\,2\,1}$ l $4\overline{)4\,2\,4}$ m $5\overline{)5\,2\,5}$ n $6\overline{)6\,2\,4}$ o $7\overline{)7\,2\,8}$

p $8\overline{)8\,3\,1}$ q $4\overline{)4\,3\,5}$ r $6\overline{)6\,2\,7}$ s $8\overline{)8\,3\,9}$ t $7\overline{)7\,4\,3}$

2 Complete these divisions.

a $3\overline{)7\,2\,6}$ b $5\overline{)3\,5\,9}$ c $4\overline{)7\,2\,6}$ d $6\overline{)8\,5\,4}$ e $7\overline{)6\,9\,3}$

f $8\overline{)8\,3\,4}$ g $9\overline{)6\,7\,9}$ h $7\overline{)7\,2\,9}$ i $8\overline{)9\,9\,9}$ j $6\overline{)7\,5\,4}$

k $10\overline{)8\,0\,0}$ l $10\overline{)7\,6\,0}$ m $10\overline{)7\,8\,5}$ n $10\overline{)6\,2\,9}$ o $10\overline{)5\,8\,5}$

3 Calculate the average distance between railway stops over 728 km.

a If the train stopped at 4 stations _____

b If the train stopped at 8 stations _____

c If the train stopped at 6 stations _____

4 Another train's average distance between railway stops was between 20 km and 30 km. If the train stopped at 7 stops what could the total distance have been?

Negative numbers

There are many instances in the real world where we need negative numbers.
Negative numbers are numbers **less than zero** written with a minus sign (−) in
front of them. Positive numbers greater than zero are the numbers you have been
dealing with so far and can be written with or without a (+) sign.

5 There are many places around the world and in Australia where temperatures below
zero exist. Look carefully at the thermometers below and record the temperatures.

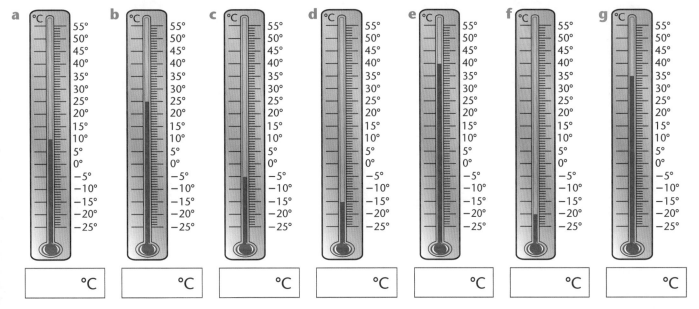

| | °C | | °C | | °C | | °C | | °C | | °C | | °C |

6 Look carefully at this diagram representing
sea levels, then estimate
an answer to each question.

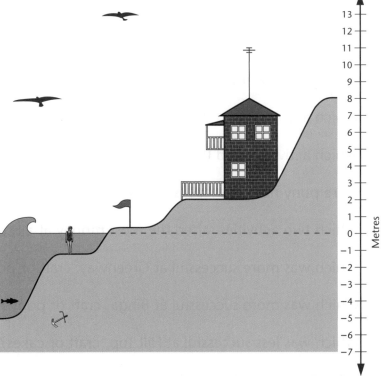

a How far above sea level
is the top of the flag? _____

b How far below sea
level is the fish? _____

c How far above sea level
is the aerial on the house? _____

d How far below sea level
is the swimmer's foot? _____

e How far above sea level
is the top of the house? _____

f Give the height of
both birds. _____

g Give the height of
the top of the wave. _____

h Give the height of
the top of the fence. _____

Interpreting graphs

Three primary schools each raised the same amount of money at their fetes.

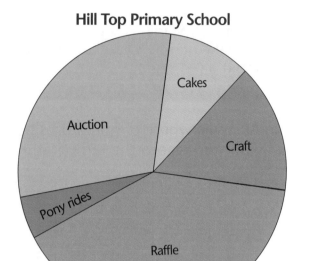

Hill Top Primary School

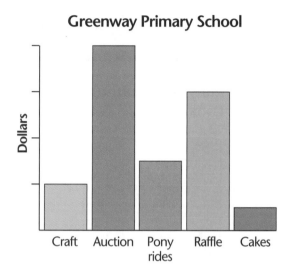

Greenway Primary School

Binga Primary School

Cakes	Craft	Auction	Raffle	Pony rides

7 Answer these questions.

a Which activity raised the most money at Hill Top School? _____

b Which activity raised the most money at Greenway School? _____

c Which activity raised the most money at Binga School? _____

d Which activity raised the least amount at Binga Primary School? _____

e Which activity raised the least amount at Hill Top Primary School? _____

f Which activity raised the least amount at Greenway Primary School? _____

g Were pony rides the least successful at all schools? _____

h Which two activities raised the most money at all schools? _____

i Which was more successful at Greenway, craft or pony rides? _____

j Which was more successful at Binga, craft or pony rides? _____

k Which was less successful at Hill Top, craft or cakes? _____

l If $300 was raised at Hill Top's auction, is it reasonable to say that
the raffle raised about $350? _____

8 Which measurement in the advertisements is easier to understand? _____

a

49 950 square metre farm for sale.

b

50 hectare farm for sale.

Large areas of land can be measured in **hectares**.
1 hectare = 10 000 m²
Two soccer fields are about 1 hectare.
The symbol for hectare is **ha**.
A square metre can be any shape, so can a hectare.

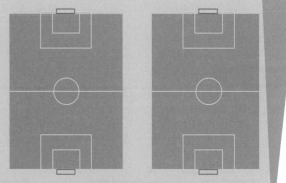

9 Is your school less than a hectare, about a hectare or more than a hectare?

a Use suitable measuring instruments to mark a hectare within your school.

b Place markers at the corners so that it is roughly the shape of a rectangle or square.

c Use a calculator to make your calculations.

Length		Breadth		Area
	m	×	m	=	m²

d Tick the correct box.

☐ My school is about one hectare.

☐ My school is less than one hectare.

☐ My school is more than one hectare.

10 Colour the pictures which represent areas of one hectare or more. (Pictures are not drawn to scale.)

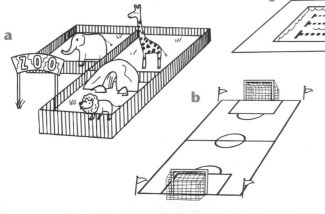

WMS3.2

MS3.2 Selects and uses the appropriate unit to calculate area, including the area of squares, rectangles and triangles

113

Diagnostic review 3

PART 1 Isabel Cox (5R) 53 NS3.2

a
```
    3 5 7 9
  + 2 3,1 6
    5 8 9 5 ✓
    2 1 4
```

b
```
    3 6 7 0 7
  +,1 5 6,4 7
    4 2 3 5 4 ✓
```

c
```
    3 5,7 8 9
  -    8 8 0 9
    2 6 9 8 0 ✓
```

d
```
    6 8 7 8 9 0
  -      6 9 5 3
    6 0 9 3 7 ✓
```

PART 2 NS3.3

Calculate the answer to each algorithm.

a
```
    3 7 4
  ×   3 2 5
    1 8 7 0 ✓
```

b
```
    5 6 5
  ×   1 1 3
    1 6 9 5 ✓
```

c
```
    2 3 8
  ×   1 3 4
      9 5 2 ✓
```

d
```
    1 4 7
  ×   2 6 0
    8 8 2 0 ✓
```

e
```
      3 6
  ×   2 5
      1 8 0
    1 7 2 0 ✓
      9 0 0
```

f
```
      4 7
  ×   2 3 6
    1 4 1 0
      2 8 2
    1 6 9 2 ✓
```

g $4)\overline{17^16}$ 44 ✓

i $5)\overline{27^25}$ 55 ✓

k $8)\overline{9^10^27}$ 113 ✗

h $3)\overline{17^24}$ 58 ✓

j $6)\overline{25^18}$ 43 ✓

l $10)\overline{64^43}$ 64 r3 ✓

m | Mr Brown planted 381 seeds in 3 boxes. How many seeds were in each box? | 127 | seeds. ✓

$3)\overline{381}$ 127

PART 3 NS3.1

Write this number.

a Six million, two hundred and twenty-one thousand, four hundred and six.   6,221,406 ✓

Rewrite the numbers with the correct spaces so they can be read.

b 3579603   3,579,603 ✓

c 27697408   27,697,408 ✓

PART 4 NS3.4

Shade the largest value in each set.

a | 33% | 0.31 | $\frac{35}{100}$ ✓ |

b | $\frac{75}{100}$ | 80% | $\frac{90}{100}$ ✓ |

c | 0.5 | 49% | $\frac{53}{100}$ ✓ |

d | $\frac{9}{10}$ | 0.89 | 99% ✓ |

Find the percentages.

e 10% of 20 = 2 ✓   h 25% of 40 = 10 ✓

f 10% of 80 = 8 ✓   i 20% of 10 = 2 ✓

g 50% of 100 = 50 ✓   j 75% of 20 = 15 ✓

Add these fractions.

k $\frac{1}{6} + \frac{3}{6} = \frac{4}{6}$ ✓   m $\frac{7}{12} + \frac{8}{12} = \frac{15}{12}$ ✓

l $\frac{3}{6} + \frac{5}{6} = \frac{8}{6}$ ✓   n $\frac{9}{10} + \frac{7}{10} = \frac{16}{10}$ ✓

Write each improper fraction as a mixed number. ✳

o $\frac{5}{4} = 1\frac{1}{4}$ ✓   p $\frac{13}{6} = 2\frac{1}{6}$ ✓   q $\frac{11}{8} = 1\frac{3}{8}$ ✓

Write the place value of the bold digits.

r 37.**5**6   5 tenths ✓

s 3**5**9.763   3 tens ✗

t 28.2**7**9   7 tenths ✗

PART 5 PAS3.1a

Continue the patterns.

a
First number	1	2	3	4	5	6
Second number	5	10	15	20	25	30	✓

b
First number	1	2	3	4	5	6
Second number	9	18	27	32	40	48

114

PART 6 SGS3.2a

a Enlarge this shape by doubling its dimensions (sides).

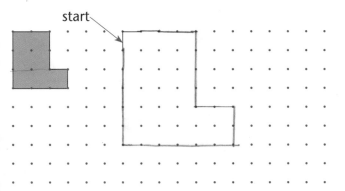
start

b How many times larger is the shape's area? 2x

PART 7 SGS3.1

Circle the model that belongs to the three views.

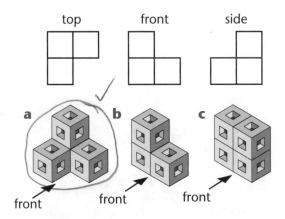
top   front   side

a   b   c
front   front   front

PART 8 SGS3.2b

Measure the angles.

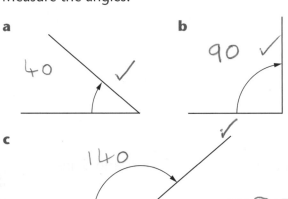

a 40 ✓

b 90 ✓

c 140 ✓

Ella got 53 correct!

PART 9 MS3.1

Measure the perimeter in millimetres.

70

P = 170 mm ✓   15

PART 10

Calculate the area of the rug in m².

34 m² ✗

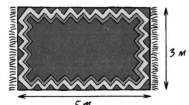
3 m
5 m

PART 11 MS3.4

Write how many kilograms in each of these. ✗ ✓

a 1 t = 1000 kg ✓   **c** 1.25 t = 1,250 kg ✓

b 1.5 t = 1500 kg ✓   **d** 2.75 t = 2,750 kg ✓

PART 12 MS3.4

Bus timetable

Boogie St	1100 hours	1205 hours	1255 hours
Rap St	1107 hours	1215 hours	1302 hours
Mad Donna St	1113 hours	1221 hours	1308 hours
Rock St	1120 hours	1228 hours	1315 hours
Lion St	1125 hours	1233 hours	1320 hours

a If you caught the bus at 1255 hours from Boogie St, when would you arrive at Lion St?   1320 ✓

b If you caught the bus at 1107 hours from Rap St, when would you arrive at Rock St?   1120 ✓

PART 13 DS3.1

Takeaway food   40 children were surveyed about their favourite takeaway food.

Hamburgers
Chickens
Chips
Pies

a About how many liked hamburgers? 20 ✓

b Do more like pies than like chips? Yes ✓

Adding decimals

1 Adding decimals.

a	b	c	d	e
3 . 5 7	6 . 7 4	6 . 4 7	7 . 4 4	3 . 6
+ 1 . 2 1	+ 2 . 1 6	+ 2 . 6	+ 7 . 8	+ 5 . 7 6

f	g	h	i	j
2 . 1 9 6	2 . 3 1 2	3 . 1 2 8	2 . 7 2 1	2 . 1 8 6
3 . 3 4 4	3 . 2 9 1	4 . 2 5	4 . 3 9 6	4 . 3 5 4
+ 6 . 2 1 5	+ 5 . 4 5 0	+ 9 . 6 0 8	+ 7 . 8 5	+ 5 . 9 0 6

k	l	m	n	o
4 . 9 5	4 . 5 1 5	4 . 4 0 4	2 . 4 8	4 . 5 3
3 . 2 8 7	3 . 2 0 9	2 . 7 2 1	2 . 4 1 7	2 . 4 9 6
+ 4 . 2 5 6	+ 4 . 2 5 6	+ 4 . 6 6 6	+ 5 . 3 1	+ 9 . 9

2 Calculate the shortest distances beween the towns. The first one is done for you.

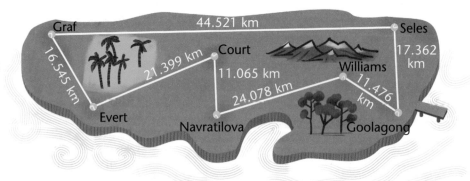

a	b	c	d

Graf and Goolagong
 	
  4 4 . 5 2 1 km
+ 1 7 . 3 6 2 km
―――――――
  6 1 . 8 8 3 km
	Graf and Court	Navratilova and Seles	Goolagong and Court

e	f	g	h
Evert and Seles	Evert and Williams	Navratilova and Graf	Court and Seles

Using the memory function

| $4.55 | $5.50 | $4.75 | $8.50 | $7.35 |

Sample problem

Sue bought 3 pairs of socks, 2 staplers and 3 balls. How much did she spend?

Step 1: Enter $4.55 × 3 on your calculator and press M+

Step 2: Enter $5.50 × 2 on your calculator and press M+

Step 3: Enter $8.50 × 3 on your calculator and press M+

Step 4: Press MR on your calculator to find the total of $50.15

3 What do you think M+ means? _____

4 What do you think MR means? _____

5 Use the memory function to calculate the totals of:

a 7 pairs of socks, 3 golf magazines and 2 packets of textas $

b 3 staplers, 6 balls and 5 pairs of socks $

c 4 balls, 9 pairs of socks and 6 golf magazines $

d 7 golf magazines, 5 staplers and 7 packets of textas $

e 6 balls, 3 golf magazines and 12 staplers $

6 Play the 'Zero in Five' game.
You have a maximum of five moves to turn the numbers into zero. You can only use one digit at a time (digits 1–9). You can use any operation. One has been done for you.

a	185	÷ 5 = 37	+ 3 = 40	÷ 8 = 5	− 5 = 0	
b	168	=	=	=	=	=
c	460	=	=	=	=	=
d	373	=	=	=	=	=

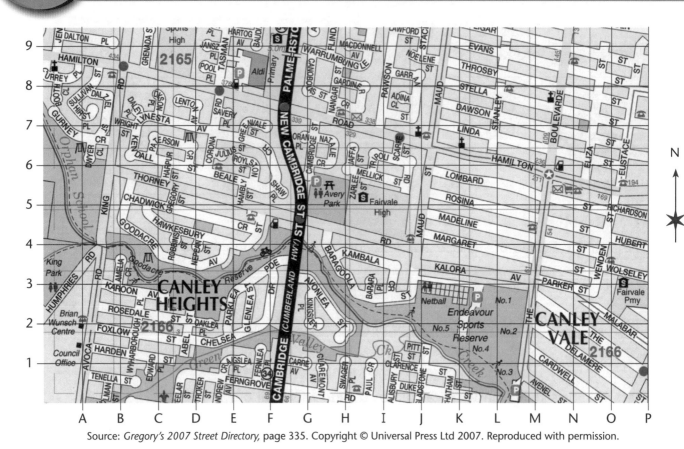

Source: *Gregory's 2007 Street Directory*, page 335. Copyright © Universal Press Ltd 2007. Reproduced with permission.

7 Put a cross on the following locations.

a Chadwick Cr (D5)

b Ferngrove Rd (D1)

c Thorney Rd (F5)

d The Boulevarde (M3)

e Throsby St (N8)

f Lombard St (K6)

g Evans St (L9)

h Hamilton Rd (E8)

l Gurney Cr (A7)

8 Give one set of coordinates for these locations.

a Fairvale High ☐

b Hamilton Rd ☐

c Endeavour Sports Reserve ☐

d Fairvale Primary ☐

9 Write a clear set of directions to describe how to get from Greenvale St (F7) to Delamere St (O1).

_____

_____

_____

10 Draw a path on the map to show how to get from Edward Pl (C1) to Hubert St (P4).

11 Use the scale to calculate the approximate length of these streets to the nearest 100 m.

a Thornley Rd (F5) _____

b Margaret St (K4) _____

c Gladstone St (J1) _____

d Eliza St (O9) _____

Scale 1 cm = 200 m

Timelines are used to place events in a sequence.

12 Make your own personal timeline. Make sure to include important events in your life, such as your birth.

I WAS BORN

1998 | 2000 | 2002 | 2004 | 2006 | 2008 | 2010 | 2012 | 2014

AD means Anno Domini which means in the 'Year of our Lord'.
BC means 'Before Christ'.

13 Draw a line to match each event to a place on the timeline.

1 000 BC   500 BC   Birth of Christ   AD 500   AD 1 000   AD 1 500   AD 2 000

First Olympic Games 776 BC

Great Wall of China finished 500 BC

Battle of Hastings AD 1066

Discovery of America AD 1492

First Fleet arrives in Australia AD 1788

Federation of Australia AD 1901

14 Answer these questions.

a How many years between the Battle of Hastings and the First Fleet? _____

b How many years between the first Olympics and the completion of the Great Wall of China? _____

c How many years between the first Olympics and the Battle of Hastings? _____

d How many years between the completion of the Great Wall of China and the Federation of Australia? _____

e How many years between the Federation of Australia and the year you were born? _____

f Put a cross on the timeline to estimate AD 1250.

g Tick the timeline where you think 750 BC would be.

h Put C on the timeline for 1770 to mark the visit of Captain Cook.

i Put an O on the timeline to mark the Sydney Olympics in AD 2000.

1 Complete these algorithms.

a	b	c	d	e
2 8	3 4	2 6	3 8	4 5
× 1 5	× 1 6	× 1 7	× 1 8	× 1 2

f	g	h	i	j
5 2	4 3	3 7	6 4	7 8
× 1 2	× 3 6	× 2 5	× 3 2	× 1 9

k	l	m	n	o
4 7	4 2	5 8	6 5	9 3
× 3 8	× 3 5	× 2 6	× 3 4	× 3 7

2 Thirty-two children from our class went on a three-day adventure camp.

SCHOOL BUS

a How much did the bus cost if the charge was $17 per child?

b How much did the camp cost if each child was charged $57?

3 Solve these problems.

a How much water did the campers take if they took fifteen 4 litre bottles with them?

b How much money was spent at the souvenir shop if the average amount of money spent by the 32 children was $12?

c How many meals would 24 campers eat if they were away for 4 days and ate 3 meals a day?

4 Complete the decimal subtraction algorithms. Remember to keep the decimal points in a straight line.

a
```
   5 . 3 6
 - 2 . 3 4
 _____
```

b
```
   6 . 5 7
 - 3 . 4 6
 _____
```

c
```
   7 . 8 7
 - 5 . 3
 _____
```

d
```
   8 . 6 2
 - 3 . 4
 _____
```

e
```
   7 . 3 4
 - 5 . 1 6
 _____
```

f
```
   2 6 . 3 5
 - 1 3 . 1 4
 _____
```

g
```
   3 4 . 5 6
 - 1 2 . 3
 _____
```

h
```
   6 5 . 8
 - 2 3 . 0 6
 _____
```

i
```
   8 7 . 3 4
 -    2 . 5
 _____
```

j
```
   3 9 . 2
 - 1 3 . 8 6
 _____
```

k
```
   3 . 5 3 0
 - 2 . 7 5 1
 _____
```

l
```
   2 . 7 3 4
 - 0 . 2 5 5
 _____
```

m
```
   3 . 9 5 3
 - 0 . 8 0 7
 _____
```

n
```
   8 . 3 2 6
 - 6 . 6 0 7
 _____
```

o
```
   9 . 3 3 7
 - 3 . 4 4 3
 _____
```

5 Eight children in Than's group recorded their heights.

| Than 1.27 m | Melissa 1.43 m | Soula 1.35 m | Sam 1.57 m |
| Jon 1.30 m | Cathy 1.54 m | Pablo 1.50 m | Alexis 1.49 m |

Calculate the difference in heights between:

a Sam and Than   ___.___ m   d Cathy and Than ___.___ m   g Pablo and Jon   ___.___ m

b Alexis and Melissa ___.___ m   e Alexis and Cathy ___.___ m   h Cathy and Jon   ___.___ m

c Sam and Alexis   ___.___ m   f Pablo and Soula ___.___ m   i Melissa and Soula ___.___ m

6 Solve these problems.

a Peter's mass is 47.5 kg and Kim's mass is 36.4 kg. What is the difference in their masses?

d Garry needed to cut a 4.75 m piece of timber from a 6 m length. How much timber was left over?

b Jill can run 76.34 m in 10 seconds and Lauren can run 73.55 m in 10 seconds. How much further can Jill run in 10 seconds?

e Karo is 1.37 m tall. How tall will she be by the end of next year if she grows another 0.09 m?

c Kelly saved $37.80 but spent $29.50 on a CD. How much did she have left?

f Danielle wanted to cut 4 lengths of timber measuring 1.67 m each from a length of timber measuring 6.5 m. Is it possible for Danielle to do this?

7 **Finding all possible combinations.**

A witness remembers seeing a car speed away from a bank robbery. She remembers the two letters that were on the car's number plate (TR), and the three numbers (1 2 3), but not the order they were in.

a Predict how many possible number plates can be made from the combinations of the three numbers. _____

b Write in the box all possible combinations of the three numbers. It has been started for you.

> TR-132

8 **Shaking hands.**

At the end of a doubles tennis match each player shook hands with every other player. How many handshakes took place?

9 Complete the tree diagram to show all the possible combinations when the spinner is spun three times.

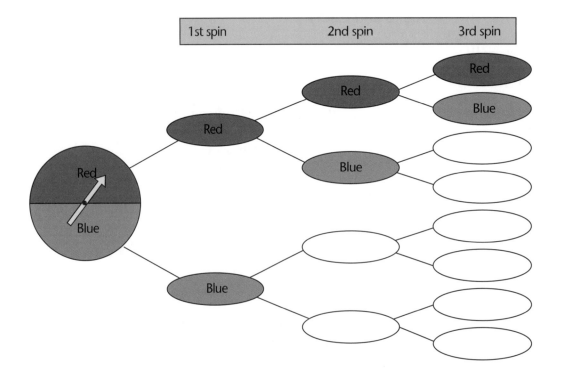

1st spin	2nd spin	3rd spin	Outcome
		Red	R, R, R
	Red		
Red		Blue	R, R, B
	Blue		
Blue			

NS3.5 Orders the likelihood of simple events on a number line from zero to one

WMS3.2, WMS3.3

10 Draw a line to match each object to its net.

a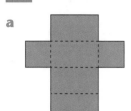

b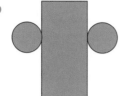

c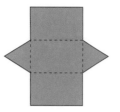

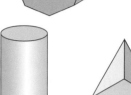

d

e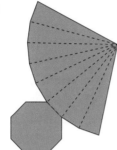

f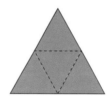

11 A pin box is displayed and another identical box had been pulled apart to show the net.

a Colour yellow the top view on the net.

b Colour red the front view on the net.

c Colour blue the side view on the net (be careful).

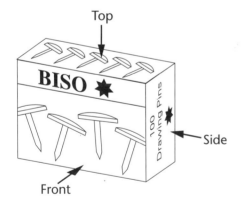

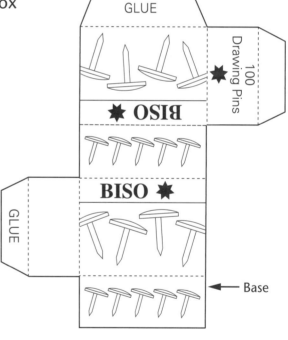

12 Mr Bing makes cube puzzles for children. Study the net to answer the questions.

Mr Bing's cube

a If **B** was the base, what letter would be on the top? _____

b If **A** was the front face what letter would be on the back face? _____

c What letter do you think is on the opposite side to **E**? _____

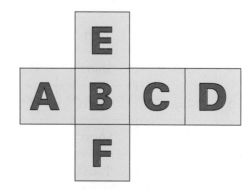

WMS3.2,
WMS3.3

SGS3.1 Identifies three-dimensional objects, including particular prisms and pyramids, on the basis of their properties, and visualises, sketches and constructs them given drawings of different views

123

1 Complete these subtractions.

a
```
  6 5 4 2 7
-   7 1 9 3
_____
```

b
```
  9 1 7 1 5
- 7 2 4 6 2
_____
```

c
```
  5 0 8 5 6
- 4 7 2 9 0
_____
```

d
```
  8 2 7 0 3
- 2 7 5 3 2
_____
```

e
```
  1 6 8 4 0
-   7 4 9 0
_____
```

f
```
  6 0 2 0 5
- 5 4 8 1 9
_____
```

g
```
  9 3 4 1 1
- 4 7 5 8 4
_____
```

h
```
  7 2 4 0 0
-   3 4 3 1
_____
```

i
```
  3 5 7 2 3
- 2 5 8 5 9
_____
```

j
```
  8 4 1 2 2
- 3 6 5 4 3
_____
```

k
```
  $ 7 2 4 . 9 7
-     6 3 . 6 7
_____
```

l
```
  $ 2 6 3 . 7 5
-   1 8 3 . 0 5
_____
```

m
```
  $ 7 6 9 . 2 6
-   6 7 3 . 4 3
_____
```

n
```
  $ 3 4 6 . 7 4
-   2 8 3 . 2 5
_____
```

2 Solve these problems.

a Jenny had an amount of $4 773 in the bank but spent $2 765 at the travel agency. How much does she have left?

c Tina's new car cost $27 834. If she was given a trade-in for her old car of $12 477, how much more money does she need?

b Tony left Sydney on a trip, to the USA, of 11 920 km. How far does he still need to travel if he has already covered 6 577 km?

d There were 18 654 spectators at the football match. If 11 076 of them were adults, how many were children?

3 Complete the spreadsheet for the Dolphins Soccer Club. It has been started for you.

	A	B	C	D
1	Date	Item	Cost	Balance
2	May 3	Opening		$987.90
3	May 7	Balls	$126.00	(D2-C3) $861.90
4	May 9	Shirts	$120.32	(D3-C4)
5	May 12	Shorts	$144.22	(D4-C5)
6	May 18	Socks	$35.28	(D5-C6)
7	May 22	Pads	$34.65	(D6-C7)

Spreadsheets organise and calculate data.

NS3.2 Selects and applies appropriate strategies for addition and subtraction with counting numbers of any size

WMS3.2

4 Negative numbers can be easily displayed on a number line.

Complete the number line to −10 and +10.

−3 −2 −1 0 1 2 3 4

5 Solve the problem.

John stood on the landing which has been labelled step 0. He had to move up and down the steps as his sister gave him positive and negative numbers to follow. She said: +2, −3, +4, −5, +2 and −3. Put an X on the step where John finished.

6 Answer the questions about the table.

a Which is the hottest city? _____

b Which is the coolest city? _____

c Which city has the greatest range of temperature between its high and low? _____

7 What is the difference between the highest and lowest temperatures of:

a Bangkok? _____

b Copenhagen? _____

c Montreal? _____

d Moscow? _____

e Sydney? _____

f Stockholm? _____

8 What is the difference between the lowest temperatures of:

a Amsterdam and Bangkok? _____

b Berlin and Auckland? _____

c Copenhagen and San Francisco? _____

d Moscow and Christchurch? _____

City	High	Low
Amsterdam	18°	4°
Bangkok	34°	27°
Berlin	10°	−5°
Chicago	14°	0°
Copenhagen	7°	−4°
Auckland	22°	16°
Sydney	25°	17°
Montreal	3°	−10°
New York	12°	−1°
Wellington	17°	14°
Moscow	10°	−2°
San Francisco	22°	8°
Stockholm	7°	−3°
Christchurch	15°	13°

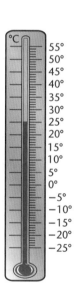

Choosing length units

9 Shade the box to select the most appropriate unit of length to measure each of the following.

	Item	mm	cm	m	km
a	The length of a sultana packet				
b	The length of a calculator				
c	The thickness of a mouse pad				
d	The length of a grasshopper				
e	The length of a pool				
f	The width of your home				
g	The length of a fingernail				
h	The length of the Hume Highway				

Choose the best unit (millimetres, metres, centimetres or kilometres).

10 Choose an appropriate measuring device from the ones given to measure each of the following.

	Length	Device
a	The length of a pencil	
b	The length of a room	
c	The circumference of a bin	
d	The length of the playground	
e	The circumference of a bottle	
f	The perimeter of a large curved garden	
g	The distance between two towns	
h	The perimeter of a book	
i	The perimeter of your school	

30 cm ruler

Odometer

Tape measure

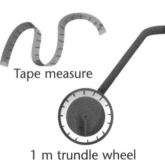
1 m trundle wheel

1 m ruler

11 Convert these measurements to the length unit given.

a 5 cm = _____ mm

b 26 cm = _____ mm

c 37 cm = _____ mm

d 30 mm = _____ cm

e 60 mm = _____ cm

f 8 m = _____ cm

g 9 m = _____ cm

h $5\frac{1}{2}$ m = _____ cm

i 200 cm = _____ m

j 700 cm = _____ m

k 2 000 m = _____ km

l 6 000 m = _____ km

m 4 000 m = _____ km

n 6 km = _____ m

o $8\frac{1}{2}$ m = _____ cm

12 Estimate and measure the length of this knife in millimetres.

Estimate: _____ mm

Length: _____ mm

MS3.1 Selects and uses the appropriate unit and device to measure lengths, distances and perimeters

WMS3.2, WMS3.5

13 The column graph below has been made with blocks to show Jason's spelling scores over 8 weeks.

Jason's spelling scores

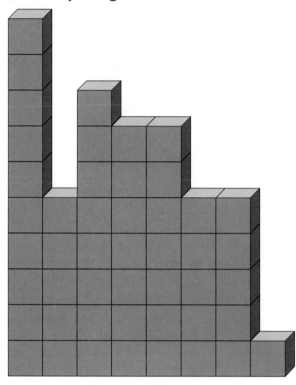

a To calculate his mean score (average) you can move the blocks around until all columns are the same height.

Do this for Jason using concrete materials and record the mean height of the columns in your column graph.

Mean = ☐

b The mean can also be found by adding all the scores and then dividing by the number of scores.

Complete this operation to find Jason's mean score.

$(10 + 5 + 8 + 7 + 7 + 5 + 5 + 1) \div 8 =$ _____

14 Did your mean score match the height of the columns in your graph? _____

15 Find the mean of these sets of numbers.

	Scores			Mean
a	3	5	7	
b	7	9	11	
c	12	10	14	
d	10	20	15	
e	16	30	20	
f	13	20	15	

	Scores				Mean
g	2	4	6	8	
h	3	5	7	9	
i	8	12	10	14	
j	7	5	9	11	
k	5	10	13	20	
l	10	20	15	15	

30 kg   30 kg   40 kg   35 kg   35 kg

16 What is the mean for the mass of these girls from the Green Point netball club?

Mean = ☐ kg

Multiplication of decimals

Step 1: Multiply 3 tenths by 4 which equals 12 tenths.

Step 2: 12 tenths is equal to 1 whole and 2 tenths. Trade the one whole to the ones column and record the 2 tenths in the tenths column.

Step 3: Multiply 2 ones by 4 which gives 8, then add the 1 that has been traded to give 9. Record the 9 in the ones column.

Ones	Tenths
¹2 .	3

×   4

9 . 2

I estimated the answer to be about 8 because 4 × 2 = 8.

1 Complete these multiplications.

a
```
    3 . 4
×       4
_____
```

b
```
    4 . 5
×       5
_____
```

c
```
    4 . 6
×       4
_____
```

d
```
    5 . 2
×       5
_____
```

e
```
    3 . 6
×       6
_____
```

f
```
  6 . 2 3
×       3
_____
```

g
```
  7 . 1 8
×       4
_____
```

h
```
  8 . 2 1
×       5
_____
```

i
```
  7 . 4 3
×       3
_____
```

j
```
  5 . 2 4
×       6
_____
```

k
```
  4 5 . 5
×       3
_____
```

l
```
  3 6 . 7
×       4
_____
```

m
```
  4 8 . 3
×       6
_____
```

n
```
  2 9 . 2
×       2
_____
```

o
```
  3 1 . 7
×       5
_____
```

p
```
2 5 . 2 3
×       6
_____
```

q
```
2 1 . 2 9
×       5
_____
```

r
```
3 1 . 8 2
×       6
_____
```

s
```
7 4 . 2 3
×       7
_____
```

t
```
1 3 . 7 5
×       9
_____
```

$3.45

$7.65

$8.05

$12.35
Textas
10 Colours

$45.8

2 Calculate the cost of these purchases.

a 7 scissors

b 5 calculators

c 6 staplers

d 9 texta sets

e 4 sunglasses

NS3.4 Compares, orders and calculates with decimals, simple fractions and simple percentages

WMS3.3, WMS3.2

Number patterns

3 Complete the number patterns then write a rule for each.

a

First number	1	2	3	4	5	6	7
Second number	7		9		11		

Rule: _____

b

First number	1	2	3	4	5	6	7
Second number	4		12		20		

Rule: _____

c

First number	1	2	3	4	5	6	7
Second number	5		15		25		

Rule: _____

d

First number	2	4	6	8	10	12	14
Second number	12		36		60		

Rule: _____

e

First number	2	4	6	8	10	12	14
Second number	14		42		70		

Rule: _____

f

First number	35	32	29	26	23	19	16
Second number	23		17		11		

Rule: _____

4 Create a number pattern using addition, and a number pattern using multiplication.

a Addition

First number	11	12	13	14	15	16	17	18
Second number								

b Multiplication

First number	1	2	3	4	5	6	7	8
Second number								

5 Write a rule for each function machine. (Question 5d uses two operations.)

a

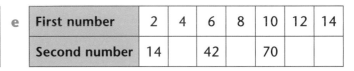

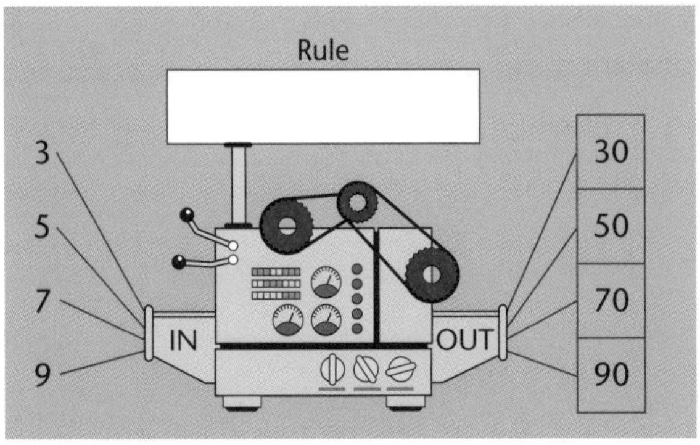

Rule

IN	OUT
3	30
5	50
7	70
9	90

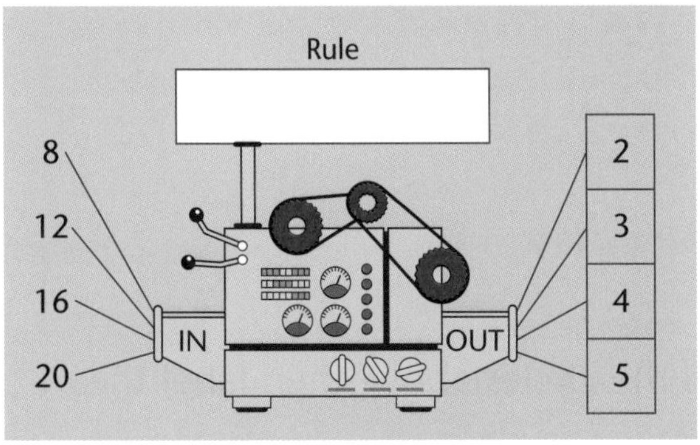

c

Rule

IN	OUT
3	15
5	25
7	35
9	45

b

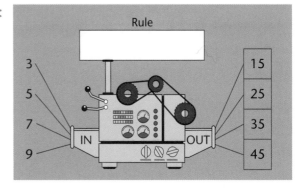

Rule

IN	OUT
8	2
12	3
16	4
20	5

d

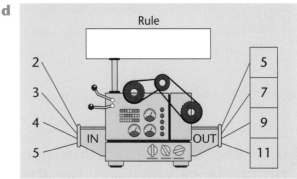

Rule

IN	OUT
2	5
3	7
4	9
5	11

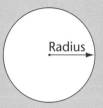

The **radius** is a line reaching from the centre of a circle to its circumference.

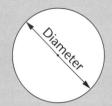

The **diameter** is a line that passes through the centre point of a circle to the circumference on each side.

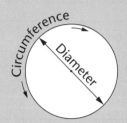

The **circumference** is a circle's perimeter.

Constructing circles

When we draw circles, we must accurately set the compasses to the exact radius. This is done by placing the point of the compasses and the pencil point accurately on a ruler.

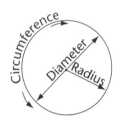

6 Use the centre point below to draw circles with a 3 cm radius and a 35 mm radius.

a A 3 cm radius.

b A 35 mm radius.

•

•

7 Draw lines to mark the diameter and radius on the circles above then label the circumference, radius and diameter.

Areas of land larger than a hectare can be measured in **square kilometres** (km²), e.g. 100 ha equals 1 km², or a square 1 000 m × 1 000 m = 1 km².

8 List the states and territories in order of size (largest first) and then use a calculator to work out the total area of Australia.

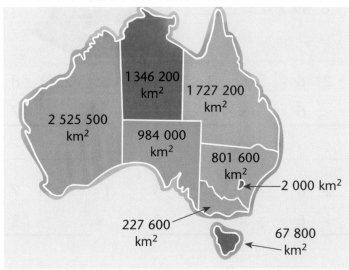

State	Area in km²
Total	

9 Use the scale to mark an area of 1 km² on the street directory page.

Scale	1 cm = 200 m

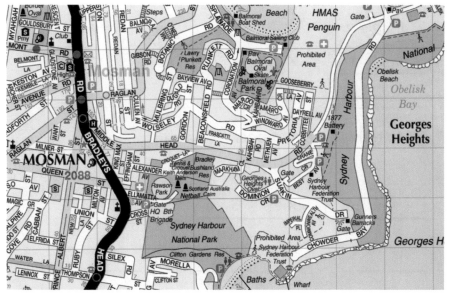

Source: *Gregory's 2007 Street Directory*, page 317.
Copyright © Universal Press Ltd 2007. Reproduced with permission.

10 Would you use square metres (m²), hectares (ha) or square kilometres (km²) to measure these areas?

a cricket oval

b tennis court

c Royal National Park

d Wollongong

e golf course

f soccer field

g Old McDonald's Farm

h your school

i Canberra

WMS3.3

MS3.2 Selects and uses the appropriate unit to calculate area, including the area of squares, rectangles and triangles

131

Multiplication methods

1 Mentally calculate the answers to these multiplications.

23 x 4.
Think 4 x 20
plus 4 x 3.

a 7 × 4 = _____

b 3 × 30 = _____

c 4 × 40 = _____

d 5 × 60 = _____

e 7 × 70 = _____

f 20 × 20 = _____

g 20 × 30 = _____

h 30 × 30 = _____

i 30 × 40 = _____

j 50 × 60 = _____

k 24 × 3 = _____

l 25 × 5 = _____

m 27 × 6 = _____

n 28 × 8 = _____

o 39 × 4 = _____

2 Complete these multiplications.

a
```
    2 4 2
×         4
_____
_____
```

b
```
    2 3 5
×         5
_____
_____
```

c
```
    1 2 6
×         6
_____
_____
```

d
```
    3 2 5
×         4
_____
_____
```

e
```
    2 1 8
×         7
_____
_____
```

f
```
    1 3 5
×         4
_____
_____
```

g
```
    2 4 6
×         5
_____
_____
```

h
```
    4 2 8
×         6
_____
_____
```

i
```
    3 1 5
×         8
_____
_____
```

j
```
    2 4 7
×         3
_____
_____
```

3 Multiply these numbers by a multiple of 10.

a
```
    1 2 3
×     3 0
_____
_____
```

b
```
    4 2 5
×     4 0
_____
_____
```

c
```
    3 6 0
×     5 0
_____
_____
```

d
```
    2 7 3
×     6 0
_____
_____
```

e
```
    5 7 4
×     7 0
_____
_____
```

4 Multiply these numbers.

a
```
      2 5
×     2 5
_____
_____
_____
```

b
```
      4 7
×     3 6
_____
_____
_____
```

c
```
    1 8 5
×     4 4
_____
_____
_____
```

d
```
    2 6 7
×     5 6
_____
_____
_____
```

e
```
    3 7 4
×     6 8
_____
_____
_____
```

5 Solve these mentally by multiplying the hundreds, tens and ones separately then adding them.

a 235 × 6

b 326 × 5

c 254 × 7

NS3.3 Selects and applies appropriate
strategies for multiplication and division

WMS3.2, WMS3.3

Rounding for estimation

6 Round each number to the nearest 10. Remember numbers ending in 5 are rounded up.

a 12 = _____   c 33 = _____   e 49 = _____   g 56 = _____   i 35 = _____

b 91 = _____   d 88 = _____   f 77 = _____   h 85 = _____   j 99 = _____

7 Round each number to the nearest 100. Remember numbers ending in 50 are rounded up.

a 96 = _____   d 307 = _____   g 427 = _____   j 701 = _____   m 450 = _____

b 111 = _____   e 341 = _____   h 599 = _____   k 909 = _____   n 990 = _____

c 137 = _____   f 369 = _____   i 625 = _____   l 350 = _____   o 891 = _____

8 Round each number to the nearest 1 000. Remember numbers ending in 500 are rounded up.

a 960 = _____   d 3 230 = _____   g 3 074 = _____   j 7 500 = _____

b 740 = _____   e 5 690 = _____   h 6 099 = _____   k 9 701 = _____

c 1 212 = _____   f 2 748 = _____   i 7 259 = _____   l 5 026 = _____

$117 $213 $795 $95 $389

9 Over the year, Bill ordered the following items from his supplier. Estimate how much he spent by rounding each item to $100.

a Two tennis racquets and an iPod. $

b Four phones and a tennis racquet. $

c A table and a guitar. $

d A guitar and four iPods. $

e Three tennis racquets and a table. $

f Two guitars and two phones. $

10 List three different ways you could spend between $1 600 and $1 700.

Making a map

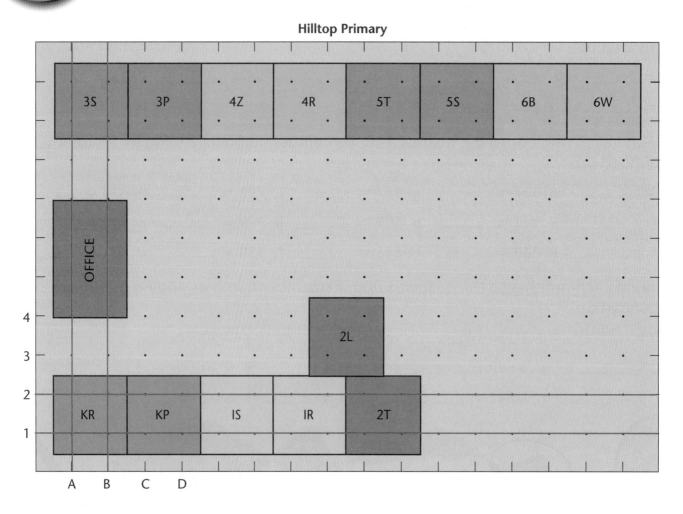

Hilltop Primary

11 Complete the map.

a Use the marks on the map to draw vertical and horizontal lines to make a coordinate grid.

b Complete the labelling of the coordinates.

c Draw a shade area by joining the coordinate points C3, G3 and C7.

d Draw the school hall by joining the coordinates L5, L6, K6, K7, L7, L8, P8 and P5.

e Draw the toilets by joining the coordinates L1, L2, P2 and P1.

f Find a place for the canteen, draw it on the map and list its coordinate points. _____

g Draw any object you like on the map and give its coordinate points. _____

12 What can be found at these coordinate points?

a B2 _____ **b** G10 _____ **c** A5 _____ **d** D4 _____

13 Give a set of coordinate points for:

a Class 5S _____ **b** The hall _____ **c** Class KP _____ **d** Class 2L _____

14 If the school's office is 9 m long, make up a suitable scale for the map.

Scale	1 cm =

To convert tonnes to kilograms, multiply by 1 000.

15 Convert these measurements from tonnes to kilograms without the use of a calculator. Then use a calculator to check your conversions.

Tonnes	5.055	4.259	6.385	5.634	7.500	6.900	25	50
Kilograms	5 055							

16 A group of 11-year-old children recorded their mass at the Technology Park. Place them in order of mass from lightest to heaviest.

I'm the heaviest!

Name	Mass
Will	32 kg
Ellen	29.8 kg
Connie	30.5 kg
Fran	29.585 kg
George	35.005 kg
Alice	36 kg

Name						
Mass						

17 Whose mass is closest to 30 kilograms? _____

A television set would be measured in kilograms.

18 Choose the appropriate mass unit to measure the mass of:

a a matchbox _____   e an elephant _____   i a glue stick _____

b a dog _____   f a ruler _____   j a desk _____

c a pencil _____   g a ship _____   k a whale _____

d a person _____   h a pony _____   l a building _____

Write g, kg or t for your answers.

19 Solve these problems.

a Eve weighed 29.5 kg last year and is now 2.4 kg heavier. What is her mass now?

b For each wash, I use 100 grams of washing powder. How many washes will I get out of a 1.5 kg pack?

c A truck has a mass of 4.205 t. What will be the truck's total mass if a load of 750 kg of wheat is packed onto the truck?

Dividing decimals

Example: Share 85.8 among 6.

Step 1: The 8 tens are shared 6 ways, with each person receiving one ten. The remaining 2 tens are traded to 20 ones.

Step 2: There are now 25 ones divided by 6, which gives each person 4 with a remainder of 1. The 1 remainder is traded to become 10 tenths.

Step 3: There are now 18 tenths to be divided by 6 which gives 3 tenths.

$$6 \overline{)8^25.^18} = 14.3$$

1 Calculate the answers to the following divisions.

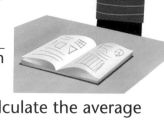

Use a calculator to check your answers.

a $3\overline{)63.9}$ b $4\overline{)84.8}$ c $2\overline{)86.4}$ d $3\overline{)96.3}$

e $4\overline{)96.8}$ f $2\overline{)72.8}$ g $5\overline{)75.5}$ h $3\overline{)75.9}$

i $5\overline{)56.5}$ j $6\overline{)67.2}$ k $3\overline{)67.2}$ l $4\overline{)89.6}$

m $5\overline{)\$6.85}$ n $3\overline{)\$5.76}$ o $2\overline{)\$3.66}$ p $6\overline{)\$9.12}$

q $8\overline{)10.96\,m}$ r $4\overline{)5.04\,m}$ s $5\overline{)7.65\,m}$ t $4\overline{)6.56\,m}$

2 The total distance jumped by some long jumpers is given. Calculate the average length of each jump.

a Jai jumped a total distance of 24.69 m in three attempts. What was the average length of his jumps?

b Teagan jumped a total distance of 27.68 m in four attempts. What was the average length of her jumps?

3 Calculate how much each person's share of the bill was at these restaurants.

a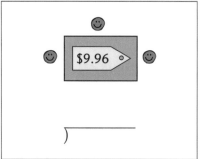
$9.96

b
$84.56

c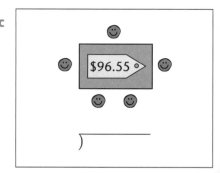
$96.55

4 Display how these number sentences can be done on a number line. The first one is done for you.

a $4 + 2 - 6 - 2 = \boxed{-2}$

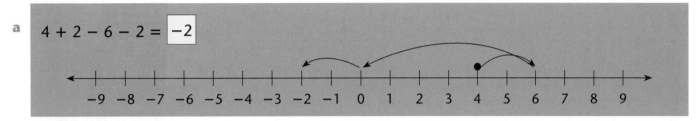

b $5 + 2 - 4 - 3 - 6 = \boxed{}$

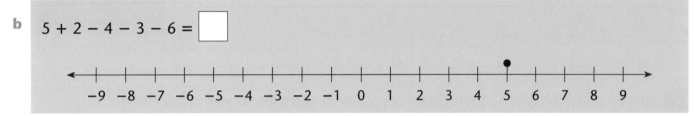

c $0 + 4 + 3 - 9 + 2 = \boxed{}$

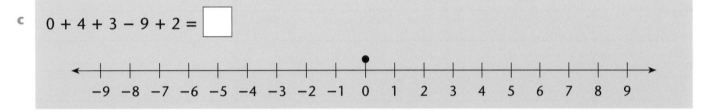

d $-6 + 2 + 8 - 4 = \boxed{}$

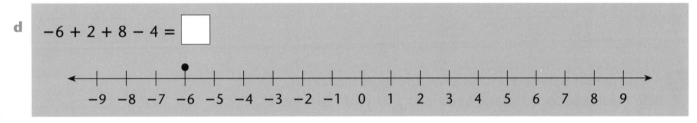

e In the spelling quiz, Frank scored 3 points, lost 7 points and scored 3 points. What was his final score?

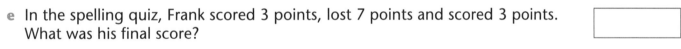

f Mary went on a diet and lost 3 kg, then lost another 4 kg before putting on 2 kg. What was her final weight loss? $\boxed{}$ kg

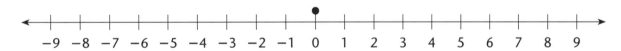

5 Write a number sentence or story of your own and solve it on the number line.

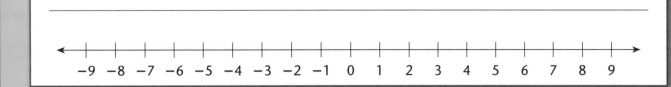

Collecting data/questionnaires

6 Design three survey questions to improve your school canteen. You could consider such things as days it is open and types of food.

a _____

_____

b _____

_____

c _____

_____

7 Survey some children, then report on their responses to your questions.

a _____

_____

b _____

_____

c _____

_____

8 Write a statement about a possible improvement the canteen could make according to your survey. _____

_____

9 Do you think that you surveyed enough children to make a fair sampling of children in your school? Why? _____

_____

10 Does the oldest person run the fastest?

a Order eight children in your class, from youngest to oldest.

b Number them from 1 to 8, then record their dates of birth and sprinting times over 50 m in the table below.

Child	D.O.B.	Time	Child	D.O.B.	Time
1			5		
2			6		
3			7		
4			8		

c Did the oldest person run the fastest? _____

11 Sally has a choice of the three sultana packs below. Discuss with a friend how you could use cubic centimetre blocks to decide which one has the greatest volume.

12 Record the volume of each pack below its picture and colour the largest pack.

a

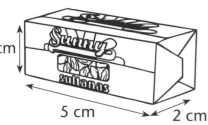

2 cm

5 cm 2 cm

Volume _____ cm³

b

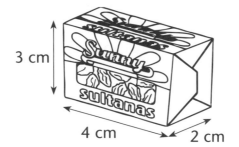

3 cm

4 cm 2 cm

Volume _____ cm³

c

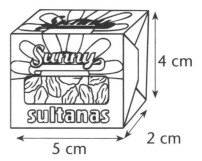

4 cm

5 cm 2 cm

Volume _____ cm³

Cubic metres are used to measure the volume of large objects and containers. A cubic metre (**m³**) is 1 metre long, 1 metre wide and 1 metre high.

---

13 How to make a cubic metre.

Materials
- six 1-metre squares of cardboard
- scissors
- tape
- metre rules or metre length sticks.

Procedure
- Arrange the squares in the form of a net.
- Join all pieces using tape.
- Metre rules may be used to support the edges.
- Fold to form a cube.
- Tape along the edges, but leave the top open.

To take it from room to room, you will probably need to undo one or two edges, because doorways are less than 1 metre wide.

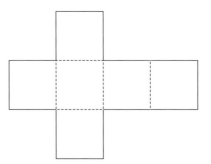

14 Name three objects in your school and at home, such as washing machines and dog kennels, that are about 1 cubic metre, less than 1 m³ and greater than 1 m³.

About 1 m³			
Less than 1 m³			
Greater than 1 m³			

Calculator problems

Fred's Fruit Barn

Bananas
$3.99 a kg

Oranges
$2.49 a kg

Rockmelon
$1.95 each

Avocado
$0.90 each

Mushrooms
$3.85 a kg

1 Use the memory function on your calculator as outlined in unit 28 on page 117 to calculate these purchases.

a Ms Cook bought 3 kg of bananas, 2 kg of mushrooms and 6 avocados. How much did she spend? $ _____

c Mr Tom bought 17 avocados and 15 kg of mushrooms for his catering business. How much did he spend? $ _____

b Trent bought 5 avocados, 4 rockmelons and 7 kg of oranges. How much did he spend? $ _____

d Kelly bought 4 kg of bananas, 3 kg of oranges, 2 avocados and 7 rockmelons. How much change did she receive from $50? $ _____

2 Write and solve two memory function problems using the shopping items above.

a

b

3 Draw a line to match each number sequence with its correct problem then solve the problems.

a Twenty-seven children attended the movies. If it cost them $6.50 each, what was the total amount charged by the theatre?

$(6 \times \$7) + (3 \times \$9) + (7 \times \$5) =$

b Mrs Kent bought six books at $7 each, three books at $9 each and seven books at $5 each. How much did she spend?

$(\frac{1}{4} \text{ of } 24) \times \$0.60 =$

c Sarah bought $\frac{1}{4}$ of a box of 24 apples. If she paid 60c for each apple, how much did she spend?

$27 \times \$6.50 =$

d Trevor bought five tins of dog food at 90c each and a magazine at $5.60. How much did he spend?

$6 \times 8 \times \frac{1}{4} =$

e Mrs Hill planted 6 rows of 8 flowers. $\frac{1}{4}$ of them died. How many flowers died?

$(\$0.90 \times 5) + \$5.60 =$

WMS3.2 Selects and applies appropriate problem-solving strategies, including technological applications, in undertaking investigations

WMS3.2, WMS3.1

Multiplying and dividing decimals

4 Use your calculator to answer these questions.

I multiplied 3.23 x 100 and got 323.

a 0.45 × 1 ☐

b 0.45 × 10 ☐

c 0.45 × 100 ☐

d 0.45 × 1 000 ☐

e 3.16 × 1 ☐

f 3.16 × 10 ☐

g 3.16 × 100 ☐

h 3.16 × 1 000 ☐

5 Answer these questions about what happened in question 4.

a What happened to the numbers when they were multiplied by 10?

_____

b What happened when the numbers were multiplied by 100?

_____

6 Multiply these numbers mentally.

a 2.35 × 10 ☐

b 3.62 × 10 ☐

c 5.75 × 10 ☐

d 4.74 × 10 ☐

e 3.6 × 100 ☐

f 5.753 × 100 ☐

g 3.63 × 1 000 ☐

h 8.7 × 100 ☐

i 6.796 × 1 000 ☐

7 Use your calculator to answer these questions.

I divided 6.74 by 100 and got 0.0674.

a 0.47 ÷ 1 ☐

b 0.47 ÷ 10 ☐

c 0.47 ÷ 100 ☐

d 0.47 ÷ 1 000 ☐

e 5.46 ÷ 1 ☐

f 5.46 ÷ 10 ☐

g 5.46 ÷ 100 ☐

h 5.46 ÷ 1 000 ☐

8 What happened when the numbers were divided by 100?

_____

9 Divide these numbers mentally.

a 0.45 ÷ 10 ☐

b 0.45 ÷ 100 ☐

c 0.45 ÷ 1 000 ☐

d 3.16 ÷ 10 ☐

e 3.16 ÷ 100 ☐

f 3.16 ÷ 1 000 ☐

10 In the space provided, draw the cross-section of each object. All objects are cut parallel to their bases. You may need to model some of these objects from soft substances to discover the shape of the cross-section.

a
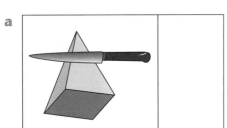

e
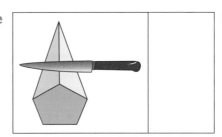

i
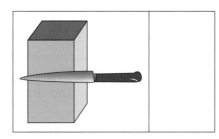

b
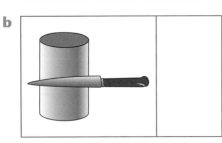

f
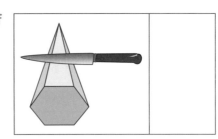

j
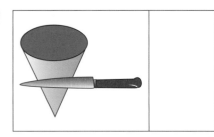

c
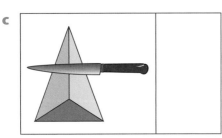

g
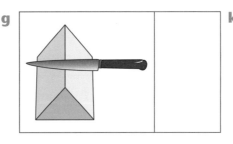

k
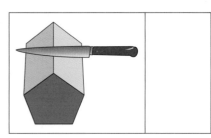

d
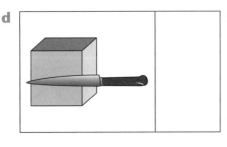

h
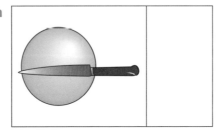

l
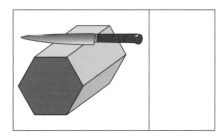

11 What objects could these shapes be the cross-sections of? **Note:** You can have more than one answer.

a

c

b

d

The **mean** is the average of a collection of numbers or set of scores.
It is found by finding the total of the scores then dividing that number by the number of scores.
For example the mean of 2, 3, 4, 5, 6 = $\frac{2 + 3 + 4 + 5 + 6}{5}$ = 4

12 Find the mean score of these cricketers over four innings.

a Sam 3, 7, 8, 2 _____

b Kelly 6, 4, 7, 7 _____

c Jessica 10, 15, 10, 5 _____

d Con 1, 3, 5, 3 _____

e Matthew 10, 20, 5, 5 _____

f Billy 12, 13, 11, 12 _____

g Susan 20, 0, 5, 3 _____

h Harry 26, 14, 25, 15 _____

i Than 13, 17, 27, 15 _____

j Max 35, 40, 5, 8 _____

13 Kimberley went to five shops to find the best price for a pair of hockey boots. These are the prices she was quoted.

$24 $30 $36 $26 $24

What is the mean price of the hockey boots? $ _____

14 Eight students in the top maths class sat for a special exam. Their marks out of 10 are in the table. Study the table, then answer the questions.

Tom	Louise	Ken	Kelly	Jade	Peita	Kahu	Sonia
7	8	6	4	8	9	8	6

a What is the mean score? _____

b How many students scored below the mean? _____

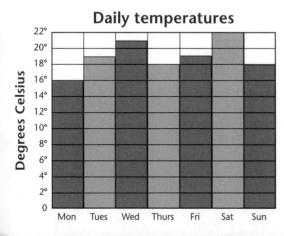

Daily temperatures

15 Answer these questions.

a What was the lowest temperature recorded? _____

b What was the highest temperature recorded? _____

c What is the mean temperature? _____

d Which days recorded temperatures above the mean?

_____

1 Use multiplication to check these divisions. Use the box to tick the correct answers and write the correct answer for those that you think are incorrect.

a 12 ÷ 4 = 3 ☐   e 24 ÷ 6 = 4 ☐   i 36 ÷ 4 = 8 ☐   m 45 ÷ 9 = 3 ☐

b 20 ÷ 4 = 4 ☐   f 28 ÷ 7 = 3 ☐   j 36 ÷ 6 = 5 ☐   n 42 ÷ 7 = 6 ☐

c 20 ÷ 5 = 4 ☐   g 32 ÷ 4 = 8 ☐   k 40 ÷ 5 = 8 ☐   o 48 ÷ 8 = 6 ☐

d 24 ÷ 4 = 4 ☐   h 27 ÷ 9 = 3 ☐   l 21 ÷ 3 = 7 ☐   p 48 ÷ 3 = 12 ☐

2 Use an inverse operation, such as multiplication, to check these statements. Answer by stating true or false.

30 ÷ 5 = 6
300 ÷ 5 = 60

a 50 ÷ 10 must be more than 3 _____

b 60 ÷ 5 is less than 15 _____

c 100 ÷ 4 is greater than 20 _____

d 80 ÷ 4 must be more than 25 _____

e 100 ÷ 5 is less than 15 _____

f 160 ÷ 4 is more than 50 _____   k 1 000 ÷ 5 is more than 250 _____

g 200 ÷ 5 is more than 30 _____   l 900 ÷ 6 is more than 130 _____

h 250 ÷ 5 is more than 45 _____   m 1 500 ÷ 5 is more than 30 _____

i 500 ÷ 3 is more than 120 _____   n 2 000 ÷ 4 must be more than 50 _____

j 800 ÷ 5 is less than 120 _____   o 2 400 ÷ 6 must be more than 50 _____

3 Check the answers to these division questions using multiplication. The first one is done for you.

a	b	c	d	e
$\frac{14}{4\overline{)56}}$ ✓	$\frac{13}{6\overline{)78}}$	$\frac{123}{3\overline{)369}}$	$\frac{144}{6\overline{)864}}$	$\frac{131}{7\overline{)917}}$
$\begin{array}{r} 14 \\ \times 4 \\ \hline 56 \\ \hline \end{array}$	× _____ _____	× _____ _____	× _____ _____	× _____ _____

4 Estimate an answer to each problem by rounding the larger number.

a 58 sheep were shared among 3 paddocks. Estimate how many sheep per paddock. _____

b $789 was shared among 4 people. Estimate each person's share. $ _____

c 309 books were shared among 10 shelves. Estimate the number of books per shelf. _____

d $3 987 was shared among 8 people. Estimate each person's share. $ _____

PAS3.1b Constructs, verifies and completes number sentences involving the four operations with a variety of numbers   **WMS3.2, WMS3.4**

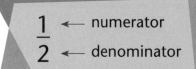

Calculator division

UNIT 35

5 Use your calculator to change the given fractions to decimals. You will need to divide the numerator by the denominator.

$$\frac{1}{2} \quad \begin{array}{l}\leftarrow \text{numerator} \\ \leftarrow \text{denominator}\end{array}$$

a $\frac{27}{100} = 0.$　　　d $\frac{1}{2} = 0.$　　　g $\frac{90}{100} = 0.$　　　j $\frac{1}{8} = 0.$

b $\frac{4}{100} = 0.$　　　e $\frac{1}{5} = 0.$　　　h $\frac{3}{5} = 0.$　　　k $\frac{3}{8} = 0.$

c $\frac{4}{10} = 0.$　　　f $\frac{3}{4} = 0.$　　　i $\frac{4}{5} = 0.$　　　l $\frac{1}{4} = 0.$

6 Solve these divisions using a pen-and-paper method.

a $5\overline{)756}$　　b $4\overline{)247}$　　c $8\overline{)979}$　　d $8\overline{)445}$　　e $5\overline{)777}$

7 Now repeat the divisions using a calculator, and record the answers.

a $5\overline{)756}$　　b $4\overline{)247}$　　c $8\overline{)979}$　　d $8\overline{)445}$　　e $5\overline{)777}$

The reason for the **decimal remainder** is that the calculator has put the remainder over the divisor and created a decimal as you did in activity 5 on this page.

For example

$$\begin{array}{r}45\ r3 \\ 8\overline{)363}\end{array}$$

becomes $45\frac{3}{8} = 45.375$

8 Solve these divisions using a calculator. Write exactly what you see on your calculator display. You may be surprised when dividing by 3, 6, 7 or 9.

a $8\overline{)3595}$　　b $8\overline{)2981}$　　c $8\overline{)1703}$

d $3\overline{)1060}$　　e $8\overline{)8989}$　　f $3\overline{)1061}$

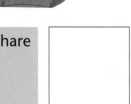

$$\begin{array}{r}6.1666666 \\ 6\overline{)37} \quad ??? \end{array}$$

g $6\overline{)7267}$　　h $7\overline{)1492}$　　i $9\overline{)3890}$

9 Solve these problems using a calculator.

a Ms Hill has 363 rare stamps that she wants to share among her 4 children. How many stamps will each receive?

c Jim had 2 345 books to share among 4 libraries. How many books would each library receive?

b Monica bought 567 beads that she wanted to put on 5 necklaces. How many beads are there for each necklace?

d Peter travelled 1 445 km. If he stopped 8 times, what was the average distance between stops?

WMS3.2, WMS3.3

NS3.3 Selects and applies appropriate strategies for multiplication and division

145

Diagonals

A **diagonal** is a line that joins two non-adjacent vertices (corners) of a polygon.
A square has two diagonals.

10 Draw the diagonals on these quadrilaterals then record the number of diagonals for each.

a
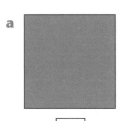
☐

b

☐

c

☐

d
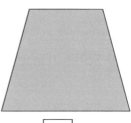
☐

e
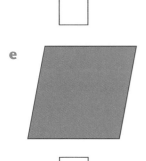
☐

f
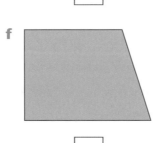
☐

g
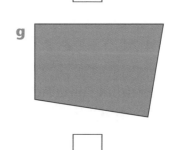
☐

h
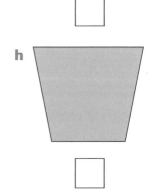
☐

11 What did you notice about the number of diagonals on quadrilaterals?

_____

12 Draw the diagonals on these shapes and record the number of diagonals on each. The pentagon has been started for you.

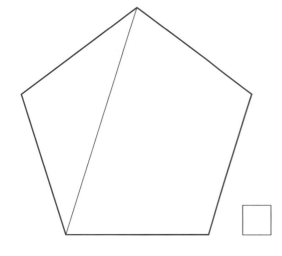
☐

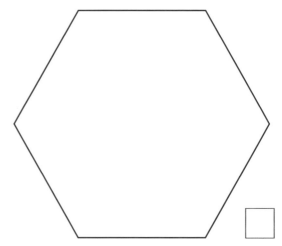
☐

13 Why do you think the hexagon has more diagonals than the pentagon?

_____

_____

SGS3.2a Manipulates, classifies and draws two-dimensional shapes and describes side and angle properties

WMS3.3, WMS3.4

Study the map that shows Australia's three time zones.

Key
White: Eastern standard
Yellow: Central standard
Green: Western standard

Central standard time is $\frac{1}{2}$ an hour behind Eastern standard time.

Western standard time is 2 hours behind Eastern standard time.

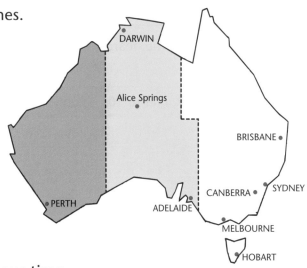

14 Complete the time zone tables using 24-hour time.

	Western standard time	Central standard time	Eastern standard time
a	0800	0930	1000
b			1100
c		1130	
d	1100		

	Western standard time	Central standard time	Eastern standard time
e			1600
f		1630	
g			1800
h			1900

15 Complete the clocks to show the time in each location.

a  Perth

b  Darwin

c 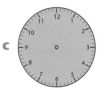 Adelaide

d  Brisbane

e  Sydney

f 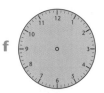 Hobart

In summer in NSW we have **daylight saving**. This has the effect of making the days seem longer, with more daylight hours in the evenings.

16 In addition to NSW, the ACT, Victoria, Tasmania, South Australia and Western Australia also have daylight saving. This means that clocks are moved forward one hour on the first Sunday in October and moved back again on the last Sunday in April the following year. Complete the clocks to show the times in the other capital cities compared to Sydney during daylight saving.

a  Sydney

b Darwin

c  Adelaide

d Brisbane

e Perth

f Hobart

Diagnostic review 4

PART 1 — NS3.1

Round each number to the nearest 10 and nearest 100.

	Number	Round to 10	Round to 100
a	91	90	100
b	229	230	200
c	356	360	400
d	497	500	500
e	986	990	1000

PART 2 — NS3.1

Write the missing positive and negative numbers below the number line.

a

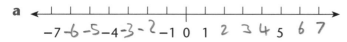

−7 −6 −5 −4 −3 −2 −1 0 1 2 3 4 5 6 7

Record the temperature in degrees Celsius.

b
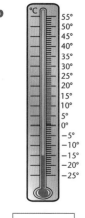

−15 °C

c
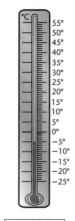

−5 °C

PART 3 — NS3.2

Solve the algorithms.

a
```
      2
  5 4 3 1 6
- 3 2 1 9 4
  _____
  2 2 1 2 2
```

b
```
    7   5
  8 2 6 2 4
- 1 7 2 8 3
  _____
  6 5 3 4 1
```

c
```
  6 3 4 8 2
- 3 1 7 4 9
```

d
```
  $ 9 6 3 . 2 8
- $ 2 8 1 . 9 5
```

PART 4 — NS3.3

Calculate the answer to each algorithm.

a
```
      4 7
  ×    6
    _____
    2 8 2
      4
```

b
```
    3 5 2
  ×    7
  _____
  2 4 6 4
    3 1
```

c
```
      3 9
  ×  4 0
  _____
  1 5 6 0
      3
```

d
```
      5 9
  ×  2 4
  _____
    2 3 6
  1 1 8 0
  _____
  1 4 1 6
```

e
```
      7 5
  ×  3 7
  _____
    5 2 5
  2 2 5 0
  _____
  2 7 7 5
```

f
```
    2 6 3
  ×   4 8
  _____
  2 1 0 4
  1 0 5 2 0
  _____
  1 2 6 2 4
```

PART 5 — NS3.4

Solve the algorithms. ✳

a
```
    6 8 . 7 4
  + 1 2 . 5 3
  _____
    8 1 . 2 7
```

b
```
  $ 6 5 . 8 9
 +$ 2 4 . 0 7
  _____
  $ 8 9 . 9 6
```

c
```
         4
    3 5 . 4 9
  - 2 0 . 8 6
  _____
    1 4 . 6 3
```

d
```
    5 4 . 5 0
  + 4 2 . 5 8
  _____
    9 7 . 0 8
```

e
```
       8
  $ 9 0 . 4 6
 -$ 2 8 . 3 5
  _____
  $ 6 2 . 1 1
```

f
```
       5 9
  $ 6 0 . 4 9
 -$ 4 6 . 8 5
  _____
  $ 1 3 . 6 4
```

g
```
    3 . 2 6
  ×      3
  _____
    3 . 2 3
```

h
```
    8 . 1 7
  ×      4
  _____
    8 . 1 3
```

i
```
  $ 2 . 8 1
  ×      5
  _____
  $ 2 . 7 6
```

Use your calculator to solve these.

j 5.64 ÷ 10 = .564

k 5.64 ÷ 100 = .0564

l 7.63 ÷ 100 = .0763

m 7.63 ÷ 1000 = .00763

PART 6 — PAS3.1a

Complete these number patterns.

a

1st number	3	4	5	6	7	8	9	10	11
2nd number	18	24	30	36	42	48	54	60	66

b

1st number	26	25	24	23	22	21	20	19	18
2nd number	13	12	11	10	9	8	7	6	5

Diagnostic review 4

PART 7
DS3.1

Find the mean score for the scores in each row.

	Scores					Mean
a	9	8	7	6	5	7
b	9	11	13	7	5	9
c	16	13	10	7	4	10
d	14	11	2	5	8	8
e	14	12	10	11	13	12

PART 8
SGS3.1

Name the shapes these nets form.

a

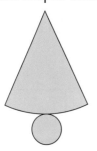

cone

c

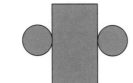

cylinder

b

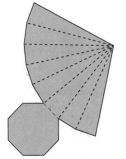

octaganal pyramid

d

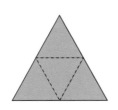

pyramid

PART 9
SGS3.2a

a Label the radius, diameter and circumference of this circle.

circle

Diameter
radius
circumference

b This circle has a diameter of 30 mm. What is its radius?

Radius = 15mm

PART 10
SGS3.3

Write the letter found at each coordinate point to discover the secret word.

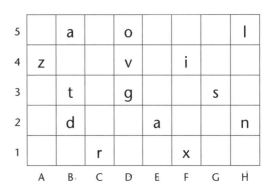

5		a		o				l
4	z			v		i		
3		t		g			s	
2		d			a			n
1			r			x		
	A	B	C	D	E	F	G	H

B2 F4 E2 D3 D5 H2 B5 H5

d i a g o n a L

PART 11
MS3.1

Convert these measurements to the units given.

a 6 cm = 60 mm   d 3 000 m = 3 km

b 40 mm = 4 cm   e 5 km = 5 000 m

c 9 m = 900 cm   f 1.5 km = 1 500 m

PART 12
MS3.2

How many square kilometres of land does this section of parkland occupy?

14 km²

3 km

4 km

PART 13
MS3.5

Complete the time zone grid using 24-hour time.

Western standard time	Central standard time	Eastern standard time
1000 hours	1130 hours	1200 hours
1100	1230	1300 hours
1200	1330 hours	1400
1300 hours	1430	1500
1400	1530 hours	1600
1500	1630	1700 hours

149

Dictionary

acute angle
An angle less than 90°.

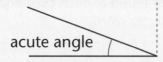

acute angle

addend
Any number which is added to obtain the sum.

$$3 + 7 + 8 = 18$$
(addends)   (sum)

adjacent
Next to; adjacent sides of a triangle have a common vertex.

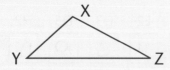

XY and YZ are adjacent because they have a common vertex, Y.

algebra
Where letters are substituted for numbers in a number sentence.

$$3 \times b = 15 \quad (b = 5)$$

Where letters are grouped together with numbers it means that you multiply them.

$$2b \text{ means } 2 \times b$$
$$5c + 4 = 14 \quad (c = 2)$$

algorithm
The calculation procedure for setting out a mathematical problem in a certain way.

$$
\begin{array}{ccc}
324 & 874 & 364 \\
+\ 207 & -\ 23 & \times\ 30
\end{array}
$$

am
Abbreviation from the Latin words *ante meridiem* (the morning). Any time from midnight to noon.

apex
The highest point of a solid (3D) shape from its base.

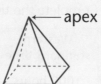

apex

associative property
When using addition and multiplication, it doesn't matter how the numbers are grouped. The answers will always remain the same.

$$
\begin{array}{cc}
5 \times 4 \times 2 = 40 & 3 + 6 + 7 = 16 \\
\text{and} & \text{and} \\
5 \times 2 \times 4 = 40 & 7 + 3 + 6 = 16
\end{array}
$$

average
The total of a series of numbers divided by the amount of numbers in the group.

Average of 3, 5, 7, 9:
- add $3 + 5 + 7 + 9 = 24$
- divided 24 by the number of scores

$$24 \div 4 = 6$$
The average is 6.

axis
A line which divides a shape symmetrically in half.

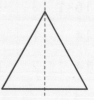

Lines of reference for a graph.

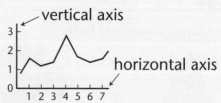

vertical axis

horizontal axis

axis of symmetry
Each imaginary line that divides a shape in half.

bar graph
A graph where bars or columns are used to show quantity.

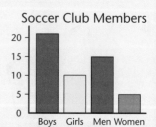

Soccer Club Members

Celsius
A scale for measuring temperature.

0°C	→	ice begins to melt
100°C	→	boiling point of water
36.9°C	→	human body temperature

circumference
The distance around a circle.

CIRCUMFERENCE

Dictionary

commutative law
Numbers can be added or multiplied in any order.

$$5 + 6 \text{ is equal to } 6 + 5$$
$$5 \times 7 \text{ is equal to } 7 \times 5$$

complementary
Two angles whose sum is 90°.

congruent
Two shapes that are identical in all ways.

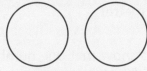

congruent circles

coordinates
Coordinates show position on a grid. The first column refers to the horizontal position (x-axis). The second coordinate refers to the vertical position (y-axis).

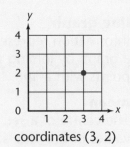

coordinates (3, 2)

cubic metre
A metre cube has a volume equal to one cubic metre.

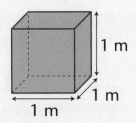

denominator
The bottom number of a fraction that tells how many parts in the whole.

$\dfrac{1}{4}$ → numerator
→ denominator

diameter
A straight line touching both sides of a circle which passes through the centre point.

diameter

edge
The intersection of two faces.

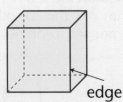

edge

equilateral triangle
A triangle that has three equal sides and three equal angles.

equivalent fractions
Fractions that have the same value.

$$\frac{70}{100} = \frac{7}{10}$$

faces
The surfaces of a three-dimensional (solid) shape.

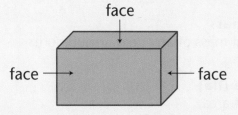

face

face → ← face

factor
Any whole number that can be multiplied with another to make a given number.

Factors of 12: 12, 6, 4, 3, 2, and 1

factor tree
A diagram that displays factors of a number.

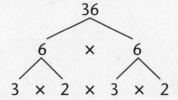

frequency
In a collection of data, the frequency of a category is the number of occurrences for that category.

Animal	Frequency
Sheep	＼＼＼ ＼＼＼ ＼＼＼
Horses	＼＼＼ ＼＼
Cows	＼＼＼ ＼＼＼ ＼＼＼
Dogs	＼＼

The frequency of the horses in the table is 7.

Dictionary

front view
The view of a 3D object seen from the front.

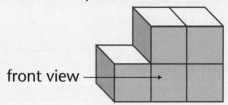

front view

greater than (>)
Symbol used to show that one number has a value greater than the other number.

27 > 15

gross mass
The total mass of any item, including its packaging.

hectare (ha)
A unit of area.
1 ha = 10 000 m^2

hemisphere
One half of a sphere.

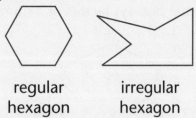

hexagon
A 2D shape with six sides.

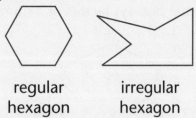

regular hexagon   irregular hexagon

horizontal
A straight line at right angles to the vertical and parallel to the horizon.

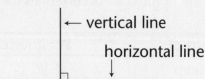

← vertical line

horizontal line

improper fraction
A fraction where the numerator is greater than the denominator. Improper fractions have a value greater than one whole.

$\frac{5}{3}$ → numerator
 → denominator

isosceles triangle
A triangle that has two sides of equal length and two angles the same size.

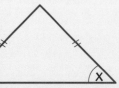

kilogram (kg)
A mass unit.
1 kg = 1 000 grams.

kilolitre (kL)
A capacity unit.
1 kL = 1 000 litres

kilometre (km)
A length unit.
1 km = 1 000 metres

less than (<)
Symbol used to show that one number has a value less than the other number.

240 < 420

line graph
Information represented on a graph by joining plotted points with a line.

mean
The centre of a set. It is found by adding all the values in the data sample, then dividing the total by the number of values in the set.

8 is the mean for the scores:
6, 8, 6, 9, 10 and 9

$$\frac{6 + 8 + 6 + 9 + 10 + 9}{6} = 8$$

metre (m)
The basic SI unit of length.

1 metre = 1 000 mm
1 metre = 100 cm

millilitre (mL)
A measurement of capacity.
1 000 mL = 1 litre

millimetre (mm)
A measurement of length.
1 mm = 1 thousandth of a metre
10 mm = 1 centimetre

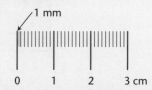

Dictionary

million
1 000 000

$$1\,000 \times 1\,000 = 1\,000\,000$$
or
$$10 \times 100\,000 = 1\,000\,000$$

mixed numerals
A number that consists of a whole number and a fractional part.

For example: $4\frac{1}{2}$

negative numbers
Numbers that have a value less than zero.
A minus sign is placed in front of a number to identify it as negative.

For example: The temperature was −5°C

net
A flat shape which can be folded to make a 3D shape.

Net of a triangular prism

net mass
The mass of any shape without its packaging.

obtuse angle
An angle larger than 90° but less than 180°.

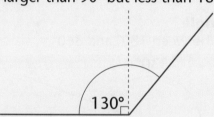

130°

order of rotational symmetry
The number of times a shape matches the original as it completes one full rotation.

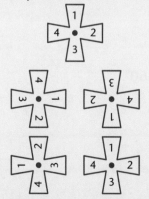

Order of rotation of 4

outcome
The result of a mathematical investigation. For example, when three coins are tossed there are 8 possible outcomes.

per cent (%)
A fraction of 100.

87% means 87 out of 100

i.e. $\frac{87}{100} = 87\% = 0.87$

perimeter
The distance around the outside of a shape.

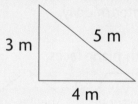

3 m   5 m

4 m

Perimeter = 3 m + 4 m + 5 m
Perimeter = 12 m

perpendicular
A vertical line forming a right angle with the horizontal.

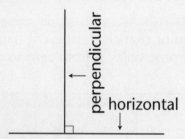

perpendicular

horizontal

perpendicular lines
Lines which meet at right angles.

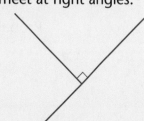

Dictionary

pie graph
A circular graph whose parts look like portions of a pie.

plan
A diagram from above, showing the position of objects. Also known as the top view of a 3D object.

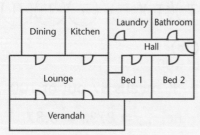

pm
Abbreviation for the Latin words *post meridiem* which means after midday.

polygon
A 2D shape with plane faces.

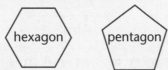

prime number
A number that is divisible only by itself and 1.

Examples:
2, 3, 5, 7, 11, 13, 17, 19, 23, 29

probability
The likelihood or chance of an event happening. The range of probability is from zero to one.

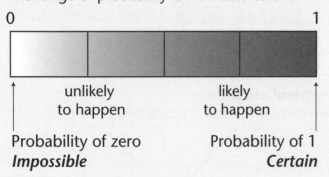

quadrilateral
A 2D shape with four sides.

Examples:

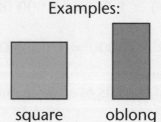

square   oblong

radius
A straight line extending from the centre of a circle to the outside.

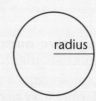

ray
A line that has a starting point but does not end.

rectangle
A four-sided figure with four right angles and two pairs of parallel sides.

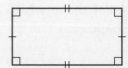

rectangular prism
A 3D shape which consists of six rectangular faces.

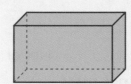

reflective symmetry
A mirror image of a shape.

reflex angle
An angle between 180° and 360°.

Example: 330°

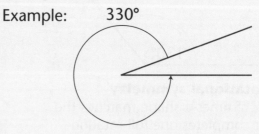

revolution
A full turn of 360°.

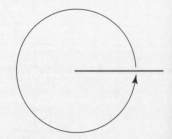

Dictionary

rhombus
A four-sided shape with four equal sides. Opposite angles are equal and it has two sets of parallel lines.

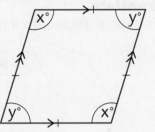

Roman numerals
Number system devised by the ancient Romans.

Examples:

I = 1   D = 500
V = 5   M = 1 000
X = 10
L = 50   XCV = 95
C = 100   MMX = 2010

rotation
To turn an object through a fixed point.

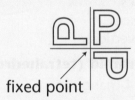

fixed point

rotational symmetry
When a shape maps onto itself after being rotated less than 360° it is said to have rotational symmetry.

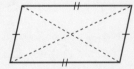

Parallelograms have rotational symmetry about the point of intersection of their diagonals

scalene triangle
A triangle with sides of different lengths and angles of different size.

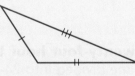

sequence
An order of numbers or objects arranged according to a rule:

Example:

Number	1	2	3	4
$	$5	$10	$15	$20

square centimetre (cm²)
A unit for measuring area.

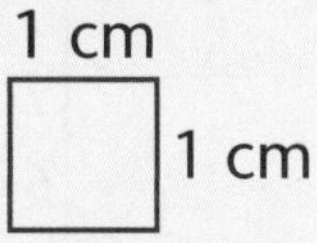

1 cm × 1 cm = 1 cm^2

square kilometre (km²)
A unit for measuring area.

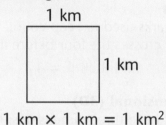

1 km × 1 km = 1 km^2

square metre (m²)
A unit for measuring area.

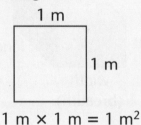

1 m × 1 m = 1 m^2

square number
The product of a number multiplied by itself.

Examples:

$2^2 = 2 \times 2 = 4$
$3^2 = 3 \times 3 = 9$
$4^2 = 4 \times 4 = 16$

supplementary angles
Two angles which have a total of 180°.

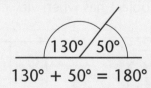

130° + 50° = 180°

Dictionary

surface area
The total area of all faces of a 3D object.

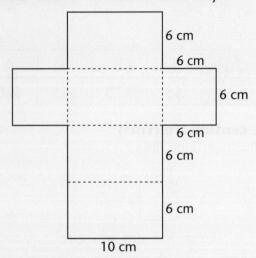

6 cm
6 cm
6 cm
6 cm
6 cm
6 cm
10 cm

A rectangular prism has six surfaces.

tally marks
Groups of marks used to keep count. Every fifth mark usually crosses the four before it.

‖‖ ‖‖ ‖‖ ‖ = 17

three-dimensional (3D)
Solid objects have three dimensions: height, length, width (or breadth).

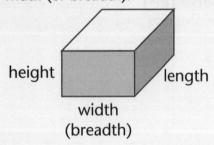

height   length
width
(breadth)

timeline
A line which represents a span of time.

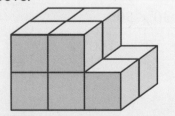

| 1985 | 1990 | 1995 | 2000 | 2005 |
| Born | School | High school | | Work |

tonne
1 000 kilograms.

top view
The shape an object has when viewed from above.

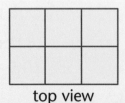

top view

translate
To slide a shape into a new position.

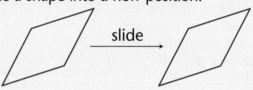

slide

trapezium
A four-sided figure with only one pair of parallel sides.

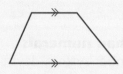

triangular numbers
Numbers that can be arranged as a triangular pattern.

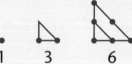

1   3   6

triangular prism
A prism with two congruent triangles as bases, 3 rectangular faces, 9 edges and 6 vertices.

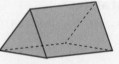

triangular pyramid (tetrahedron)
3D shape with 4 triangular faces, 6 edges and 4 vertices.

turn
To rotate a shape around a point.

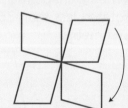

twelve-hour time
Analog clocks break the day into two lots of 12 hours:
am (midnight–midday)
pm (midday–midnight)

twenty-four hour time
Time divided into 24-hour intervals, so as to distinguish between am and pm.

Dictionary

two-dimensional (2D)
Plane shapes have only two dimensions length and width (breadth).

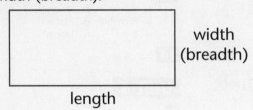

unit fraction
Fractions with a numerator of 1.

Examples:
$$\frac{1}{2}, \frac{1}{3}, \frac{1}{4}, \frac{1}{5}, \frac{1}{10}$$

vertex
The point where two or more lines meet to form an angle.

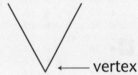

vertical
Vertical lines are at right angles to the horizontal.

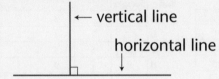

vertices
Plural of vertex.

A triangle has 3 vertices.

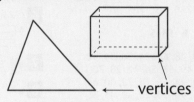

A rectangular prism has 8 vertices.

volume
The amount of space an object occupies.
Formula:
Volume = length × width × height

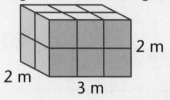

Volume = 3 m × 2 m × 2 m = 12 m^3

Basic units = cubic metre (m^3),
cubic centimetre (cm^3), litre and millilitre.

whole numbers
The counting numbers from one to infinity.

1, 2, 3, 4, → infinity

Answers

Unit 1

1
a 364   e 624   i 883   m 91°C
b 595   f 476   j 868   n 948 mL
c 650   g 958   k 750 g   o $26.14
d 765   h 776   l 761 cm

2
a 497   b $845

3
a 12, 18, 30, 48, 60, 24, 36, 54, 42
b 7, 21, 35, 49, 63, 56, 42, 28, 70
c 32, 48, 40, 24, 56, 16, 72, 80, 64
d 10, 25, 15, 40, 50, 20, 30, 45, 35
e 36, 54, 45, 27, 72, 63, 81, 18, 90
f 12, 4, 20, 28, 36, 32, 24, 16, 40

4
a 6 × 5 = 30, 30 ÷ 5 = 6 or 30 ÷ 6 = 5
b 7 × 6 = 42, 42 ÷ 6 = 7 or 42 ÷ 7 = 6
c 8 × 9 = 72, 72 ÷ 9 = 8 or 72 ÷ 8 = 9
d 8 × 4 = 32, 32 ÷ 4 = 8 or 32 ÷ 8 = 4
e 9 × 6 = 54, 54 ÷ 6 = 9 or 54 ÷ 9 = 6
f 7 × 9 = 63, 63 ÷ 9 = 7 or 63 ÷ 7 = 9

5
a $72   c $56   e $40
b $70   d $54   f $32

6 Hands on.

7

Shape	Name	Sides	Angles	Types of angles	Lines of symmetry
triangle	triangle	3	3	acute	3
rectangle	rectangle	4	4	right angle	2
trapezium	trapezium	4	4	right angle obtuse acute	0
pentagon	pentagon	5	5	obtuse	5
octagon	octagon	8	8	obtuse	8
hexagon	hexagon	6	6	obtuse	6

8 a   b   c   d   e

9 1 000 clicks

10 Hands on.   **11** Hands on.

12
a 433 km   c 396 km   e 378 km
b 368 km   d 245 km

13 Hands on.

Unit 2

1
a 77   h 85   o 559
b 85   i 58   p 888
c 30   j 91   q 879
d 68   k 21   r 799
e 96   l 111   s 111
f 74   m 458   t 925
g 32   n 497   u 633

2
a 62   g 39   m 154
b 74   h 59   n 273
c 62   i 59   o 403
d 72   j 38   p 303
e 102   k 39   q 327
f 87   l 35   r 258

3
a 800   h 700   o 1 300
b 500   i 600   p 500
c 1 000   j 300   q 400
d 1 000   k 600   r 1 300
e 400   l 1 000   s 400
f 1 000   m 1 200   t 1 400
g 700   n 200   u 1 400

4
a 92 m   b $25

5
a $\frac{2}{3}$ c $\frac{7}{12}$ e $\frac{3}{12}$ g $\frac{5}{12}$
b $\frac{4}{6}$ d $\frac{5}{6}$ f $\frac{4}{6}$ h $\frac{2}{6}$

6 Possible solutions:
a $\frac{2}{3}$ b $\frac{5}{12}$ c $\frac{5}{6}$ d $\frac{9}{12}$

7
a $\frac{5}{6}$ b $\frac{2}{3}$ c $\frac{7}{12}$

8
a $\frac{1}{3}, \frac{2}{3}$ b $\frac{1}{6}, \frac{2}{6}, \frac{3}{6}, \frac{4}{6}, \frac{5}{6}$
c $\frac{1}{12}, \frac{2}{12}, \frac{3}{12}, \frac{4}{12}, \frac{5}{12}, \frac{6}{12}, \frac{7}{12}, \frac{8}{12}, \frac{9}{12}, \frac{10}{12}, \frac{11}{12}$

9 $\frac{4}{6}$

10
a Obtuse angle   g Obtuse angle
b Acute angle   h Reflex angle
c Right angle   i Right angle
d Acute angle   j Acute angle
e Straight angle   k Straight angle
f Right angle   l Obtuse angle

11

a I have four right angles. — B
b I have one obtuse angle, one acute angle and two right angles. — C
c I have three acute angles. — E
d I have three right angles and two obtuse angles. — D
e I have six obtuse angles. — A

12 Hands on.   **13** Hands on.

14

	Length	Breadth	Array
a	3 cm	2 cm	6 cm²
b	4 cm	2 cm	8 cm²
c	4 cm	3 cm	12 cm²
d	6 cm	3 cm	18 cm²

15
a 12 cm²   b 28 cm²   c 40 cm²

Unit 3

1 a 622   b 641   c 521   d 445   e 235

2 a 418   b 317   c 207   d 318   e 327

3 a 385   b 565   c 493   d 685   e 585

4 a 360   b 13   c 177   d 78

5
a 2, 4, 3, 6, 8   d 2, 4, 3, 5, 7
b 2, 4, 6, 9, 7   e 6, 9, 3, 7, 10
c 2, 4, 3, 5, 7

6
a 6 r 1   e 7 r 2   i 7 r 3
b 4 r 1   f 5 r 4   j 7 r 2
c 2 r 1   g 5 r 2   k 8 r 1
d 5 r 1   h 5 r 2   l 9 r 3

7
a 16 r 1   c 5 r 3   e 4 r 1
b 8 r 1   d 6 r 3

8 Hands on.

9
a 50   c 95   e 15
b 55   d 25   f No, there are 225 animals only.

10
a 24   c 26   e 4th   g 4th   i 188
b 28   d 34   f 6th   h 6

Unit 4

11 a, b, c, f   **12** They stack without gaps.

13
a 3 cm³   e 10 cm³   i 24 cm³
b 6 cm³   f 16 cm³   j 18 cm³
c 8 cm³   g 24 cm³
d 8 cm³   h 16 cm³

14 Hands on.

Unit 4

1
a 15   e 140   i 1 300
b 150   f 90   j 250
c 1 500   g 1 000   k 330
d 130   h 400   l 300

2
a 41   h 31   o 172
b 62   i 97   p 101
c 88   j 114   q 171
d 58   k 102   r 131
e 23   l 169   s 161
f 21   m 179   t 330
g 128   n 176   u 393

3
a 63   e 69   i 369
b 64   f 91   j 283
c 75   g 68   k 194
d 96   h 79   l 572

4
a 36   e 34   i 159
b 33   f 14   j 228
c 47   g 27   k 138
d 24   h 35   l 225

5 Hands on.

6

	Ten thousands	Thousands	Hundreds	Tens	Ones
a			3	6	7
b		1	4	5	4
c	2	5	3	0	9
d	8	7	9	3	6
e	9	0	2	3	5
f	3	7	2	9	4

7
a 345, 665, 5 867, 6 745
b 567, 3 576, 6 987, 9 453
c 22 899, 22 998, 23 567, 32 567
d 45 678, 45 876, 49 887, 54 876
e 5 999, 12 898, 21 889, 45 887
f 12 335, 12 553, 21 335, 21 553

8

	Cards	Largest number	Smallest number
a	3 7 4 5 9	9 7 5 4 3	3 4 5 7 9
b	9 6 8 3 7	9 8 7 6 3	3 6 7 8 9
c	1 3 2 9 8	9 8 3 2 1	1 2 3 8 9

9
a 237   Two hundred and thirty-seven
b 1 379   One thousand, three hundred and seventy-nine
c 25 327   Twenty-five thousand, three hundred and twenty-seven
d 36 000   Thirty-six thousand

10
a Sydney I3   d Whyalla F3
b Alice Springs E5   e Tasmania H1
c Cairns H7   f Darwin E7

11
a North   e South-east
b South   f North-west
c North-east   g South-west
d North-east   h South-east

12 a to c Hands on.   d Stegal

Answers

13 Hands on. **14** Hands on.

15 a 12 **b** 4 **c** 20 **d** 60

16 a Spring scale **d** Weighbridge
b Kitchen scales **e** Bathroom scales
c Displacement tank

Unit 5

1 a 90 **d** 180 **g** 210 **j** 400
b 120 **e** 240 **h** 320 **k** 540
c 200 **f** 300 **i** 280 **l** 490

2 a 1 000 **f** 2 400 **k** 2 800
b 1 200 **g** 3 000 **l** 4 900
c 1 600 **h** 2 500 **m** 3 500
d 1 500 **i** 2 100 **n** 6 400
e 2 000 **j** 3 600 **o** 5 600

3 a 96 **d** 91 **g** 126 **j** 204
b 115 **e** 136 **h** 136 **k** 152
c 150 **f** 114 **i** 144 **l** 215

4 a $180 **c** $200 **e** $184
b $180 **d** $130

5 Hands on.

6 a 13 **c** $4.91 **e** 75 **g** $206
b 16 **d** $315 **f** 264 **h** $1 650

7 Hands on.

8 a, b, c, d all Hands on. **9** Hands on.

10–11 Discussion. Six combinations give 7 but only one combination gives 12.

12 a (R) 15 Y 8 G 5 (O) 2 **d** Orange
b Red **e** No
c Hands on (fair, 50/50, even) **f** Yes

13

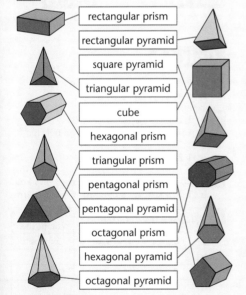

rectangular prism
rectangular pyramid
square pyramid
triangular pyramid
cube
hexagonal prism
triangular prism
pentagonal prism
pentagonal pyramid
octagonal prism
hexagonal pyramid
octagonal pyramid

Unit 6

1 a 5 **d** 4 **g** 6 **j** 8 **m** 9
b 5 **e** 7 **h** 5 **k** 3 **n** 5
c 5 **f** 3 **i** 6 **l** 7 **o** 8

2 a 5 r1 **d** 5 r5 **g** 8 r2 **j** 7 r3 **m** 7 r1
b 7 r1 **e** 7 r2 **h** 7 r3 **k** 4 r2 **n** 5 r3
c 6 r3 **f** 4 r2 **i** 5 r2 **l** 6 r3 **o** 6 r2

3 a 24 **c** 15 **4** 3
b 18 **d** 6

5

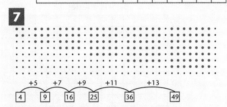

a	15	20	25	30	35	40	45
b	12	16	20	24	28	32	36
c	4	7	10	13	16	19	22
d	5	12	19	26	33	40	47

e	536	532	528	524	520	516	512
f	213	227	241	255	269	283	297
g	3	6	12	24	48	96	192
h	198	191	184	177	170	163	156

6

	Rule	Sequence						
a	Minus 3	43	40	37	34	31	28	25
b	Plus 4	53	57	61	65	69	73	77
c	Plus 0.5	3.5	4	4.5	5	5.5	6	6.5
d	Doubling	1	2	4	8	16	32	64
e	Halving	128	64	32	16	8	4	2
f	Multiply by 3	1	3	9	27	81	243	729
g	Add 1 extra number each time	1	2	4	7	11	16	22
h	Add the two previous numbers	1	1	2	3	5	8	13

7

+5 +7 +9 +11 +13

4 9 16 25 36 49

8

| Square numbers | 4 | 9 | 16 | 25 | 36 | 49 | 64 | 81 | 100 | 121 | 144 | 169 |

9 a

(graph: Millimetres vs Months J F M A M J J A S O N D)

b 25 mm **e** 180 mm
c June **f** 165 mm
d February **g** Hands on.

10 a Darwin
b Hobart
c 10.5°C
d Darwin, Perth
e Sydney and Melbourne; Adelaide and Canberra

(graph: Capital city temperature — Canberra, Sydney, Melbourne, Brisbane, Adelaide, Perth, Hobart, Darwin)

11 a 1:30 am **e** 5:13 pm **i** 5:06 pm
b 11:30 am **f** 6:37 pm **j** 8:50 pm
c 6:17 am **g** 5:56 am **k** 9:17 am
d 10:28 pm **h** 7:47 pm **l** 7:58 pm

12 a 3:00 am 3:00 pm 6:00 pm
b 8:27 am 8:30 am 9:03 pm
c 1:15 am 2:06 am 2:03 pm
d 7:15 am 7:36 pm 8:34 pm
e 7:51 am 7:53 am 7:52 pm

13 a 3:35 am **b** 4:53 am **c** 12:10 pm

Unit 7

1 a 81 **d** 185 **g** 240 **j** 504 **m** 196
b 92 **e** 184 **h** 444 **k** 336 **n** 230
c 87 **f** 252 **i** 203 **l** 392 **o** 256

2 a 261 flights **c** 612 kg
b 364 sultanas

3 Hands on.

4 a 4 **e** 3 **i** 9 **m** 3 **q** 10
b 8 **f** 7 **j** 20 **n** 4 **r** 9
c 6 **g** 5 **k** 5 **o** 10 **s** 6
d 2 **h** 2 **l** 6 **p** 5 **t** 30

5 a 16 **b** 8 **c** 6 **d** 12

6 a 9 **b** 20 **c** 8 **d** 8

7 a 10 **b** 6

8 a

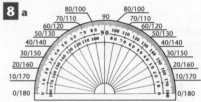

b So angles can be read from either direction.

9 a acute 70° **d** obtuse 120°
b right angle 90° **e** obtuse 135°
c acute 45° **e** acute 50°

10 a 50° **c** 90° **e** 120° **g** 90°
b 70° **d** 130° **f** 80° **h** 20°

11

| Metres | 1 525 | 2 399 | 3 514 | 4 786 | 2 905 | 4 567 | 2 063 | 2 560 |
| Kilometres | 1.525 | 2.399 | 3.514 | 4.786 | 2.905 | 4.567 | 2.063 | 2.560 |

12 2.905

13

| Kilometres | 3.505 | 2.459 | 8.355 | 7.684 | 9.502 | 6.349 | 82 | 35 |
| Metres | 3 505 | 2 459 | 8 355 | 7 684 | 9 502 | 6 349 | 82 000 | 35 000 |

14

	Distance	Metres	Kilometres
a	A to B to C	6 815	6.815
b	C to D to E	9 405	9.405
c	E to F to G	5 320	5.320
d	H to G to F	6 236	6.236
e	F to E to D	9 455	9.455
f	D to C to B to A	8 665	8.665

15 Hands on.

Unit 8

1 a 8 689 **c** 9 888 **e** 7 589
b 4 688 **d** 6 999

2 a 5 370 **c** 5 883 **e** 8 981
b 6 793 **d** 7 082

3 a 5 634 **c** 8 830 **e** 8 743
b 5 846 **d** 6 540

4 He forgot to trade in the thousands column. The answer should be 10 277.

5 Hands on.

Answers

6
a 8 e 15 i 6 m 4
b 7 f 9 j 9 n 5
c 13 g 3 k 4 o 7
d 15 h 4 l 12

7 △ = 7   △ = 5

a ⑦ + ⑧ = 15   b ⑤ × ⑦ = 35
⑧ + ⑨ = 17   ⑦ × ⑥ = 42
⑨ − △ = 2   ⑥ × ⑤ = 30
⑨ + △ = 16   37 − ⑥ = 31
△ × ⑧ = 56   42 − ⑥ = 36
△ + ⑧ + ⑨ = 24   (⑤ + ⑦) × ⑥ = 72

8
a 19 oranges c $70
b $77 d 7 books

9 Hands on – some examples below:

a ④ × ⑤ + ⑥ = ㉖
b ⑤ × ⑥ + ④ = ㉞
c ④ × ⑥ + ⑤ = ㉙
d ⑥ × ④ − ⑤ = ⑲

10 Hands on. **11** Hands on.

12 Hands on. **13** Hands on.

14
a Mondays and Wednesdays
b 450 e 650
c 650 f 3 250
d Sunday

15 Hands on. **16** Hands on.

17 Hands on.

Unit 9

1
a 10 d 8 g 8 j 100 m 40
b 10 e 5 h 10 k 50 n 50
c 5 f 5 i 100 l 50 o 60

2
a 3 d 2 g 30 j 60
b 30 e 20 h 40 k 60
c 300 f 200 i 60 l 70

3
a 6 d 12 g 19 j 60
b 8 e 15 h 30 k 45
c 10 f 20 i 50 l 55

4
a 5 c 8 e 15 g 30 i 60
b 4 d 10 f 25 h 40

5 Hands on.

6
a $\frac{3}{6}$ d $\frac{3}{12}$ g $\frac{8}{12}$ j $\frac{8}{12}$ m $\frac{6}{6}$
b $\frac{6}{12}$ e $\frac{4}{12}$ h $\frac{2}{3}$ k $\frac{9}{12}$ n $\frac{12}{12}$
c $\frac{2}{6}$ f $\frac{4}{6}$ i $\frac{4}{12}$ l $\frac{3}{3}$ o $\frac{4}{4}$

7
a > d < g > j >
b > e < h < k =
c > f > i = l <

8
a 3 b 12 c 6 d 15

9

10

Shape	Name	Faces	Edges	Vertices
a	 Cube	6	12	8
b	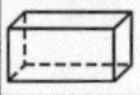 Rectangular prism	6	12	8
c	 Square pyramid	5	8	5
d	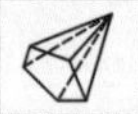 Pentagonal pyramid	6	10	6
e	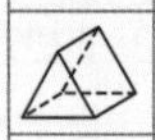 Triangular prism	5	9	6
f	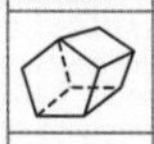 Pentagonal prism	7	15	10
g	 Triangular pyramid	4	6	4

11 Hands on.

12 One example shown below.
a
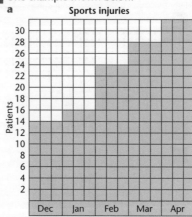

b April
c December

DIAGNOSTIC REVIEW 1

Part 1
a 76 532
b Sixty-three thousand, one hundred and twenty-five.
c 167 412, 617 241, 617 412, 716 241

Part 2
a 782 d 301 g 172 j 47
b 7 421 e 611 h 59 k 142
c 18.4 f 703 i 172

Part 3
Possible solutions:
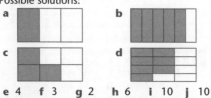

e 4 f 3 g 2 h 6 i 10 j 10

Part 4
a | 10 | 15 | 25 | 35 | 30 | 40 | 45 |
b | 14 | 21 | 35 | 49 | 42 | 56 | 63 |
c | 16 | 24 | 40 | 56 | 48 | 64 | 72 |

---

d 6 g 6 j 320 m 5 r2 p 375
e 6 h 6 r2 k 600 n 7 r3 q 216
f 6 i 9 r2 l 9 o 256

Part 5
a 23 b 9 c 6 d 7
e 27, 30, 33, 36, 39, 42, 45
f 147, 152, 157, 162, 167, 172, 177
g 1, 2, 4, 8, 16, 32, 64

Part 6
a Acute angle b Right angle
c Obtuse angle

Part 7
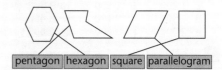

pentagon | hexagon | square | parallelogram

Part 8
a 8 b 5 c 5 d Square pyramid

Part 9
a North c East e West
b North-east d South-west f South-east

Part 10
a 1:25 am b 10:37 pm c 3:57 am

Part 11
Possible solutions:
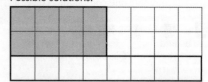

Part 12
a 8 cm³ b 20 cm³

Part 13
a 30 b 45

Unit 10

1
a 2 947 c 3 124 e 1 228
b 4 428 d 3 608

2
a 1 182 e 2 355 i 7 186
b 138 f 4 257 j 6 418
c 1 281 g 5 148
d 1 278 h 5 159

3
a 585 km c 2 018 km e 3 683 km
b 1 138 km d 3 098 km f 1 313 km

4

	Number	Factors	Prime or composite
a	8	1, 2, 4, 8	Composite
b	7	1, 7	Prime
c	9	1, 3, 9	Composite
d	11	1, 11	Prime
e	18	1, 2, 3, 6, 9, 18	Composite
f	16	1, 2, 4, 8, 16	Composite
g	23	1, 23	Prime
h	17	1, 17	Prime

5
a Prime
b Composite
c Prime
d Composite
e Prime
f Composite
g Prime
h Composite
i Composite
j Prime
k Composite
l Composite

6 a Hands on (No). b Hands on (Yes).

7 16, 36, 64, 100

8
a Equilateral triangle
b Isosceles triangle
c Equilateral triangle
d Isosceles triangle
e Scalene triangle
f Scalene triangle

9 A, B, D

10 Hands on.

11
a A = 6 cm²   d A = 18 cm²
b A = 8 cm²   e A = 18 cm²
c A = 9 cm²   f A = 12 cm²

12 Hands on.   **13** Hands on.

Unit 11

1
a 15   e 14   i 16   m 19
b 13   f 18   j 14   n 17
c 13   g 16   k 26   o 23
d 12   h 14   l 24   p 14

2
a 6 × 4 = 24, 24 ÷ 6 = 4
b 7 × 5 = 35, 35 ÷ 7 = 5 or 35 ÷ 5 = 7
c 8 × 6 = 48, 48 ÷ 8 = 6 or 48 ÷ 6 = 8
d 9 × 7 = 63, 63 ÷ 9 = 7 or 63 ÷ 7 = 9

3
a 9 cards   c 8 r2 lollies
b 5 r2 stickers   d 4 runs

4
a 0.48   c 0.25   e 0.63
b 0.77   d 0.66   f 0.99

5 0.28, 0.43, 2.50, 2.57, 4.35, 4.45, 8.22

6
a 1.27 m   d 5.63 m   g 8.42 m
b 3.52 m   e 7.42 m   h 9.06 m
c 4.27 m   f 8.90 m   i 14.23 m

7
a Trent   c Catherine
b Sarah   d Hands on.

8
a False   d False   g True
b True   e False   h False
c True   f True   i False

9
a 0
b 0.1, 0.2, 0.3 or 0.4
c 0.5
d 0.6, 0.7, 0.8 or 0.9
e 1

10 Hands on.   **11** Hands on.

12
a 400 km   c 700 km   e 550 km
b 600 km   d 450 km   f 225 km

13
a 140 km   e 350 km
b 90 km   f 280 km
c 300 km   g 380 km
d 160 km

14 a 360 km   b 160 km

Unit 12

1
a 7 485   c 8 948   e 5 924
b 5 773   d 5 631

2
a 6 386   c 7 599   e 8 878
b 8 495   d 6 189

3
a 5 844   c 8 756   e 9 541
b 7 456   d 9 642

4
a 278 km   c 670 km   e 849 km
b 471 km   d 610 km   f 697 km

5 Possible solution: Wollongong to Port Macquarie.

6 Possible solution: Sydney to Grafton and return.

7
a XXXIII   h XXIII   o CXX
b XX   i LVI   p CL
c XXVIII   j LXXIV   q CLXXII
d VI   k LXIX   r CCXXVII
e XXXVI   l XLVII   s CCXXIII
f XLVI   m LXVI   t CCCXXXIV
g XIX   n LXXXVI   u CCCLXV

8
a
X	III	VIII
V	VII	IX
VI	XI	IV

b
IV	IX	II
III	V	VII
VIII	I	VI

c
VIII	III	IV
I	V	IX
VI	VII	II

9 a
Litres	6	12	18	24	30	36	42
Kilometres	50	100	150	200	250	300	350

b
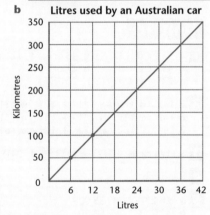
Litres used by an Australian car

c 200 km   e 75 km   g 42 L
d 300 km   f 30 L   h 48 L

10 a
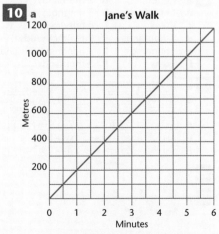
Jane's Walk

b 2 000 metres   c 500 metres

11
Prism	Length	Breadth	Height	Volume
Sarah	6 cm	2 cm	3 cm	36 cm³
John	9 cm	2 cm	2 cm	36 cm³
Alisha	4 cm	3 cm	3 cm	36 cm³

12 All 36 cm³

13
	Length	Breadth	Height	Tally	Volume (cm³)
a	4 cm	2 cm	2 cm	⳩⳩⳩ I	16 cm³
b	4 cm	3 cm	3 cm	⳩⳩⳩⳩⳩⳩⳩ I	36 cm³
c	6 cm	2 cm	3 cm	⳩⳩⳩⳩⳩⳩⳩ I	36 cm³
d	6 cm	1 cm	4 cm	⳩⳩⳩⳩ IIII	24 cm³
e	4 cm	2 cm	4 cm	⳩⳩⳩⳩⳩⳩ II	32 cm³
f	8 cm	1 cm	4 cm	⳩⳩⳩⳩⳩⳩ II	32 cm³

Unit 13

1
a 705   f 1 815   k 1 280
b 3 388   g 1 488   l 2 443
c 4 500   h 3 318   m 2 568
d 4 560   i 2 632   n 2 184
e 5 999   j 2 367   o 3 320

2 a 1 825   b 2 020 km   c 1 125 mL

3 5, 6, 7 or 8

4
a 7   d 18   g 9   j 88
b 32   e 5   h 12   k 250
c 50   f 6   i 24   l 7

5 a 3   b 24   c 7

6
a 4 × 2 + 6 = 14   e 6 × 4 ÷ 3 = 8
b 4 × 3 − 7 = 5   f 3 + 5 × 7 = 56
c 7 − 5 + 8 = 10   g 30 − 15 ÷ 5 = 3
d 20 ÷ 5 + 3 = 7

7–9 Hands on.

10
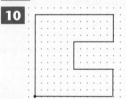

11
a 0300   g 2200
b 0800   h 0600
c 1600   i 2000
d 1800   j 1930
e 1400   k 0730
f 2300   l 2115

12
Analog						
Digital	3:00 AM	6:15 PM	5:40 PM	11:45 AM	9:35 PM	10:05 AM	12:45 PM
24-hour	0300	1815	1740	1145	2135	1005	1245

13
a Home shopping
b Channel 6, 1930, 30 min
c Bewitched
d No
e Channel 6, 2230, 1 hour 30 minutes

161

Unit 14

1 a 2 814 c 1 631 e 4 532
 b 3 722 d 713

2 a 1 634 e 4 471 h 7 175
 b 4 172 f 3 278 i 9 658
 c 1 838 g 2 867 j 4 684
 d 1 751

3 a 3 013 c 376 e 1 574
 b 1 815 d 398 f 774

4

Estimate	Answer
$1 900	$1 880
1 400	1 403
300	299
$8 800	$8 748

5 a 14 r1 e 14 r1 i 13 r2 m 12 r1
 b 13 r1 f 15 r2 j 14 r2 n 13 r1
 c 16 r1 g 13 r5 k 14 r1 o 18 r2
 d 15 r3 h 15 r2 l 14 r1 p 24 r1

6 a 12 d 12 r1 g 5 j 4
 b 10 e 7 h 13 k 12 r4
 c 14 r4 f 8 i 21 r1 l 15
Top Bingo card wins.

7 Hands on.

8

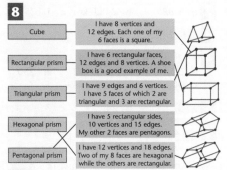

Cube — I have 8 vertices and 12 edges. Each one of my 6 faces is a square.

Rectangular prism — I have 6 rectangular faces, 12 edges and 8 vertices. A shoe box is a good example of me.

Triangular prism — I have 9 edges and 6 vertices. I have 5 faces of which 2 are triangular and 3 are rectangular.

Hexagonal prism — I have 5 rectangular sides, 10 vertices and 15 edges. My other 2 faces are pentagons.

Pentagonal prism — I have 12 vertices and 18 edges. Two of my 8 faces are hexagonal while the others are rectangular.

9 Hands on.

10 a 12 cm c 12 cm e 14 cm
 b 16 cm d 16 cm

11 a 16 cm b 18 cm c 13 cm

12 a 12 cm perimeter b 16 cm perimeter

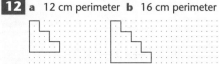

13 a 20 m b 12 m c 24 m

Unit 15

1 a 1 304 e 4 284 i 3 642 m 2 142
 b 2 410 f 1 748 j 3 105 n 3 370
 c 1 185 g 4 830 k 6 020 o 3 496
 d 5 664 h 3 650 l 3 648

2 a 1 722 m b 1 096 m

3 Hands on. (625)

4 a $\frac{4}{6}$ c $\frac{7}{12}$ e $\frac{5}{6}$ g $\frac{9}{12}$
 b $\frac{7}{10}$ d $\frac{3}{4}$ f $\frac{6}{8}$ h $\frac{8}{10}$

5 a $\frac{7}{12}$ d $\frac{6}{8}$ g $\frac{5}{6}$ j $\frac{4}{6}$
 b $\frac{3}{4}$ e $\frac{4}{5}$ h $\frac{7}{8}$ k $\frac{5}{6}$
 c $\frac{7}{10}$ f $\frac{3}{6}$ i $\frac{3}{6}$ l $\frac{6}{12}$

6 a $\frac{3}{10}$ e $\frac{3}{10}$ i $\frac{3}{8}$ m $\frac{2}{6}$
 b $\frac{2}{12}$ f $\frac{3}{6}$ j $\frac{2}{4}$ n $\frac{3}{6}$
 c $\frac{4}{12}$ g $\frac{1}{5}$ k $\frac{1}{3}$ o $\frac{1}{6}$
 d $\frac{4}{12}$ h $\frac{2}{12}$ l $\frac{3}{6}$

7 Possible solutions:
$\frac{6}{12} + \frac{3}{12}$, $\frac{7}{12} + \frac{2}{12}$, $\frac{5}{12} + \frac{4}{12}$, $\frac{8}{12} + \frac{1}{12}$

8

	First name	Surname	Date of birth	Suburb	Telephone
	Telephone list				
13	Brett	Sattler	21/9/94	Kensington	948 6098
14	Lauren	Lockett	2/9/93	Kensington	948 4788
15	Catherine	Laws	5/6/94	Maroubra	941 5671

9 a Zena, Brett, Lauren
 b Julia, John, Mark
 c Helen, Zena, Lauren
 d Jessica, Brett, Catherine
 e Jessica, Helen
 f Taryn, Mark

10 a 9 × 6 = 54 m² b 8 × 6 = 48 m²

11 a 5 × 3 = 15 m² c 9 × 3 = 27 m²
 b 3 × 2 = 6 m² d 6 × 2 = 12 m²

12 a $240 b 90 m, 450 m²

Unit 16

1 a 134 d 132 g 432 r1 j 121 r3
 b 432 e 121 h 212 r1
 c 231 f 232 r1 i 231 r2

2 a 142 d 152 g 121 j 121 m 131
 b 142 e 132 h 171 k 131 n 141
 c 164 f 162 i 172 l 121 o 161

3 a 174 r2 b 104 r1 c 151 d 241

4 Hands on.

5 a 26 237 d 35 009
 b 42 713 e 50 204
 c 67 360

6 a 4 ones g 2 thousands
 b 3 hundreds h 3 ten thousands
 c 3 tens i 8 hundreds
 d 6 thousands j 9 ten thousands
 e 7 hundreds k 3 hundred thousands
 f 5 tens l 3 thousands

7 a 200 000 + 30 000 + 5 000 + 200 + 40 + 7
 b 300 000 + 60 000 + 4 000 + 300 + 80 + 2
 c 400 000 + 90 000 + 1 000 + 400 + 50 + 6
 d 600 000 + 70 000 + 200 + 90 + 1
 e 700 000 + 80 000 + 2 000 + 8
 f 800 000 + 90 000 + 9 000 + 90 + 9

8 5 987

9 a

b

Triangles	1	2	3	4	5	6	7
Matches	3	6	9	12	15	18	21

c Hands on (triangles × 3 = matches).
d 45

10 a

b

Pentagons	1	2	3	4	5	6	7
Sides	5	10	15	20	25	30	35

c Hands on (pentagons × 5 = sides).
d 50

11 a

b

Squares	1	2	3	4	5	6	7
Sides	4	8	12	16	20	24	28

c Hands on (squares × 4 = sides).
d 48

12 Colour a, b, c, f, h, i and l.

13 a Hands on. b 64 c 16

14 a Hands on (H, I, N, O, S, X or Z).

Unit 17

1 a 27 c 25 e 88 g 47 i 97
 b 63 d 66 f 27 h 86

2 a 28 c 18 e 60 g 36 i 12
 b 10 d 36 f 54 h 16

3 a 15 c 48 e 75 g 216 i 900
 b 24 d 93 f 168 h 202

4 a 17 d 15 g 40 j 4
 b 10 e 36 h 73 k 130
 c 4 f 200 i 193 l 50

5 Hands on.

6 a $\frac{4}{5}$ b $\frac{3}{4}$ c $\frac{7}{8}$ d $\frac{5}{6}$ e $\frac{9}{10}$

7 a $1\frac{2}{3}$ b $1\frac{4}{5}$ c $2\frac{1}{2}$

8 a $\frac{3}{4}$ b $\frac{2}{3}$ c $1\frac{3}{4}$ d $1\frac{2}{3}$ e $2\frac{3}{4}$
 f $2\frac{2}{3}$ g $3\frac{3}{4}$ h $3\frac{2}{3}$ i $4\frac{2}{3}$

9 a B b A c D d C

10 a Yes b B c C d B and D e C

11 a red, blue, green b yellow, blue, red
 c red, green, yellow, blue

12

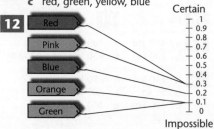

Certain
1
0.9
0.8
0.7
0.6
0.5
0.4
0.3
0.2
0.1
0
Impossible

Red
Pink
Blue
Orange
Green

Answers

13 Hands on—some examples below:

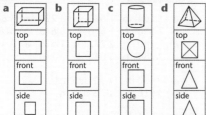

a | b | c | d
top | top | top | top
front | front | front | front
side | side | side | side

14
a
b
c

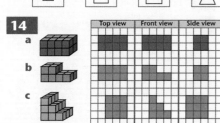

| | Top view | Front view | Side view |

Unit 18

1
a	77 989	f	88 094	k	94 481
b	78 465	g	94 670	l	32 620
c	55 744	h	67 203	m	87 289
d	84 515	i	119 452	n	79 384
e	85 233	j	123 432	o	44 285

2
| a | 1 316 km | c | 4 031 km | e | 3 310 km |
| b | 2 849 km | d | 5 166 km | f | 3 459 km |

3
a	XXVII	h	LXXVIII	o	CCLII
b	XXXIV	i	LXXIV	p	CCLXIII
c	XXVI	j	LIX	q	CCCLXIV
d	XXXVIII	k	XXXVII	r	CDLXIV
e	XLII	l	CXXVI	s	DXXI
f	LIII	m	CXV	t	DCXXXII
g	LXIV	n	CXXXV	u	DCCXXIV

4
a	V	VI	VII	**VIII**
b	XV	XVI	XVII	**XVIII**
c	XXI	XXII	XXIII	**XXIV**
d	XV	XX	XXV	**XXX**
e	XXIV	XXIII	XXII	**XXI**
f	LIII	LIV	LV	**LVI**
g	LXI	LXII	LXIII	**LXIV**
h	LXXV	LXXX	LXXXV	**XC**

5
a	Oberon	200 km	b	Dubbo	410 km
	Blackheath	130 km		Blackheath	130 km
		70 km			280 km

c	Ivanhoe	650 km	d	Orange	275 km
	Dubbo	410 km		Oberon	200 km
		240 km			75 km

6 Hands on.

7
a	32°C	d	About 31.5°C	g	About 33°C.
b	29°C	e	About 26.5°C
c	23°C	f	6°C

8 a

Seconds	10	20	30	40	50	60	70	80	90	100	110	120	130	140	150	160
Litres	2	4	6	8	10	12	14	16	18	20	22	24	26	28	30	32

b 14 L   c 17 L   d 200 seconds

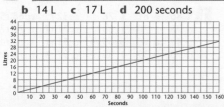

---

9 Hands on.

10 New levels are:
a About 35 mL
b About 40 mL
c About 45 mL
d and
e Each cubic centimetre displaces 1 mL.

11 100

DIAGNOSTIC REVIEW 2

Part 1
a	4 tens	e	10	i	36
b	5 hundreds	f	18	j	44
c	3 thousands	g	71
d	3 hundred thousands	h	20

Part 2
| a | 597 | c | $60.25 | e | 3 265 |
| b | 7 274 | d | 7 193 | f | 1 199 |

Part 3
a	762	h	4 r3	o	12
b	2 450	i	9 r4	p	11
c	2 136	j	121	q	Composite
d	8	k	172	r	Prime
e	3	l	121	s	Prime
f	7	m	50	t	Composite
g	9 r5	n	38

Part 4
a $\frac{23}{100}$, 0.23 c $\frac{37}{100}$, 0.37 e $\frac{2}{12}$ g $\frac{11}{12}$

b $\frac{46}{100}$, 0.46 d $\frac{5}{6}$ f $\frac{3}{6}$

$0 \quad \frac{1}{4} \quad \frac{1}{2} \quad \frac{3}{4} \quad 1 \quad 1\frac{1}{4} \quad 1\frac{1}{2} \quad 1\frac{3}{4} \quad 2 \quad 2\frac{1}{4}$

$\frac{1}{8}$ $1\frac{1}{4}$ $2\frac{1}{4}$

Part 5
0.5

Part 6
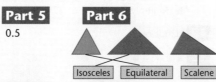

Isosceles | Equilateral | Scalene

Part 7
Hands on.

Part 8
a and c

Part 9
a 700 m   b 650 m

Part 10
a A square with sides of 5 cm.
b No (25 cm²)

Part 11
b

Part 12
a 0936 hours   c 2025 hours
b 1535 hours

Part 13
a 2:00 pm   b 15°C   c 25°C

Unit 19

1
a	153	f	185	k	148 r1	p	118 r7
b	144	g	177	l	194 r1	q	166 r3
c	163	h	125	m	168 r1	r	162 r5
d	135	i	184	n	123 r1	s	118 r2
e	188	j	124	o	131	t	139 r6

2
a	74	h	56 r5	n	107 r1	t	101 r1
b	75	i	45 r6	o	85 r4	u	203
c	77	j	48 r3	p	102 r1	v	132
d	66	k	93 r3	q	101	w	155 r2
e	63	l	75 r5	r	100 r6	x	61 r1
f	84 r3	m	98 r3	s	100 r2	y	128 r1
g	84 r7

3 Hands on.

4
| a | b | c | d | e |
| 52% | 94% | 63% | 88% | 5% |

5
a $\frac{1}{10}, \frac{10}{100}$, 0.10, 10% g $\frac{6}{10}, \frac{60}{100}$, 0.60, 60%

b $\frac{2}{10}, \frac{20}{100}$, 0.20, 20% h $\frac{7}{10}, \frac{70}{100}$, 0.70, 70%

c $\frac{1}{4}, \frac{25}{100}$, 0.25, 25% i $\frac{3}{4}, \frac{75}{100}$, 0.75, 75%

d $\frac{3}{10}, \frac{30}{100}$, 0.30, 30% j $\frac{8}{10}, \frac{80}{100}$, 0.80, 80%

e $\frac{4}{10}, \frac{40}{100}$, 0.40, 40% k $\frac{9}{10}, \frac{90}{100}$, 0.90, 90%

f $\frac{1}{2}, \frac{50}{100}$, 0.50, 50% l $1, \frac{100}{100}$, 1.0, 100%

6 a 23% b 25% c 50% d 70% e 75%

7
	Room	Length	Breadth
a	Bathroom	3 m	2 m
b	Lounge	5 m	4 m
c	Kitchen	3 m	2 m
d	Bedroom	4 m	$3\frac{1}{2}$ m

8 Hands on.   **9** Hands on.

10
a	4WD 2 t	d	Submarine 2 456 t
b	Truck 14 t	e	Frigate 3 921 t
c	Semi-trailer 36 t	f	Destroyer 4 788 t

11 a 2 332 t b 11 165 t c 22 t d 3 919 t

12
a	1 000 kg	d	500 kg	g	2 500 kg
b	2 000 kg	e	250 kg	h	3 500 kg
c	3 000 kg	f	750 kg	i	1 250 kg

Unit 20

1 a 25 595 b 15 083 c 29 426 d 38 756

2
a	Reasonable	e	Unreasonable
b	Unreasonable	f	Unreasonable
c	Unreasonable	g	Reasonable
d	Reasonable

3
	Travel agent	Father	Mother	Son	Daughter	Total
a	Juz Flights	$2 080	$2 080	$1 020	$1 020	$6 200
b	Jet Travel	$2 494	$2 494	$1 308	$1 308	$7 604
c	Whisper Travel	$3 170	$3 170	$0	$0	$6 340
d	Fly High Travel	$1 457	$1 457	$1 457	$1 457	$5 828

e Jet Travel   f Fly High Travel

Answers

4

	Numbers	Total of scores	Number of scores	Average
a	4, 5, 6, 7, 8	30	5	6
b	8, 10, 12, 14, 16	60	5	12
c	7, 9, 13, 11, 5	45	5	9
d	18, 6, 9, 15, 12	60	5	12
e	30, 10, 15, 25	80	4	20
f	40, 36, 32	108	3	36
g	12, 15, 18, 21, 24, 27, 30	147	7	21

5 **a** 11 seconds   **b** $8   **c** 11 years
d 22ºC   **e** 30 minutes

6–9 Hands on.

10 **a** 48   **c** 24   **e** Yes
b 12   **d** Pineapple and mango

11 **a** 9 hours   **c** Yes
b 6 hours   **d** Sport, eating and studying

12 Hands on.

Unit 21

1 **a**
```
254 × 5 =
200 × 5 = 1 000
 50 × 5 =   250
  4 × 5 =    20
            1 270
```
f
```
326 × 8 =
300 × 8 = 2 400
 20 × 8 =   160
  6 × 8 =    48
            2 608
```

b
```
467 × 6 =
400 × 6 = 2 400
 60 × 6 =   360
  7 × 6 =    42
            2 802
```
g
```
707 × 4 =
700 × 4 = 2 800
  7 × 4 =    28
            2 828
```

c
```
493 × 3 =
400 × 3 = 1 200
 90 × 3 =   270
  3 × 3 =     9
            1 479
```
h
```
854 × 6 =
800 × 6 = 4 800
 50 × 6 =   300
  4 × 6 =    24
            5 124
```

d
```
365 × 7 =
300 × 7 = 2 100
 60 × 7 =   420
  5 × 7 =    35
            2 555
```
i
```
732 × 9 =
700 × 9 = 6 300
 30 × 9 =   270
  2 × 9 =    18
            6 588
```

e
```
284 × 4 =
200 × 4 =   800
 80 × 4 =   320
  4 × 4 =    16
            1 136
```

2 **a** $625   **c** $3 258   **e** $2 548
b $1 296   **d** $948

3 Hands on.

4 **a** 216 426   **d** 1 518 620
b 321 216   **e** 12 270 480
c 435 560   **f** 28 378 999

5 **a** ACT, Tas, Vic, NSW, SA, NT, Qld, WA
b SA   **c** WA   **d** Qld, WA   **e** WA   **f** SA

6 **a** Yes   **b** Yes   **c** Yes   **d** 50   **e** Yes

7 BLACK | Blue | Red | Green | White

8 Blue   **b** Yes   **c** No

9 Hands on.

10 **a** 2 h 10 min   **e** 2 h 20 min
b 4 h 45 min   **f** 1 h 45 min
c 1 h 5 min   **g** 20 min
d 2 h 45 min

11 **a** 45 min   **c** 35 min
b 1 h   **d** 26 h 15 min

12 Hands on.

Unit 22

1 **a** 63 471   **f** 47 615   **k** 15 215
b 34 222   **g** 23 162   **l** 41 712
c 15 225   **h** 25 314   **m** 56 563
d 51 171   **i** 55 211   **n** 30 736
e 52 509   **j** 37 147   **o** 16 118

2 **a** 15 962   **c** 24 117   **e** 6 776
b 1 734   **d** 26 146   **f** 25 331

3 Dubbo

4 **a** 4   **d** 8   **g** 35   **j** 90   **m** 20   **p** 120
b 8   **e** 40   **h** 18   **k** 40   **n** 22
c 5   **f** 20   **i** 10   **l** 90   **o** 50

5 **a** 2   **c** 15   **e** 20   **g** 6   **i** 15   **k** 3
b 10   **d** 4   **f** 35   **h** 12   **j** 16   **l** 24

6 **a** $25   **b** $8   **c** $40   **d** $90

7 Hands on. Some examples below.
10%—$16   25%—$40
50%—$80   75%—$120

8 **a**
Hexagons	1	2	3	4	5	6	7
Sides	6	12	18	24	30	36	42

b Multiply by 6   **c** 54

9 **a**
Octagons	1	2	3	4	5	6	7
Sides	8	16	24	32	40	48	56

b Multiply by 8   **c** 88

10 **a**
Decagons	1	2	3	4	5	6	7
Sides	10	20	30	40	50	60	70

b Multiply by 10   **c** 150

11 **a**
Dodecagons	1	2	3	4	5	6	7
Sides	12	24	36	48	60	72	84

b Multiply by 12   **c** 120

12 Hands on.

13 **a**   **b**   **c**   **d**
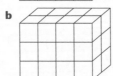

14 **a**

b

c
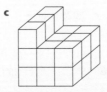

Unit 23

1 **a** 1 564   **e** 1 620   **i** 3 220   **m** 3 663
b 2 550   **f** 1 556   **j** 3 648   **n** 618
c 1 180   **g** 2 277   **k** 1 615   **o** 2 418
d 2 784   **h** 5 040   **l** 2 240

2 **a** 1 430 m   **c** 1 325 m
b 3 918 m   **d** 3 616 m

3 **a** Bosnic to Rafter or Bosnic to Judd

4

	Algorithm	Estimate	Product
a	3 × 29	3 × 30 = 90	87
b	4 × 48	4 × 50 = 200	192
c	6 × 97	6 × 100 = 600	582
d	6 × 213	6 × 200 = 1 200	1 278
e	7 × 817	7 × 800 = 5 600	5 719
f	9 × 482	9 × 500 = 4 500	4 338

5 **a** $\frac{5}{4}$ **c** $\frac{6}{5}$ **e** $\frac{10}{4}$ **g** $\frac{7}{4}$ **i** $\frac{7}{5}$
b $\frac{3}{2}$ **d** $\frac{4}{3}$ **f** $\frac{9}{6}$ **h** $\frac{5}{3}$ **j** $\frac{7}{3}$

6 **a**
A	B	C	D
$\frac{5}{4}$	$\frac{7}{4}$	$\frac{10}{4}$	$\frac{11}{4}$

b
E	F	G	H
$\frac{6}{5}$	$\frac{8}{5}$	$\frac{11}{5}$	$\frac{12}{5}$

7 **a** $\frac{5}{4}$ **b** $\frac{3}{2}$ **c** $\frac{13}{10}$ **d** $\frac{7}{5}$

8
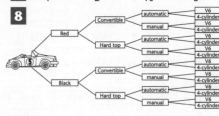

9
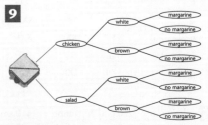

10 **a** Sporty Rd   **c** Ricky Rd   **e** Beatle St
b Savage Rd   **d** Britany Ave   **f** Mariah Rd

11 **a** N10   **b** B10   **c** K4

12 **a** E   **b** F

13 **a** A and B 1 200 m   **d** F and G 1 000 m
b B and C 900 m   **e** A and E 1 500 m
c C and D 600 m   **f** D and F 2 200 m

Unit 24

1 **a** 86   **e** 81   **i** 78   **m** 32 r5   **q** 68 r5
b 75   **f** 70   **j** 86   **n** 77 r7   **r** 79 r7
c 48   **g** 98   **k** 65 r4   **o** 51 r1   **s** 87 r4
d 90   **h** 39   **l** 35 r7   **p** 97 r4   **t** 78 r9

Answers

2

Question	Answer	Estimate	Reasonable	Unreasonable
a	388 ÷ 4	97	100	✓	
b	318 ÷ 6	53	50	✓	
c	776 ÷ 4	94	200		✓
d	1 590 ÷ 8	198 r6	200	✓	
e	2 417 ÷ 4	404 r1	600		✓

3 a 11   b 11   c 140 cm

4 Possible solutions:
6 people = $48   8 people = $64
7 people = $56   9 people = $72

5 a $\frac{5}{3}$, $1\frac{2}{3}$ e $\frac{9}{4}$, $2\frac{1}{4}$ i $\frac{15}{6}$, $2\frac{3}{6}$

b $\frac{3}{2}$, $1\frac{1}{2}$ f $\frac{8}{5}$, $1\frac{3}{5}$ j $\frac{7}{3}$, $2\frac{1}{3}$

c $\frac{5}{3}$, $1\frac{2}{3}$ g $\frac{7}{4}$, $1\frac{3}{4}$

d $\frac{6}{4}$, $1\frac{2}{4}$ h $\frac{12}{5}$, $2\frac{2}{5}$

6 a $\frac{6}{5}$ b $\frac{8}{5}$ c $\frac{12}{5}$ d $\frac{14}{5}$ e $\frac{16}{5}$

7 a $1\frac{2}{5}$ b $1\frac{4}{5}$ c $2\frac{1}{5}$ d $2\frac{3}{5}$ e $3\frac{2}{5}$

8 a Angle A = 60°   c Angle A = 40°
Angle B = 60°   Angle B = 100°
Angle C = 60°   Angle C = 40°
b Angle A = 60°   d Angle A = 90°
Angle B = 80°   Angle B = 60°
Angle C = 40°   Angle C = 30°

9 They are all equal.

10 They are all different.

11 Hands on.

12 a 128 mm b 170 mm c 172 mm

13 Hands on.
(a 12 cm b 14 cm c 24 cm d 30 cm)

14 a Bedroom 16 m c Bathroom 10 m
b Lounge 22 m   d Kitchen 14 m

15 a 13.6 m b 16.4 m c 12.9 m

Unit 25

1 a 47 795 e 78 093 i 78 086
b 69 797 f 59 586 j 82 222
c 49 917 g 57 051
d 79 779 h 57 969

2 a
```
 5 2 1 3 4
 2 1 7 2 4
+1 4 0 2 5
─────────
 8 7 8 8 3
```
c
```
 1 3 1 3 3
 3 0 2 1 4
+2 8 1 3 2
─────────
 7 1 4 7 9
```
e
```
 3 3 4 5 6
 2 7 1 2 3
+3 1 8 2 7
─────────
 9 2 4 0 6
```
b
```
 2 4 0 2 3
 2 1 1 3 2
+3 4 4 7 1
─────────
 7 9 6 2 6
```
d
```
 2 7 2 9 4
 4 0 3 2 3
+2 7 2 2 1
─────────
 9 4 8 3 8
```

3 a $92 298 c $111 853
b $47 443 d $82 742

4 a 30, 300, 3 000
b 50, 500, 5 000
c 60, 600, 6 000
d 70, 700, 7 000
e 90, 900, 9 000

f 100, 1 000, 10 000
g 180, 1 800, 18 000
h 250, 2 500, 25 000
i 310, 3 100, 31 000
j 440, 4 400, 44 000
k 560, 5 600, 56 000
l 780, 7 800, 78 000

5 Estimates are:
a 700   e 400   i 1 400
b 300   f 200   j 1 800
c 100   g 1 200 k 2 000
d 300   h 1 250 l 6 400

6 a 480 e 900 i 7 080 m 19 250
b 1 040 f 2 540 j 12 400 n 19 040
c 1 050 g 6 750 k 13 800 o 40 230
d 1 080 h 5 120 l 27 780

7 a 9, 10, 11, 12, 13, 14, 15
b 2nd number is 8 more than the 1st number.
c 18
d 3, 6, 9, 12, 15, 18, 21
e 2nd number is 3 times the value of the 1st number.
f 30
g 9, 18, 27, 36, 45, 54, 63
h 2nd number is 9 times the value of the 1st number.
i 90
j 18, 19, 20, 21, 22, 23, 24
k 2nd number is 17 more than the 1st number.
l 27
m 99, 90, 81, 72, 63, 54, 45
n 2nd number is 9 times the value of the 1st number.
o 18
p 14, 24, 34, 44, 54, 64, 74
q 2nd number is 13 less than the 1st number.
r 104

8 a Food b Clothes c Yes d No

9 $160

10 a Pottery b Art c Metalwork d 15

11 Shoe sizes of children
| SIZE 4 | SIZE 5 | SIZE 6 | SIZE 7 |

Unit 26

1 a 575   f 999   k 2 679
b 1 224 g 2 520 l 1 512
c 1 125 h 2 184 m 2 494
d 1 260 i 756
e 1 334 j 1 365

2 864 cans

3 Between 13 and 18 people

4 a 2 hundredths f 8 hundredths
b 7 tenths   g 6 thousandths
c 4 tens   h 3 tenths
d 6 ones   i 7 tenths
e 6 thousandths j 9 thousandths

5 a 1.256 kg e 3.499 m
b 1.378 m   f 4.649 L
c 2.372 L   g 6.296 kg
d 5.109 kg h 7.759 m

6 a 0.236 d 0.678 g 0.834 j 0.023
b 0.475 e 0.279 h 0.994 k 0.088
c 0.259 f 0.352 i 0.074 l 0.096

7 a 0.111, 0.123, 0.423, 0.456
b 0.567, 0.657, 0.756, 0.765
c 0.978, 1.459, 1.999, 2.234
d 3.555, 4.077, 4.098, 5.006

8 Hands on.   **9** Hands on.

10
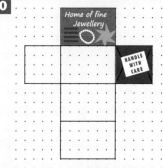

11 Hands on. **12** Hands on.
13 Hands on. **14** Hands on.

Unit 27

1 a 103 f 105 k 107 p 103 r7
b 102 g 105 l 106 q 108 r3
c 104 h 103 m 105 r 104 r3
d 102 i 104 n 104 s 104 r7
e 103 j 102 o 104 t 106 r1

2 a 242 e 99 i 124 r7 m 78 r5
b 71 r4 f 104 r2 j 125 r4 n 62 r9
c 181 r2 g 75 r4 k 80 o 58 r5
d 142 r2 h 104 r1 l 76

3 a 182 km c 121 r2 km (or 121.33 km)
b 91 km

4 Any distance between 140 km and 210 km.

5 a 10°C c −5°C e 40°C g 35°C
b 25°C d −15°C f −20°C

6 a 2 m d −1 m g 1 m
b −4 m e 8 m h 3 m
c 11 m f 8 m, 13 m

7 a Raffle   g No
b Auction   h Auctions and raffles
c Auction   i Pony rides
d Cakes   j Craft
e Pony rides   k Cakes
f Cakes   l Yes

8 a 50 hectare farm for sale. **9** Hands on.

10 Hands on. (a zoo and d shopping mall would normally be larger than a hectare.)

DIAGNOSTIC REVIEW 3

Part 1
a 5 895 b 42 354 c 26 980 d 60 937

Answers

Part 2

a	1 870	e	900	i	55	m	127 seeds
b	1 695	f	1 692	j	43		
c	952	g	44	k	113 r3		
d	8 820	h	58	l	64 r3		

Part 3

a 6 221 406   b 3 579 603   c 27 697 408

Part 4

a	$\frac{35}{100}$	h	10	o	$1\frac{1}{4}$
b	$\frac{90}{100}$	i	2	p	$2\frac{1}{6}$
c	$\frac{53}{100}$	j	15	q	$1\frac{3}{8}$
d	99%	k	$\frac{4}{6}$	r	5 tenths
e	2	l	$\frac{8}{6}$ or $1\frac{2}{6}$	s	3 thousandths
f	8	m	$\frac{15}{12}$ or $1\frac{3}{12}$	t	7 hundredths
g	50	n	$\frac{16}{10}$ or $1\frac{6}{10}$		

Part 5

a 5, 10, 15, 20, 25, 30
b 9, 18, 27, 36, 45, 54

Part 6

a Hands on.
b 4 times

Part 7

Model a

Part 8

a 40°   b 90°   c 140°

Part 9

170 mm

Part 10

15 m²

Part 11

a	1 000 kg	c	1 250 kg
b	1 500 kg	d	2 750 kg

Part 12

a 1320 hours
b 1120 hours

Part 13

a 20
b Yes

Unit 28

1
a	4.78	e	9.36	i	14.967	m	11.791
b	8.90	f	11.755	j	12.446	n	10.207
c	9.07	g	11.053	k	12.493	o	16.926
d	15.24	h	16.986	l	11.980		

2

a
```
   44.521
 +17.362
  61.883 km
```

e
```
   44.521
 +44.521
  61.066 km
```

b
```
   16.545
 +21.399
  37.944 km
```

f
```
   21.399
   11.065
 +24.078
  56.542 km
```

c
```
   24.078
   11.476
 +17.362
  52.916 km
```

g
```
   11.065
   21.399
 +16.545
  49.009 km
```

d
```
   11.476
   24.078
 +11.065
  46.619 km
```

h
```
   11.065
   24.078
   11.476
 +17.362
  63.981 km
```

3 Hands on.   **4** Hands on.

5
a	$60.80	c	$103.45	e	$131.25
b	$90.25	d	$112.20		

6 Hands on.   **7** Hands on.

8 Possible solutions:
a I 5
b D 8, E 8, I 7, J 7, N 6
c J 2, J 3, K 2, K 3, L 1, L 2, L 3
d P 3

9 Hands on.   **10** Hands on.

11 a 1 700 m b 1000 m c 300 m
d 700 m

12 Hands on.

13

```
1000 BC   500 BC   Birth of Christ   AD 500   AD 1000   AD 1500   AD 2000
```
First Olympic Games 776 BC
Great Wall of China finished 500 BC
Battle of Hastings AD 1066
Discovery of America AD 1492
First Fleet arrives in Australia AD 1788
Federation of Australia AD 1901

14 a 722 years   d 2 288 years
b 276 years   e–i Hands on.
c 1 842 years

Unit 29

1
a	420	e	540	i	2 048	m	1 508
b	544	f	624	j	1 482	n	2 210
c	442	g	1 548	k	1 786	o	3 441
d	684	h	925	l	1 470		

2 a $544   b $1 824

3 a 60 L   b $384   c 288 meals

4
a	3.02	e	2.18	i	84.84	m	3.146
b	3.11	f	13.21	j	25.34	n	1.719
c	2.57	g	22.26	k	0.779	o	5.894
d	5.22	h	42.74	l	2.479		

5
a	0.30 m	d	0.27 m	g	0.20 m
b	0.06 m	e	0.05 m	h	0.24 m
c	0.08 m	f	0.15 m	i	0.08 m

6
a	11.1 kg	c	$8.30	e	1.46 m
b	2.79 m	d	1.25 m	f	No

7 a Hands on.
b TR123, TR321, TR213, TR312, TR231, TR132

8 6 handshakes

9
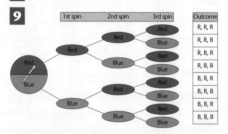

10
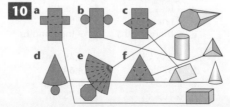
a b c
d e f

11

GLUE   Blue
Drawing Pins
BISO   Yellow
BISO   Red
GLUE   Base

12 a D   b C   c F

Unit 30

1
a	58 234	f	5 386	k	$661.30
b	19 253	g	45 827	l	$80.70
c	3 566	h	68 969	m	$95.83
d	55 171	i	9 864	n	$63.49
e	9 350	j	47 579		

2
a	$2 008	c	$15 357
b	5 343 km	d	7 578

3

	A	B	C	D
1	Date	Item	Cost	Balance
2	May 3	Opening		$987.90
3	May 7	Balls	$126.00	(D2-C3) $861.90
4	May 9	Shirts	$120.32	(D3-C4) $741.58
5	May 12	Shorts	$144.22	(D4-C5) $597.36
6	May 18	Socks	$35.28	(D5-C6) $562.08
7	May 22	Pads	$34.65	(D6-C7) $527.43

4
```
-10-9-8-7-6-5-4-3-2-1 0 1 2 3 4 5 6 7 8 9 10
```

5 John finished on step −3.

6 a Bangkok 34°C   c Berlin 10°C to −5°C
b Montreal −10°C

7
a	7°C	c	13°C	e	8°C
b	11°C	d	12°C	f	10°C

8 a 23°C   b 21°C   c 12°C   d 15°C

9

	Item	mm	cm	m	km
a	The length of a sultana packet				
b	The length of a calculator				
c	The thickness of a mouse pad				
d	The length of a grasshopper				
e	The length of a pool				
f	The width of your home				
g	The length of a fingernail				
h	The length of the Hume Highway				

10

	Length	Device
a	The length of a pencil	30 cm ruler
b	The length of a room	metre ruler/ trundle wheel
c	The circumference of a bin	tape measure
d	The length of the playground	trundle wheel
e	The circumference of a bottle	tape measure
f	The perimeter of a large curved garden	trundle wheel/ tape measure
g	The distance between two towns	odometer
h	The perimeter of a book	30 cm ruler
i	The perimeter of your school	trundle wheel

11
a	50 mm	f	800 cm	k	2 km
b	260 mm	g	900 cm	l	6 km
c	370 mm	h	550 cm	m	4 km
d	3 cm	i	2 m	n	6 000 m
e	6 cm	j	7 m	o	850 cm

12 Estimate = Hands on.
Length = 131 mm

13 a Hands on, mean = 6 b 48 ÷ 8 = 6

14 Discussion: The mean score of 6 should match the height of the columns.

15 a 5 d 15 g 5 j 8
b 9 e 22 h 6 k 12
c 12 f 16 i 11 l 15

16 34 kg

Unit 31

1 a 13.6 f 18.69 k 136.5 p 151.38
b 22.5 g 28.72 l 146.8 q 106.45
c 18.4 h 41.05 m 289.8 r 190.92
d 26 i 22.29 n 58.4 s 519.61
e 21.6 j 31.44 o 158.5 t 123.75

2 a $24.15 c $48.30 e $183.40
b $38.25 d $111.15

3   Rule

a 7, 8, 9, 10, 11, 12, 13   +6

b 4, 8, 12, 16, 20, 24, 28   ×4

c 5, 10, 15, 20, 25, 30, 35   ×5

d 12, 24, 36, 48, 60, 72, 84   ×6

e 14, 28, 42, 56, 70, 84, 98   ×7

f 23, 20, 17, 14, 11, 7, 4   −12

4 Hands on.

5 a ×10 b ÷4 c ×5 d ×2, +1

6 Hands on.

7 Hands on.

8

State	Area in km²
WA	2 525 500
Qld	1 727 200
NT	1 346 200
SA	984 000
NSW	801 600
Vic	227 600
Tas	67 800
ACT	2 000
Total	7 681 900

9 Possible solution: A 5 cm × 5 cm square

10 a ha c km² e ha g ha i km²
b m² d km² f m² h m²/ha

Unit 32

1 a 28 e 490 i 1 200 m 162
b 90 f 400 j 3 000 n 224
c 160 g 600 k 72 o 156
d 300 h 900 l 125

2 a 968 d 1 300 g 1 230 i 2 520
b 1 175 e 1 526 h 2 568 j 741
c 756 f 540

3 a 3 690 c 18 000 e 40 180
b 17 000 d 16 380

4 a 625 c 8 140 e 25 432
b 1 692 d 14 952

5 a 1 410 b 1 630 c 1 778

6 a 10 d 90 g 60 i 40
b 90 e 50 h 90 j 100
c 30 f 80

7 a 100 d 300 g 400 j 700 m 500
b 100 e 300 h 600 k 900 n 1 000
c 100 f 400 i 600 l 400 o 900

8 a 1 000 d 3 000 g 3 000 j 8 000
b 1 000 e 6 000 h 6 000 k 10 000
c 1 000 f 3 000 i 7 000 l 5 000

9 Estimates:
a $300 d $1 200
b $900 e $700
c $1 200 f $2 000

10 Hands on
(one example: 1 of each item).

11 a, b, c, d, e

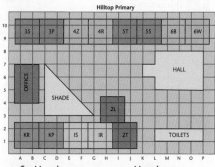

f Hands on. g Hands on.

12 a KR classroom b 4R classroom
c Office d Shade

13 Possible solutions:
a K9, K10, L9, L10
b M6, M7, N6, N7, O6, O7, P5, P6, P7
c C1, C2, D1, D2
d H3, H4, I3, I4

14 1 cm = 3 m

15

t	5.055	4.259	6.385	5.634	7.500	6.900	25	50
kg	5 055	4 259	6 385	5 634	7 500	6 900	25 000	50 000

16

Fran	Ellen	Connie	Will	George	Alice
29.585 kg	29.8 kg	30.5 kg	32 kg	35.005 kg	36 kg

17 Ellen

18 a g e t i g
b kg f g j kg
c g g t k t
d kg h kg l t

19 a 31.9 kg b 15 c 4.955 t

Unit 33

1 a 21.3 f 36.4 k 22.4 p $1.52
b 21.2 g 15.1 l 22.4 q 1.37 m
c 43.2 h 25.3 m $1.37 r 1.26 m
d 32.1 i 11.3 n $1.92 s 1.53 m
e 24.2 j 11.2 o $1.83 t 1.64 m

2 a 8.23 m b 6.92 m

3 a $3.32 b $21.14 c $19.31

4 a

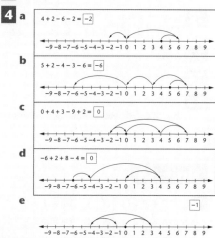

$4 + 2 - 6 - 2 = \boxed{-2}$

b $5 + 2 - 4 - 3 - 6 = \boxed{-6}$

c $0 + 4 + 3 - 9 + 2 = \boxed{0}$

d $-6 + 2 + 8 - 4 = \boxed{0}$

e $\boxed{-1}$

f

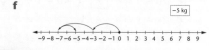

$\boxed{-5 \text{ kg}}$

5–11 Hands on.

12 a 20 cm³ c 40 cm³
b 24 cm³ (Circle pack C)

13–14 Hands on.

Unit 34

1 a $25.07 c $73.05
b $29.73 d $11.12

2 Hands on.

3 a 27 × $6.50 = $175.50
b (6 × $7) + (3 × $9) + (7 × $5)
= $104
c ($\frac{1}{4}$ of 24) × $0.60 = $3.60
d ($0.90 × 5) + $5.60 = $10.10
e 6 × 8 × $\frac{1}{4}$ = 12 flowers

4 a 0.45 d 450 g 316
b 4.5 e 3.16 h 3 160
c 45 f 31.6

5 a Decimal point moved 1 place right.
b Decimal point moved 2 places right.

6 a 23.5 c 57.5 e 360 g 3 630 i 6 796
b 36.2 d 47.4 f 575.3 h 870

7 a 0.47 c 0.0047 e 5.46 g 0.0546
b 0.047 d 0.00047 f 0.546 h 0.00546

8 The decimal point moved 2 places left.

9 a 0.045 c 0.00045 e 0.0316
b 0.0045 d 0.316 f 0.00316

Answers

10 a ▢ e ⬠ i ▢
b ◯ f ⬡ j ◯
c △ g △ k ⬠
d ▢ h ◯ l ⬡

11 Some solutions:
a Cube   c Triangular prism
b Cylinder d Rectangular prism

12 a 5 c 10 e 10 g 7   i 18
b 6   d 3   f 12 h 20 j 22

13 $28

14 a 7   b 3

15 a 16°C c 19°C
b 22°C d Wednesday and Saturday

Unit 35

1
a 12 ÷ 4 = 3 ✓   i 36 ÷ 4 = 8 [9]
b 20 ÷ 4 = 4 [5]   j 36 ÷ 6 = 5 [6]
c 20 ÷ 5 = 4 ✓   k 40 ÷ 5 = 8 ✓
d 24 ÷ 4 = 4 [6]   l 21 ÷ 3 = 7 ✓
e 24 ÷ 6 = 4 ✓   m 45 ÷ 9 = 3 [5]
f 28 ÷ 7 = 3 [4]   n 42 ÷ 7 = 6 ✓
g 32 ÷ 4 = 8 ✓   o 48 ÷ 8 = 6 ✓
h 27 ÷ 9 = 3 ✓   p 48 ÷ 3 = 12 [16]

2
a True   e False i True   m True
b True   f False j False n True
c True   g True   k False o True
d False h True   l True

3

a	b	c	d	e
$\frac{14}{4)56}$ ✓	$\frac{13}{6)78}$ ✓	$\frac{123}{3)369}$ ✓	$\frac{144}{6)864}$ ✓	$\frac{131}{7)917}$ ✓

$$\begin{array}{r} 14 \\ \times\ \ 4 \\ \hline 56 \end{array} \quad \begin{array}{r} 13 \\ \times\ \ 6 \\ \hline 78 \end{array} \quad \begin{array}{r} 123 \\ \times\ \ 3 \\ \hline 369 \end{array} \quad \begin{array}{r} 144 \\ \times\ \ 6 \\ \hline 864 \end{array} \quad \begin{array}{r} 131 \\ \times\ \ 7 \\ \hline 917 \end{array}$$

4 Estimates:
a 20 sheep b $200 c 30 books d $500

5 a 0.27 d 0.5   g 0.9 j 0.125
b 0.04 e 0.2   h 0.6 k 0.375
c 0.4   f 0.75 i 0.8 l 0.25

6
a $\frac{151\ r1}{5)756}$ or $151\frac{1}{5}$

b $\frac{61\ r3}{4)247}$ or $61\frac{3}{4}$

c $\frac{122\ r3}{8)979}$ or $122\frac{3}{8}$

d $\frac{55\ r5}{8)445}$ or $55\frac{5}{8}$

e $\frac{155\ r2}{5)777}$ or $155\frac{2}{5}$

7
a $\frac{151.2}{5)756}$ c $\frac{122.375}{8)979}$ e $\frac{155.4}{5)777}$

b $\frac{61.75}{4)247}$ d $\frac{55.625}{8)445}$

8
a $\frac{449.375}{8)3\ 595}$ f $\frac{353.66666}{3)1\ 061}$

b $\frac{372.625}{8)2\ 981}$ g $\frac{1\ 211.1666}{6)7\ 267}$

c $\frac{212.875}{8)1\ 703}$ h $\frac{213.1428571}{7)1\ 492}$

d $\frac{353.33333}{3)1\ 060}$ i $\frac{432.22222}{9)3\ 890}$

e $\frac{1\ 123.625}{8)8\ 989}$

9 a 90.75   c 586.25
b 113.4   d 180.625 km

10

a [2] b [2] c [2] d [2]

e [2] f [2] g [2] h [2]

11 Most quadrilaterals have 2 diagonals.

12 [diagram: pentagon with diagonals] 5   [diagram: heptagon with diagonals] 9

13 It has more vertices.

14

	Western standard time	Central standard time	Eastern standard time		Western standard time	Central standard time	Eastern standard time
a	0800	0930	1000	e	1400	1530	1600
b	0900	1030	1100	f	1500	1630	1700
c	1000	1130	1200	g	1600	1730	1800
d	1100	1230	1300	h	1700	1830	1900

15 a [clock] Perth c [clock] Adelaide e [clock] Sydney
b [clock] Darwin d [clock] Brisbane f [clock] Hobart

16 a [clock] Sydney c [clock] Adelaide e [clock] Perth
b [clock] Darwin d [clock] Brisbane f [clock] Hobart

DIAGNOSTIC REVIEW 4

Part 1

	Round to 10	Round to 100
a	90	100
b	230	200
c	360	400
d	500	500
e	990	1 000

Part 2
a

-7 -6 -5 -4 -3 -2 -1 0 1 2 3 4 5 6 7
b −15°C c −5°C

Part 3
a 22 122 b 65 341 c 31 733 d $681.33

Part 4
a 282   c 1 560 e 2 775
b 2 464 d 1 416 f 12 624

Part 5
a 81.27 e $62.11 h 32.68 k 0.0564
b $89.96 f $13.64 i $14.05 l 0.0763
c 14.63 g 9.78   j 0.564   m 0.00763
d 97.08

Part 6
a 18, 24, 30, 36, 42, 48, 54, 60, 66
b 13, 12, 11, 10, 9, 8, 7, 6, 5

Part 7
a 7   b 9   c 10   d 8   e 12

Part 8
a cone   c cylinder
b octagonal pyramid d triangular pyramid

Part 9
a
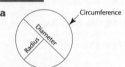
Circumference
Diameter
Radius
b Radius 15 mm

Part 10
B2 F4 E2 D3 D5 H2 B5 H5
[d] [i] [a] [g] [o] [n] [a] [l]

Part 11
a 60 mm c 900 cm e 5 000 m
b 4 cm   d 3 km   f 1 500 m

Part 12
12 km²

Part 13

Western standard time	Central standard time	Eastern standard time
1000 hours	1130 hours	1200 hours
1100 hours	1230 hours	1300 hours
1200 hours	1330 hours	1400 hours
1300 hours	1430 hours	1500 hours
1400 hours	1530 hours	1600 hours
1500 hours	1630 hours	1700 hours

Brackets ✗
Order ✗
Division ✗
Multiplacation ✗
Addition ✗
Subtraction ✗

I used this in sums like this →2×2+5×7=
You then use this → BODMAS

a. $12+8×4 = $ ④④ ✓

b. $42-24÷6 = $ ㊳ ✓

c. $(8-3)×6 = $ ㉚ ✓

d. $4×(27÷3)+14 = $ ㊿ ✓

e. $\frac{1}{2}×40 + 16 = $ ㊱ ✓

f. $\frac{1}{8}×24 + \frac{1}{4}×20 = $ ⑧ ✓

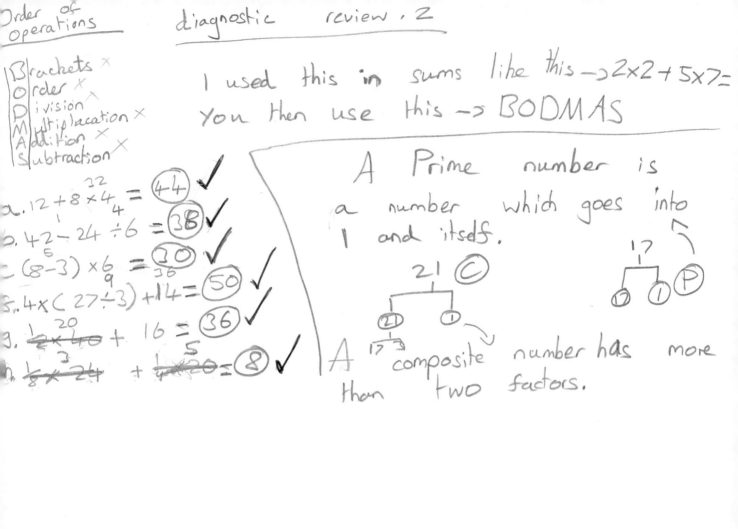

A Prime number is a number which goes into 1 and itself.

21 Ⓒ

A composite number has more than two factors.

4   8   (12)   (15)

$= \dfrac{15}{4}$

$3\tfrac{1}{8} + \tfrac{5}{4} =$

$3\tfrac{1}{8} + \tfrac{10}{8} = \tfrac{11}{8}$

$4 \tfrac{3}{8}$

$3\tfrac{1}{⑧} + \tfrac{5}{4} = 3\tfrac{3}{4} = \tfrac{15}{4}$

$3\tfrac{1}{⑧} + \tfrac{5}{8} = 3\tfrac{6}{8} \rightarrow 3\tfrac{3}{4}$

Equolatrail triangle

isocceles   scaline

right angled

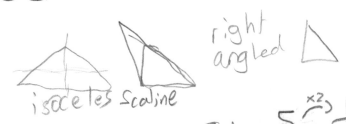

$8 \text{ in } \dfrac{5}{4} \xrightarrow[\text{×2}]{\text{×2}} \dfrac{10}{8}.$